Calvin & Marie Shenk
965 S. Dogwood Drive

S0-EGI-663

JUDAISM ON TRIAL

JUDAISM ON TRIAL

An Unconventional Discussion About Jews, Judaism and the State of Israel

NATHAN LOPES CARDOZO

URIM PUBLICATIONS
Jerusalem · New York

Judaism on Trial: An Unconventional Discussion About Jews, Judaism and the State of Israel
by Nathan Lopes Cardozo

© Copyright 2000 by Urim Publications and Nathan Lopes Cardozo
All rights reserved. Printed in Israel. No part of this book may be used or reproduced in any manner whatsoever without written permission from the copyright owners, except in the case of brief quotations embodied in reviews and articles. For further information address:
Urim Publications P.O.Box 52287 Jerusalem 91521 Israel
Tel: 02-566-0064
Email: Publisher@UrimPublications.com
Second Edition
ISBN 965-7108-28-4

Lambda Publishers, Inc.
3709 13th Avenue
Brooklyn, New York 11218 U.S.A.
Tel: 718-972-5449 Fax: 718-972-6307
mh@ejudaica.com

www.UrimPublications.com

To my brother
Jacques Eduard Lopes Cardozo

In memory of our uncle
Nico (Nathan) Lopes Cardozo *z"l*
who perished in the Holocaust
1919–1945

I carry his name with pride.
He died at the hands of the Nazis in 1945
in Blechhammer.
My mother, who saved nearly all of my father's family in the
Holocaust, told me what a wonderful man he was.
He did not merit a Jewish grave.
May his soul dwell in the Garden of Eden.

Taking fun
As simply fun
And earnestness in earnest
Shows how thoroughly thou none of the
two discernest.

Piet Hein
From "The Eternal Twins" [Dutch] in *Crooks* (1966)

CONTENTS

ACKNOWLEDGMENTS

I was blessed to sit at the feet of outstanding teachers. It were my mentors, at Gateshead Yeshiva in England, one of the bastions of rabbinic learning of the twentieth century, who taught me not only Talmud, but above all integrity and devotion. Great rabbinical personalities and thinkers influenced me in many different ways. I feel their teachings in my bones. I also had the opportunity to encounter the most outstanding Jewish and Gentile thinkers of the last few hundred years through their works and thought.

Throughout my many years of writing and teaching, many good friends have surrounded me. Words cannot describe their devotion, encouragement and interest in my work. David and Faranak Margolese have become close friends, par excellence. Stephen and Ruth Rosen, Harry and Rachel Skydell, Sean Namvar, Jeff and Helen Garden, David and Evelyne Guez are close to my heart. Steve and Lily Weiser, Kirk Douglas, Rabbi Hans Rodrigues Pereira, Els Bendheim, Norman Pomeranz, Tom Feingold, Larry and Dora Kurz, Brad and Mia Markoff, Michael and Sandy Feldmar, Jill and Rick Kahn, Jona and Tzivya Pollak, Aryeh Gallin, Larry and Lori Garon, Elan and Victoria Shasha, Peter and Susan Weintraub, Stacy and Miriam Sokol, David and Helen Scharf, David Suissa, Victor and Suzi Alhadeff, Rob Schonfeld and Dr. Herb Caskey, have all gone beyond the call of duty in assisting me. It was in the home of Mouli and Lily Spitzer that I was introduced to authentic Judaism. No words can adequately express my gratitude.

Ariella and Charles Zeloof, with their sister and brother, Bettina and David Zeloof made my stay in London a relaxing experience. Their personal interest in encouraging me to succeed in all my endeavors has exceeded the parameters of just good friendship. May they and both their parents and children carry the blessings of the Almighty. Rabbi Refoel and Loly Berish, in whose home I have so often stayed, are like real family.

Ellie and Marshall Jaffe Kulman and their sweet daughter Gilana have become family. My stay in their home in Los Angeles is the highlight of my yearly routine.

Over the years, it was my friends Rob and Elizabeth Kurtz who were always there to assist and host me. Their constant help and care for my family's well being, enabling me to teach and write, defies words. I wonder where I would have been without them. May God bless them and their lovely children. Stacy and Miriam Sokol are responsible for creating the framework of establishing the David Cardozo Academy. No words can adequately thank them. Brian and Susan Ross have proven to be loyal friends through difficult times. May God send them many blessings in their family. Adeena Karsseboom has been a great friend, organizing my lecture tours and looking after my well being while in New York. May God soon send her a life-partner. Rabbi Saul Zneimer, Daniel Soibleman and Elana Chesler are responsible for some of my most successful trips in England. To them: Thanks!

This book would not have found its way to Urim Publications without the keen assistance of my dear friends Gerry and Katy Polak. *Chazak Baruch* to them. Thanks also to Tzvi Mauer and Moshe Heller of Urim Publications for their interest in publishing this work. It was Mordechai Beck and Tzvi Mauer who dedicated time and effort in editing this work. It was especially Tzvi who offered crucial and constructive observations, many of which I included. I would like to thank Sorelle Wachmann, also of Urim Publications, for her contribution in editing the book. May they continue to publish many books of significance.

I am most thankful to Daniel Yisrael Weiss, who has guided me in many endeavors and edited many of my essays and created, with Rafi Schachar, a most successful Website.

Channi Shapiro, Elijahoe and Hadassa Phillipson, Avraham and Carry Packter, Dr. Moshe Dann, Micha Cohn, Jonathan and Ayellet Finn, Jana Chmilinsky, Bella and Avrohom Offman, Riwka and Yossi Tucker, Moise Hamaoui, Dr. Chaim Katz, Eric and Talya Brand, Jacob and Debbie Sagura, Dr. and Mrs. Michel Mazouz, Riwka Moore, Maurits and Lineke Mark, Rabbi Avi and Shelly Shapiro, Jenny Stibbe, Lex and Judith Wolff, Uriella Obst, Salomon Vaz Dias, Dr. Reuven Ben Dov, Dr. Hans Wijnfeldt, Carla Paardebek, Hans and Mechteld Meyer, Mordechai and Suzy Cohen, Joel and Rivka van Coevorden, David and Linda Emanuel, Lou and Leni Slosser, Geert Cohen Stuart, Isaac Raymond, Family Rabbi Avrohom and Cortle Katz, Family Daniel Halvon, Family Dr. Bob Friedman, Marc and Sara Hermelin, Dr. Avraham Wijler, George and Ann Mann, Henri Mashouri, Family Yisrael van Handel, Arthur Kurzweil, Eliyahu and Irena Courant, Allan and Linda Zulberg, Michael Pomeranz, Moshe and Elisheva Moskovits, Ezra and Yocheved Kahn, Simon and Aviva Keesing have been, and still are wonderful friends.

It was Dr. Nathan Cherney of Shaarei Zedek Hospital, at the recommendation of Dr. Reuven Fink of Jerusalem and Els Bendheim, who healed me of intensive pains. Special thanks to Dr. and Mrs. Alexander Duparc and to Dr. Yvonne Heitner. My gratitude to them is eternal.

To my many rabbinical and academic friends, a salute for assisting, advising and inviting me to speak at their congregations and programs: Rabbis Salomon Maimon, Chief Rabbi Professor Yonathan Sacks, Dr. Norman Lamm, Dayan Chanoch Ehrentrue, Dayan Ivan Binstock, Dr. Marc Angel, Dr. Avraham Levy, Shlomo Riskin, David Brodman, Yitschak Jeshurun, Dr. Emanuel Quint, Alan Kimche, Avraham Czapnik, Dr. Yehudah Coperman, Yacov Homnick, Dr. Aaron Rakeffet-Rothkoff, Family Dr. Ivan Lerner, Dr. David Refson, Dr. Raph Evers, Berel Wein, Moshe Cohen, Shaya Karlinsky, Yitschak Hirschfeld, Yitzchak Shurin, Joel Zevor, Dr. Emanuel Feldman, Aaron Feldman, Dr. Sholom Gold, Moshe Katz, Dr. Hillel Goldberg, Shmuel Spiero, Benyomin Bamberger, Yehoshua Karsch, Yehoshua Freilich, Avigdor Freilich, Joe Freilich, Chaim Rapoport, Fivel Smiles, Yisroel Roll, Danny Kirsch, Dr. Akiva Tatz, Yonathan Dov, Gedalyah Spinadel, Lody van de Kamp, Menachem Kashdan, Yerachmiel Fried, Yissachar Fried, Yacov Meyer, Moshe Krupka, Reuven Livingstone, Yacov Ishkovits, David and Avi Shapiro, Dr. Avraham Twerski, Sholem Zaiden, Hershal Becker, Phil Chernofsky, Shai Soloman, Lawrence Littlestone, Efraim Nisenbaum, Shmuel Moffson, Shlomo Porter, Jeff Seidel, Yacov Polak, Ilan Azizollahoff, Uriel Keesing, Jochanan Boosman and Dr. Wim van Dijk, Chanoch Teller and Rebbetzins Henkin, Kohn, Finson, Zornberg, Kimche and Rivka Bursteyn. Special thanks to Rabbis Schmuel Weiss, Kenneth Cohen, Rashi Simon, Harry Greenspan, Marc Wildes, Allen Schwartz, Daniel Wolff, Yaacov Fogelman, Albert Gabai and Mr. Max Weil. Professors Yehudah Cohen, Yehudah Gellman, Charles Isaacson, Yacov Ross, Meyer L.D. Lifchitz, Dr. Victor and Shulamit Bonchek, Dr. Alexander Goldschmidt, Dr. Alexander Alvares Vega, Dr. Avraham Schwartzbaum, Engineer David Ph. Cohen Paraira are the best of friends.

My special relationship with the Isralight Institute in the Old City of Jerusalem has been very rewarding. Rabbis David Aaron and Binny Freedman belong to the most outstanding category of people I know. Without Sprintzee Hershkovitz, this "trinity" of Rabbis would not be of the same caliber.

My very close friends: Rabbis Moshe, Shimon and Avraham Benzaquen are a major source of inspiration. With them, I feel part of a family. They make me proud to be a Sephardi.

My wife and I could not have hoped for better *mechutanim* than Mr. and Mrs. David Haskel Cohen, Rabbi Chaim Walkin and Rebbezin Henny and Dr. Berl Rudensky and his dear wife Dassy. May we enjoy together good friendship and *nachat* from our children and grandchildren. Our friendship with Rabbi Pesach and Rivka Rosenzweig continues to be an everlasting one. May Rivka have a *refua shelema*.

My dear mother, Bertha Lopes Cardozo, and my-mother-in-law Rosa Gnesin, together with my brother Jacques and his wife Eva, show infinite love for my family and me. My brother has been a constant support while I found my way to Judaism. May God grant them all many years of health. Annemarie and Kees Zwaan, my nephew Mishael and nieces Eva en Sharon Lopes Cardozo are all close to my heart. May they and their friends be blessed.

As always, the pater familias, Rabbi Abraham Lopes Cardozo from New York and his dear wife Irma are the pride of our family. May they go from *chayil* to *chayil*. Abraham's songs together with those of professor Hans Bloemendal, a famous chazan in Amsterdam and many other *chazanim*, accompany me till deep in the night. Without them, together with Beethoven, Mozart, Johann Sebastian Bach and Leonard Bernstein, I would have been unable to write this book.

My dear daughter, Devora Sara with her husband Rabbi Michael Cohen, together with their lovely children Tzipora, Leah, Tzivya and Yacov Shlomo, called after my dear and unforgettable father; my dear son Shimon Moshe Chezkiyahu with his lovely wife Tzippora Chani and their children, Sara Ruth and Abigail Dina and my daughter Michal Abigail and her husband Yitschak Elchanan Walkin with their children Yael, Avital and Refael Zvi are a source of constant *nachat*. May they all live a life of health, success and *yirat shamayim*.

Special mention should again be made of my dear friends Aaron and Bep Spijer from The Hague, Holland, whose help has been extraordinary. My weekly correspondence with Aaron, his observations on *parashat hashavua* and other matters of importance are food for my soul. Bep's delicious food including her superb *"boerenkool"* is a *simcha* for both soul and body. May *Hakadosh Baruch Hu* bless them with good health and *arichat yamim*.

Finally, I pray that my dear wife Frijda Rachel, and our two daughters who are still at home, Nechama Shulamith and Elisheva Yehudith, will receive infinite blessings from the Almighty. Their concern and love for me is the very air I breathe. Without them, life would be without music.

To the Almighty I say: *Chazak uBaruch* for all the thousands of things You do for my family of which I am unaware. The ways in which You guide my life are obscure, yet Your hand could not be clearer.

NLC

Dedicated to

Hilel and Sara Namvar

from all their children
with love

Dedicated to

Bruno

who has been a constant source of challenge and love

David and Evelyne Guez

With love for our dear parents

Doris and Salim Zeloof
and
Nelly and David Blanga

to whom we owe so much

Bettina and David Zeloof
Ariella and Charles Zeloof
and children

*In honor of my wife, Tziporah Pomeranz, thanks for the
constant love and devotion that you give to me and our three
precious children—we love you*
Norman

§ §

*In honor of my grandmother, Rose Feingold,
the hero in my life*
Tom Feingold

§ §

*In honor of our three blessed children,
Shoshana Avigayil, Amalyah Tamar and Avrohom Kurz,
Larry and Dora Kurz*

§ §

*In honor of my wife, Mia Markoff,
who has really mastered the art of being a great mother, wife,
organizer—and is my best friend*
Brad

To my wife, Sandy,
and my children Jackie and Victor, Joanna and David,
David, Daniel and my grandchildren Maiah and Tahli
They should learn to love Torah and Judaism as I have with
the help of great scholars like Rabbi Cardozo
Michael A. Feldmar

§   §

Dedicated by
Marshall and Ellie Jaffe Kulman
In memory of their parents,
George and Joan Jaffe, Alex and Hilda Kulman

§   §

Dedicated to our parents,
Max and Edith Kahn and Sidney and Renee Parker,
who provide endless love and support
Rick and Jill Kahn

§   §

For our children, Andrew and Bradley Garon,
Dor le Dor with much love
Mom and Dad
(Lori and Larry Garon)

In loving memory of our great-grandmother,
Sara Goldstein Klein
and beloved parents,
Lyla and Herschel Avraham Weintraub
Susan, Peter, Lauren, Ariela and Jennifer

§ §

In honor
of
Elan and Victoria Shasha

§ §

Dedicated in memory of my dear mother,
Muriel Hope Sokol,
With love
Stacy L. Sokol

§ §

In loving memory
of
HaRav Moshe Fruchter and Mr. Pinchas Pollak
Jona and Tzivya Pollak

BY WAY OF INTRODUCTION

The discussion, which follows, has taken place over several years. I put it in the written form of a one week encounter between a student and myself. In reality, there were numerous people who were keen to learn my opinions on many subjects.

No doubt this book will annoy some people, amuse others and, hopefully, be of interest to many. Its title: *Judaism on Trial* may sound presumptuous. Who can judge Judaism? The purpose of a trial, however, is not just merely confined to the convicting or acquittal; it often functions as a means through which one is able to bring out the best in the defendant. It is my sincere belief that when Judaism would face trial, its sublimity would be enhanced. The term "trial" also expresses the hope that this book will motivate readers to give Judaism a sincere and honest hearing, encouraging them to contemplate its importance and to "give it a try."

I am willing to admit that several people attempted to put some order into the contents, but to no avail and gave up. I seek solace in a statement by Henry Miller, who said that confusion is a word we have invented for an order, which is not under-stood. In that way, I display my disorderly insights flagrantly, leaving the reader with the impression that he or she is reading the work of a genius.

My enjoyment of writing this book has not been detracted by the pain I experienced due to surgery. Losing my voice entirely for a long period of time allowed me to concentrate on the book. I am sure that this bout of speechlessness was a divine hint that I should refrain from speech. It is debatable, however, if this meant that I should be writing a book instead. I bless the good Lord for having relieved me of that pain and for restoring my voice after a long time. Despite suffering such extreme pain to the extent that I was unable to sit behind the word-processor for longer than a few minutes, I thank God for mercifully assisting me in bringing this book to fruition. In those moments of pain, I would allow my mind to float freely as I recalled past discussions.

The only thing I can safely conclude from this book is its unconventional nature. Seriousness is intertwined with wit, leaving it the task of the reader to decide which is which. Some parts will appear to be simplistic, light reading while others will be challenging and terminologically complex. The readers will doubtlessly feel the sensation that they are floating on a boat, in which they periodically encounter moments of pleasant weather only to turn the page, finding themselves engulfed in a storm. Every topic should be carefully contemplated. Although I have been brief, there is more there than meets the eye. My greatest hope is that one day I will be able to write a work, which will surpass this book by far and gladden those who are now annoyed and surprise those who are now disappointed.

Now that I have violated all the rules regarding how an introduction should probably be written, I would like to wish the reader the blessings of the Lord of the Universe.

Nathan Lopes Cardozo
Shevat 5760 / January 2000
From my comfortable armchair overlooking the hills of Jerusalem

*   *   *

It is a great privilege to present to the public the second edition of *Judaism on Trial.* The first edition was sold out within a few months and received many positive responses and reviews.

Aside from the novel understandings which I introduced regarding Judaism, Jews and the Jewish State, I believe that because Israel now finds itself once more in serious conflict, my observations on the Middle East discord are more relevant than ever. It is tempting to add more insights regarding these circumstances and their possible resolution. Perhaps I will have the opportunity of doing so at a later date in another book.

I pray that the Middle East will soon witness real peace and I hope that my humble observations will make a small contribution in fulfilling this goal.

Marcheshvan 5761 / October 2000

DAY ONE

The Chimpanzees of Texas; To Be Bored Is Beastly; Robert Assagioli and the Three Stonecutters; Halacha As A Religious Behaviorism; The Chassidic Rabbi Who Did Not Fast on *Yom Kippur*; The "As If" Principle; The Tyranny of the Telephone; Chaos Breeds Life While Order Breeds Habit; Judaism on Trial?; To Blame Judaism For Its Own Defeat?; There Is Nothing More Irrelevant Than an Answer to a Question Nobody Asks; To Ignore the Claim; *Mah Nishtana*?; A Guide to Make People Perplexed; The Fear to Ask; Relevance and the Need For Change; The Need For Creativity; To Re-work the Classics; The Forgotten Masters; Halacha and Aggada; Rabbi Chaim Soloveitchik and His Grandson; Secular Thought As an Interpretation of Judaism?; World Literature Is a Commentary on the Torah; The Application of Halacha Changes Precisely Because the Torah Does Not Change; Teaching Torah to Women Is to Teach Them Folly?; The Case of the *Beth Yaacov* Revolution; The Prohibition of Applying the Wrong Halacha; To Go or Not to Go to *Beth Yaacov*; The Conversion Crisis; The Danger of Three Jewish Peoples; The Halachic Demand to Stay One Nation; A Halachic Conflict of Interest; Divine Promise?; The Case of Esther; Esther Was Permitted to Marry Achashverosh; The Actual Situation?; The Halacha Is Not Changed or Abolished; Do Women Really Want to Marry Anybody?; Another Solution to the Conversion Crisis; Marriage Yes, Divorce No; The Problem of Adultery; Only the Orthodox Will Convert; A One Way Road; A Common Denominator; "But"; Cardinal Newman; Conscience Is the Last Word; Two Ways to Compromise; To Save the Situation; Winston Churchill and Democracy

THE CHIMPANZEES OF TEXAS

Student: Rabbi Cardozo, a manufacturer in Texas was once overcome by a strange whim. He wanted to employ a few hundred chimpanzees in his furniture factory, where all the goods were produced by means of a conveyer-belt. He had hundreds of people employed to do nothing else except for this one action; repeated and executed with absolute perfection, ad nauseum. The manufacturer was suddenly overcome with a flash of inspiration. The idea that came to him was that he could employ several hundred monkeys to do the same work. All it required was the repetition of the same action from early morning till late in the afternoon; requiring neither creativity nor any special level of concentration. One person needed to drill a hole in a piece of wood, another to add a screw and the third to cut it to size.

The manufacturer thus decided to employ a large number of chimpanzees. He trained them, sent all his employees home, replaced paychecks with bananas and waited expectantly to see what would happen. For several hours, everything went smoothly, but suddenly the monkeys lost control. One hammered all the screws in the floor, another sat himself comfortably on the conveyer-belt, while yet another took a nap or hung from a lamp. The manufacturer was more than perturbed and wondered what had gone wrong. After all, this was surely work fit for monkeys. Why did they not behave the way they should?

LC (Lopes Cardozo): It seems to me that the manufacturer missed the point entirely.

Student: Why?

TO BE BORED IS BEASTLY

LC: Because this kind of monotonous work reveals one of the great qualities with which man is endowed: the ability to give a spiritual dimension to that which otherwise belongs in the animal realm. The central issue here is boredom. To overcome boredom is a quintessential human challenge. True, on a superficial level, the repetition of only one action throughout the day suggests a beastly existence, but in reality it is not. To survive boredom one must see behind a single monotonous act, something of a higher order. This may manifest itself in a feeling that one supports a loving family, or in the knowledge that one day one will be able to buy a home or contribute to a spiritual cause.

ROBERTO ASSAGIOLI AND THE THREE STONECUTTERS

I recall the great Italian psychiatrist, Roberto Assagioli, who once wrote a parable about interviewing three stonecutters, who were building a cathedral in the fourteenth century. When he asked the first stonecutter what he was doing, the man bitterly replied that he was cutting stone into blocks, one foot by one foot by three-quarters of a foot. With much frustration, he described his life as one of perpetual boredom, having to cut stone for the rest of his life. The second stonecutter had exactly the same job, but had a different attitude. He told the interviewer warmly that he was earning a living for his beloved family, so that he could clothe and feed his children, while he and his wife created a nurturing home built on love. But when the interviewer came to the third stonecutter, he heard a joyous voice telling him what a privilege it was to participate in the building of a great cathedral, so strong, that it will stand as a place of God for thousands of years to come. All three crafts-men did the same work, but only the one who looked beyond the immediate task at hand, was in love with his work.

It is important to understand the reason behind man's capa-bility and willingness to do boring work. His subconscious propels him to believe that there is a loftier, spiritual dimension to life. This enables him to look beyond the mundane nature of his daily work, and to even infuse it with spiritual meaning. Religion is at the core of this subconscious knowledge. To be placed in this world is by its very nature mysterious. It alludes to a higher order of things. This awareness is the reason why people are able to endure the most desperate and painful conditions. They know that there is more to life than meets the eye and are therefore able to tolerate what animals cannot.

In other words, man is by definition a religious creature, which manifests itself not only through his religious worship, but above all through the way in which he experiences the mundane. An animal will only work to gratify its desires. Once its desire is sated, it abandons its work. A human surpasses this level, because he or she is aware of a greater meaning.

To cultivate the mystery of existence, through which man is able to surpass his or her physical existence, is to acknowledge the presence of a transcendent meaning.

Student: But if it is indeed true that religion is the encounter with the enigmatic, why is Judaism so concerned with the external and purely physical side of human existence?

LC: What do you mean?

HALACHA AS A RELIGIOUS BEHAVIORISM

Student: Over the years I have had several discussions with my Jewish, religious friends. Whenever I spoke to them, in order to understand the Jewish tradition, I was always under the impression that Judaism is a kind of religious behaviorism, in which external compliance with thousands of laws is of supreme importance. Matters such as inner devotion, the imponderable, religious experience, and the need to belong to something noble and uplifting seemed relatively unimportant. There is really only one discipline that counts and that is Halacha, Jewish law. If you live according to its many demands you are a fine, upstanding Jew (even when there is little else that is spiritual about you). If you do not comply, you are inadequate. It reduces Judaism to a sort of sacred physics, that lacks any need for the introspective and metaphysical.

You will perhaps argue that these young men do not really know enough about Judaism to make such sweeping observations. But my problem is that when I look closely at the Orthodox Jewish community, I indeed feel that these observations are universally correct. Orthodox Jews are always occupied with the minutiae of the law, while neglecting the broader spiritual dimension. They prioritize the law over ideas, and outward action over the spiritual needs of the soul. Is this really what Judaism is all about?

THE CHASSIDIC RABBI WHO DID NOT FAST ON *YOM KIPPUR*

LC: You've touched on many issues here. So let me answer you briefly for the moment, by confessing that I myself have wrestled with this issue for many years, until somebody told me the following story.

His closest disciples once approached a great Chassidic Rebbe, known to be a holy man. They asked him how many days in the week he was actually fasting. After all, such a holy man would, no doubt, fast frequently. The Rebbe smiled and told them that he never fasted! Flabbergasted by his response, they asked him what he did on *Yom Kippur*, the holiest day of the Jewish year, the Day of Atonement, on which the Jew is forbidden to eat or drink.

The Rebbe smiled: "I do not fast on *Yom Kippur*." "You don't?" said the disciples, aghast.

"No," said the Rebbe, "you see, I just have no time to eat on *Yom Kippur*. It is the only day of the year on which we are able to do complete *teshuva*, repentance. So how has one time to eat?"

Astonished by this reply, the disciples asked him what their teacher did on *Tisha be'Av*, the ninth day of the Hebrew month of *Av*, commemorating the destruction of both Temples. Did Jewish law not demand that every Jew fast on that day? "Ah," said the Rebbe, "you do not understand. On *Tisha be'Av*, I just cannot eat. On that day I lose all appetite. So many tragedies occurred on this day. Do you really believe that I am able to eat? It is not that I fast, I simply cannot eat!" For me, this answer captures the essence of Judaism. What is it that Judaism wants to achieve? The answer is clear: the outer act should be the spontaneous reflection of man's inner emotions, so that the difference between the spirit of the Torah and the essence of the human being is no longer discernible.

A great Rabbi once wrote: "The divine Torah should become the very essence of man, so that a person can no longer be conceived as man without Torah, as little as he can be conceived as man without life."[1]

Student: I am not sure I fully understand. Could you elaborate on this a little more?

THE "AS IF" PRINCIPLE

LC: When the Torah introduces a prohibition, it does so with the hope that one day this prohibition will be internalized to the degree that external pressure in the form of this law is no longer needed. It will have become an integral part of our nature; our so-called "second nature." But we cannot achieve this on our own. It first needs to be introduced as an external force, in the form of one of the Torah's prohibitions. I call this the "as if" principle. First we listen to and observe the demands made by the Torah. This results in improved standards of our behavior, "as if" we have actually reached that level, although in reality, we have not.

The Torah, for example, prohibits the consumption of food on *Yom Kippur* because, aside from other factors, it wants us to realize that we should not really have time to eat or drink on such a day. So it tells us to act "as if" we actually operate on such a spiritual level and indeed have no time to eat. The goal, however, is that one day, after many years of observing *Yom Kippur*, we will begin to internalize the awesomeness of the day, rendering us incapable of even contemplating eating or

---

[1] Rabbi Moshe Almosnino, *Tefillat LeMoshe*, p. 11a.

drinking. The monumental importance of the day will super-sede all other concerns. What was external is now internal! What initially appeared as a prohibition is now transformed into our own will. The commandments are not given just to perform, but to transform. Jewish law is constantly trying to educate man, so that one day he will be receptive to the more subtle and refined dimensions of his spiritual existence.

Student: That sounds very nice, and makes sense for those commandments that have a clear moral message. But why are there so many rituals and prohibitions that can only cause a person to feel restricted? It is hard to imagine how a person's moral fiber could be improved under such conditions.

LC: Give me a specific example.

Student: Take the example of Shabbat. One is not even allowed to use the telephone on the Shabbat! What could be the moral purpose behind that? It clearly prevents a person from communicating with the world. He may as well revert back to the Middle Ages!

THE TYRANNY OF THE TELEPHONE

LC: Let me ask you a question: do you really consider this constraint on using the telephone on Shabbat a prohibition?

Student: What is the question? It is obviously a prohibition!

LC: I would strongly disagree with you. For me it is a positive commandment!

Student: How can that possibly be?

LC: Simply this: one of the greatest problems of this century is that our privacy is increasingly denied us. One of the more obvious disturbances to our everyday sense of self is the portable telephone. Not an hour passes without somebody calling to infringe on our privacy. Seemingly, every time I try to speak to my wife, children, or grandchildren, the phone rings and my conversation is interrupted. This has become so overwhelming, that it can result in our losing the quiet so necessary for our inner peace of mind. One manifestation of this loss may be our need to escape our own surroundings, or perhaps, even, to consult a psychologist.

On Shabbat, we are liberated from the tyranny of the telephone, so we experience some elevated tranquility. I can, at least once a week, "take revenge" on this irritating device, by "unplugging it" from my life every Friday afternoon till Saturday night. With tongue-in-cheek, I would have to ask why the Rabbis do not prescribe a blessing to be said before one performs this act?

Student: A blessing for this act?

LC: Why not, indeed? It may very well be my greatest religious act of the week! It creates an oasis of rest in a turbulent sea of worldliness. The inability to use the telephone is not a prohibition, but liberation! It gives me time for my family, allowing me to study, sing, and contemplate my life and that of my family, my community and perhaps all of mankind. It creates a completely new perspective on life. So, what you call a Shabbat prohibition is to me a positive, liberating commandment! It is not the modern, superficial "freedom" governed by spontaneous impulse, but rather genuine freedom and peace for my soul as well as my body. It is true no less of the car or the computer. We need to free ourselves of these devices before they dominate us. This is what Shabbat offers us. I dare to argue that this is true of all the prohibitions. They are all reversed positive commandments!

CHAOS BREEDS LIFE WHILE ORDER BREEDS HABIT

Student: I see your point, although I am not sure I accept it, not at least without some elaboration. I would really like you to expand on these unusual observations, but I planned a careful list of questions and issues, which I would like to raise with you in an orderly fashion.

LC: Don't worry if our discussion is chaotic. That is what is so enjoyable about a good argument. Henry Adams once said: "Chaos often breeds life when order breeds habit!"[2] But you are right, let us at least *try* to keep some order to our conversation.

Student: Okay, but forgive me if I sometimes ask you a "dislocated" question in order to hear your views on issues that confuse me.

LC: Please feel free to do so.

Student: You told me that you would like to write a book based on these discussions to be called: "Judaism on Trial." Why this title? Does one need to put Judaism on trial?

---

[2] *The Education of Henry Adams* (1907) p. 16.

JUDAISM ON TRIAL?

LC: First of all, there is a double meaning to the word trial. It could mean to try something out, as in giving it a chance. Or indeed as trying something—in the sense that one examines it for its truth or integrity.

I had both in mind when I suggested this title, but I believe that the second interpretation is of crucial importance. One has to put Judaism on trial because this is the only way one can fully appreciate its teachings. This is something I have done my whole life to great advantage. I'll tell you why. Many people today blame philosophy, science and other modern disciplines for the eclipse of Judaism and of other religions. But I do not agree with this approach. We have to blame those responsible for teaching Judaism for this distortion. There are two possible reasons why we are confronted with such a bitter rejection of authentic Judaism today. The first explanation is that we take Judaism for granted—as many people in the religious world do, thus failing to explain and understand Judaism in an adequate way. The second reason for Judaism's rejection is sheer ignorance.

Student: What do you mean?

LC: I believe that the Jewish religious community takes Judaism for granted, because it almost never questions its premises or studies its belief system with a critical eye.

Student: Why should it? Is it not wonderful when you are convinced of the authenticity of something precious? Why question it?

LC: You would be right, if such an approach would result in a greater appreciation of Judaism. But one has to realize that without questioning, one never discovers the deeper and, therefore, more sophisticated premises of that which one really cherishes. When I myself was uninvolved, intellectually or practically speaking, in the Jewish tradition, I spoke with many religious Jews only to discover that many of them were unable to explain Judaism in a coherent way. At the time, Judaism was a great puzzle for me; it made obscure claims, and demanded a very bizarre lifestyle which I felt was outrageous. When I probed for a possible deeper meaning to all I saw, I was met with complete silence.

I also found that there were some Jews who lived a religious life, not out of love, but out of habit, and that many lacked any real enthusiasm for the Jewish tradition. Several told me that they would really like to reject Judaism but were unable because their families and friends would ostracize them. I must tell you candidly that later on, when I started to practice Judaism and to appreciate its meaning, I was asked to meet some religious teachers and people whose superior knowledge of the Talmud and other classical works by far exceeded my own.

When they came to my home I was very surprised to hear that they had lost their belief in Judaism and urged me to tell them why *I* believed that it was such a great tradition!

Student: I do not understand. How can people with more knowledge than yourself come to ask you why Judaism is so wonderful? Would not their own studies have shown them that?

LC: I also would have thought that. Although it took me a long time to grasp the reason, I would venture to say that today I understand.

Student: Perhaps you can explain.

TO BLAME JUDAISM FOR ITS OWN DEFEAT?

LC: As previously mentioned, it is common to blame science and anti-religious philosophy for the eclipse of Judaism. But it would be wiser to blame Judaism for its own defeat. This is not to say that there is a flaw within Judaism. I prefer to think that the way it has been taught in "modern" times has made it appear irrelevant to the needs and problems of modern man. Not because it was refuted and out–dated, but because it was taught in ways which made it dull, oppressive and insipid. If Judaism is taught as a kind of dogmatic creed, if it can no longer contain exciting spontaneous worship, but remains formalistic and completely disciplined; if it has replaced love with habit, if it has become a tradition instead of being a flowing fountain and is only able to keep itself alive on the basis of authority, instead of reflecting deep compassion—then it becomes meaningless.

This is what I realized when I spoke with these teachers. To them, Judaism had become a dogma, a discipline, only capable of surviving on the basis of traditional authority. This is a great tragedy; a sparkling fountain robbed of its vital water source. As a result, it is unable to be responsive and meaningful to contemporary people. In many cases these are the most curious and searching individuals. It was only through questioning and struggling with Judaism that I came to realize that this was not merely an old fashioned tradition, but a living faith fired by a deep and persuasive passion. I believe that Judaism's strength is shown in its best light through constant struggle and questioning. Only through probing are the depths of Judaism revealed in all their power and beauty.

Student: What about the problem of ignorance?

LC: Well, how many secular Jews have really taken the time to study the Jewish tradition before they rejected it? A majority of the Jewish people today are secular, but it is very clear that the vast majority are not secular by conviction, but rather out of inertia. I have never understood how one can reject or ignore something, without previous study. I fully understand a person who carefully studied a tradition and concluded that it was false. But one cannot have an opinion based on ignorance.

When it comes to Judaism, many secular Jews are guilty of the very small-mindedness of which they accuse most Orthodox Jews. Moreover, they show a high degree of intolerance and irreligious extremism.

Student: Your observations put the onus on the secular community. This is an angle I had not considered before.

THERE IS NOTHING MORE IRRELEVANT THAN AN ANSWER TO A QUESTION NOBODY ASKS

LC: To be honest with oneself, one needs to address those ultimate questions, which touch on the meaning of one's own existence and that of the universe. But this means that one needs to know the art of asking and probing. I think it was the famous American Christian thinker, Reinhold Niebuhr, who once said: "There is nothing more irrelevant than an answer to a question nobody asks!" That is perhaps the greatest tragedy today within the Jewish community. Many people have rejected Judaism, not because they found Judaism really wanting, but because they failed to ask any questions relating to the meaning and purpose of their lives. Most people do not realize that no answer makes sense if it has not been preceded by a question. Judaism offers an answer. It is an answer to man's ultimate questions concerning life, existence and spirituality. But if these answers are not accompanied by questions, they become dull and meaningless. The problem is not that there are no answers, but that there are no questions!

Student: You are saying that this is a *sine qua non* (an indispensable condition)?

TO IGNORE THE CLAIM

LC: Yes, but I am saying even more. How is it possible that millions of Jews ignore Judaism when they know that, for centuries, their parents and grandparents dedicated their lives for this religion? One can even claim that one's forefathers were mistaken. But without prior further investigation one can not ignore this claim to the truth, for the sake of which millions of our forefathers died. We should never forget that today we are Jews because our ancestors believed in the eternity of Judaism. We owe it to them, but even more so to ourselves, to give it at least the benefit of the doubt. Anything less would be dishonest and inconsistent.

Student: Yet, it seems strange that Judaism is best found through questioning.

LC: I can give you an illustration of which I'm sure you are familiar. Let me put it in the form of a question: which is the most important "educational" night in the whole of the Jewish Year?

Student: Mm. I suppose *Pesach* night, the night of seder, when we tell the story of the exodus from Egypt.

LC: Right! And how do we start this night?

MAH NISHTANA?

Student: By making our children ask the famous four questions: *Mah Nishtana*? What is the difference between this night and all other nights?

LC: And why do we do this? Why don't we simply relate the story of the exodus of Egypt to our children without making them first ask questions?

Student: To make them ask even more questions?

LC: Exactly. Only when one masters the art of asking, can one appreciate an answer. The four questions of the Seder night are, in fact, only appetizers to make the children and grown-ups ask hundreds of other questions concerning the exodus of Egypt. In this way, we are able to appreciate the full message of the Exodus.

A GUIDE TO MAKE PEOPLE PERPLEXED

To return to my earlier observations, I remember that I was once asked why the Rabbis of our century did not write an updated *Guide for the Perplexed*, as Maimonides did in his

days—as you may know, this is Maimonides' great philosophical work on Judaism.

My answer may sound ludicrous, but I replied that I did not
see any reason to write another Guide for the Perplexed, since
almost nobody seems to be either philosophically or meta-
physically perplexed! If anything is needed, it is a book that
will *make* people existentially perplexed! Today, very few
people ask questions of a profound nature. Most of our questions demand immediate practical resolution. As, such I could
argue, with tongue in cheek, that the Torah made one vital
"mistake."

Student: Which is what?

LC: That it forgot to write down the big questions! Perhaps
God should have first offered a Torah of questions, and only
after the Israelites had studied and contemplated them for a
while, should He have given the Torah as we know it today:
the Torah of answers. This is the very reason why Judaism has
become so irrelevant to most people. The Torah became
irrelevant because *life* became irrelevant!

THE FEAR TO ASK

Student: Is this the reason why so few people search for the
higher meaning in life? Surely these profound questions are no
less relevant today than they were in the past, when man
grappled with them?

LC: One of the reasons for this current state of inertia is that
people are afraid to ask any existential questions because they
fear the answers. Many profound answers will not tally with
our desire for and understanding of just having a "good time."

They will highlight the truth that one can only have "a good time" when one fully understands what it is to be alive. In fact, many ultimate answers will often challenge our lifestyle and "ideologies." It is thus safer not to ask, so as not to receive the "wrong" answer!

Student: Does this mean that an individual should not reap the benefits of the luxuries that today's world has to offer?

LC: I am saying that one cannot experience the enjoyment of comfort and luxuries without seeing them in a larger context; that is, within an exalted realm of existence. There is the need to question and struggle with Judaism because otherwise it becomes irrelevant and outdated.

Student: How could Judaism become outdated when it is the word of God, and by extension, also eternal?

LC: Judaism can only claim to represent the word of God if it is eternally relevant to all generations and circumstances. It is only through challenging it that we are able to re-establish its primacy.

Student: Are you saying that Judaism needs to change so as to make it relevant to new generations?

RELEVANCE AND THE NEED FOR CHANGE

LC: It depends what you mean by relevance and change. From one perspective, the Torah is "beyond time and place" and therefore "unchangeable and immutable." It is the word of God and it is not for man to change. However, it needs to be "progressive" so as to be relevant to contemporary eras. There are two dimensions to this. One is philosophical, and the other one relates to Jewish law. Philosophically, it is more a re-statement of Judaism, which is required, not an actual change. This can only come about when we ask questions pertaining to our present situation, and when new dimensions of Judaism are displayed. The Jewish perspective of life needs to be translated to the language of each generation. This has happened throughout Jewish history. *The Guide for the Perplexed* is a prime example. In this work, Maimonides tried to communicate the great foundations of Jewish belief in the language of his time. This required his speaking in the tradition of Aristotle and some Arab thinkers, who, in the tenth century, were considered to be the representatives of the "truth."

In order for Jews to take the Jewish tradition seriously, Judaism needed to be explained in the style of teaching of people like Aristotle. It was the language of most intellectual Jews. I am convinced that had Maimonides lived today, he would have written a completely different work on the philosophy of Judaism. He would have based his work on the state of the prevalent intellectual climate. The foundations of Judaism itself would not have been altered, but merely the methods in which they were imparted. Moreover, one should not forget that Judaism has never been prepared to put all its eggs in one basket. Earlier and later works on Judaism show great diversity of opinion on how to understand the foundation of the Jewish tradition. Matters like the nature of God, revelation, reward and punishment and so on, have been explained in many different ways. I do not believe that there is one paramount rationale for them present within Jewish thought.

Rabbi Josef Albo (15th century) took a very different stand to that of Maimonides (11th century), as did Nachmanides (12th century), Maharal (17th century), Rabbi Samson Raphael Hirsch (19th century), Rabbi Kook *z"l* and Rabbi Soloveitchik *z"l*, in our own generation. These differences of opinion can be compared to those apparent in the multitude of commentaries on the Torah. Even though each thinker's approach is unique, nonetheless, all agree about the foundation, which includes the infallibility of the text of the Torah as the word of God as revealed at Sinai.

THE NEED FOR CREATIVITY

Student: But is it not true that, in this past century, little sign of creativity has been displayed in translating the Jewish tradition to the language of today?

LC: That is true. Rabbi Samson Raphael Hirsch probably made the last significant attempt in nineteenth century Germany. Rabbi Kook and Rabbi Soloveitchik, who were perhaps the most Western oriented intellectual rabbinical thinkers of our days, did not offer a comprehensive explanation of all of Judaism. They only dealt with specific areas. Interestingly, it is within the Conservative Movement that there have been some major attempts at a comprehensive reinterpretation. But these are often unacceptable from an Orthodox perspective because they reject the verbal divine transmission of the Torah and the foundations of the oral traditions as understood by traditional Judaism.

Student: Does that mean that there are only a few Orthodox scholars who have written about the foundations of Judaism in the language of our time?

LC: To my regret, yes. There are, however, some personalities of great intellectual stature who have dealt with the Jewish *weltanschauung* (worldview) in a profound way. In the yeshiva world, it was Rabbi Eliyahu Eliezer Dessler *z"l*, who made a major, and, I believe, a successful attempt.[3]

Other profound thinkers in the yeshiva world are Rabbi Yitschak Hutner *z"l*,[4] and Rabbi Shlomo Wolbe.[5] But none of them offered a comprehensive introduction to Judaism.

It should also be emphasized that these works deal more with the inner world of the yeshiva personality than with problems confronting the modern secular world. Nevertheless, there are quite a few other books which do attempt to reintroduce Orthodox Judaism to the Orthodox Jew, but very few of them carry intellectual depth or offer fresh and profound insights.

Given these limitations, it would still be possible to obtain an overall worldview of contemporary Orthodoxy from the works of Rabbis Kook and Soloveitchik. These thinkers were the most creative and comprehensive of their generation and offered many new approaches to the Jewish tradition. Even so, neither left us all–encompassing works.

Student: But there is a real need for it.

LC: Certainly. As I said before, I believe that there is a lot of room for innovations within Torah literature. I believe that there are many dimensions within traditional Judaism which are still to be revealed. Much could be done, for example, through comparative studies. It would be helpful to affirm Judaism's main belief system by comparing it to the Far Eastern religions, or to Christianity. It would accentuate Judaism's many original contributions to the universal world of

---

[3] See *Michtav Me'Eliyahu* (Jersualem, 1997).

[4] *Pachad Yitzchak* (NY, 1966).

[5] *Alei Shor*, books 1 and 2 (Jerusalem, 1998).

belief. It could show the "borderlines" of Judaism, which could generate a most fascinating and instructive literature.

The same thing, I think, can apply to discussing the differences between traditional Judaism and the Conservative and Reform movements. More time should be devoted to illustrate the intellectual differences between Orthodox Judaism and these ideologies.

Student: So there is a lot of creative work to be done?

TO RE-WORK THE CLASSICS

LC: I would say that it is one of the great contemporary challenges for traditional Judaism. Certainly, those who espouse traditional Judaism, and wish to influence the intellectual community, will have to be much more active. I believe that in this respect, there is a problem within the Orthodox communities. In today's Orthodox world, the focus is on practical Halacha, almost to the exclusion of any other branch of Judaism. Only in women's colleges and in the *yeshivot* of the *ba'al teshuva* movement is some attention given to those philosophical perspectives. Even then, this is not always done adequately, as the deeper elements within Judaism are not always properly discussed.

Another problem is that most of these institutions for the newly religious focus on the classics, such as the works of Maimonides, Yehuda HaLevi and Moshe Chaim Luzzato. While these are of the greatest importance, they were primarily written for the times in which they lived. These works need to be taken and "re-worked," so as to make them relevant for today's questioning Jews. If this is considered less desirable—because of the fear that one may lose out on the intrinsic beauty of these classic works—let there at least be comprehensive commentaries available for the Jews of this century.

THE FORGOTTEN MASTERS

It should also be observed that, apart from the works of Rabbis Kook and Soloveitchik, there are some other modern thinkers of distinction who have written some remarkable works. Disturbingly enough, most Orthodox Jewish students ignore these thinkers to a large degree. I am referring to the works of Rabbi Eliezer Berkovits,[6] Professors Michael Wyschgrod,[7] Andre Neher,[8] Norman Lamm,[9] and Shalom Rosenberg,[10] or even a radical like Professor Yeshayahu Leibowitz,[11] and others.

My impression is that the Orthodox community does not take some of them seriously, which, if true, is tragic. This is also the case with the multifaceted writings of the late Lubavitcher Rebbe, *z"l*. Hardly anybody seems to study these works (*sichot*), outside the Chabad community. This is again a great pity, because the Lubavitcher Rebbe left us with a rich legacy of ideas, which, I believe, are unprecedented.

---

[6] For example see: *God, Man and History* (NY: Jonathan David, 1959) and *Major Themes in Modern Philosophies of Judaism* (NY: Ktav, 1974).
[7] For example see: *The Body of Faith* (NJ: Jason Aronson, 1996).
[8] *The Exile of the Word* (Philadelphia: Jewish Publication Society, 1981).
[9] For example see: *Faith and Doubt* (NY: Ktav, 1998).
[10] For example see: *Good and Evil in Jewish Thought* (Tel Aviv: Ministry of Defense, 1989).
[11] For example see: *Judaism, Human Values and the Jewish State* (Cambridge, MA: Harvard University, 1992).

Strangely enough, it is the so-called ultra-Orthodox institutions that give little time to matters of philosophy and *weltanschauung*. It is particularly in these circles that there appears to be no works on these topics. It is there that Halacha reigns supreme, giving the impression, that besides pure Halacha, there is nothing else. But, as I have already argued, this narrow focus results in an inability to explain the meaning behind the halachic system, despite the fact that Orthodox students study Halacha with great care and diligence.

Do not misunderstand me, Halacha is by far the most authentic expression of traditional Judaism, but we cannot fail to recognize that its very *weltanschauung* is, to a great extent, ignored by those who are its greatest admirers. This matter is especially worrisome since it is clearly impossible to attract non-religious Jews to Judaism merely on the basis of its laws, without giving intellectual newcomers a comprehensive ideological insight into that law. I believe that this is also one of the reasons why some Orthodox youngsters leave the fold. The halachic system appears to them like a form of religious behaviorism.

Student: This echoes a point I raised at the beginning of our discussion. I mentioned then that some of my friends believe that the perfunctory obedience of the law is the essence.

LC: And what about the other aspects of Judaism? Issues related to the existence of God, His attributes, matters like transcendence and immanence, omnipotence and omniscience? What of providence, the love and fear of God, the concept of faith, the Chosen People, Judaism and its relation to other religions, the messianic hope and the hereafter—to mention just a few. What about the Aggada?

Student: What is Aggada?

HALACHA AND AGGADA

LC: Halacha can inform man how to act in any given situation. However, it cannot provide insight into the quality of a given act, or a sense of the spiritual transformation that comes as a result of the performance of, or adherence to, a specific dictate. That is the domain of Aggada. The word Aggada is derived from the Hebrew root "נגד" meaning to flow, in other words, that side of Judaism which interprets life flow and gives warmth to its halachic directives, through its symbolism. Rather than presenting Halacha in a totalitarian, dictatorial light, Aggada affords a person the ability to come to understand and love the laws that he is observing. Aggada prevents mechanical observance by liberating a person's inner spirit. While Halacha offers individuals consummation, Aggada offers them aspiration.[12]

Nachman Hayyim Bialik once said that "Halacha is the crystallization, the highest quintessence of Aggada, while Aggada is the refinement of Halacha."[13] While the Halacha is a code to all people of all times, basing itself on the capabilities of all Jews in general, the Aggada is free to suggest a greater degree of Godliness, only attainable to a select few.

While there is no other option but to follow Halacha, Aggada sometimes offers suggestions and offers individual choices to each person. It also attracts a person to the teachings of the Halacha. It allows that which is unseen to enter the visible world. It gives the opportunity to delve deep through

---

[12] For a full understanding with examples see Nathan T. Lopes Cardozo, *The Written and Oral Torah*, a comprehensive introduction (NJ: Jason Aronson, 1997) pp. 167–77.
[13] H.N. Bialik, *Halacha and Aggada* (Jerusalem, 1944) Introduction.

the realms of the definable, perceivable and demonstrable. Just as language attempts to allow us to comprehend the intangible, through the use of metaphor, Aggada allows us to begin to comprehend the infinite through the use of symbolism. It is a kind of religious metaphor, a camera that enables us to form mental images of what would otherwise be indescribable. It prevents the dogmatization of the halachic system. Without a proper understanding of this dimension of Judaism, one cannot capture its essence.

Student: This is in some way, then, a response to my earlier criticism that Halacha has been reduced to a kind of external mechanism!

LC: That is true, but this means that students of the Jewish tradition should pay the Aggada far more attention. It is a great pity that *yeshivot* in general fail to do so. Typically, many *yeshivot* skip the aggadic part of the tractate they are studying, thus missing a major dimension of their studies. After all, why should the talmudic sages have included this material if it was not for the purpose of study?

Student: Let us return to our earlier discussion, regarding the pragmatism of Halacha. In what way can we speak about changes while maintaining the authenticity of Halacha?

RABBI CHAIM SOLOVEITCHIK AND HIS GRANDSON

LC: That is a completely different story. But before I elaborate on this, it is worthwhile noting that Rabbi Soloveitchik did make a major attempt to explain the *weltanschauung* of the halachic system. He was one of the greatest halachic minds of our time. His grandfather, the famous Rabbi Chaim

Soloveitchik, created an analytic school of talmudic study, which brought about a major revolution in talmudic learning. His grandson, Rabbi Josef Ber, wrote two major works in which he discussed the world through the perspective of the Halacha.

His first book is called *Ish haHalacha* (*Halachic Man*).[14] This is a phenomenological study of the halachic system and its particular way of looking at the world. In his study, Rabbi Soloveitchik was able to show that the halachic world is not a dry, juristic discipline, but an existential and highly philosophical approach to the complexities of life—a conceptual orientation that gives rise to a very distinctive religious personality.

His second book is called *The Halachic Mind*.[15] In this work, Rabbi Soloveitchik goes even further. He explains how all philosophical and existential dispositions should derive from the Halacha, acting as a central force. This is a revolutionary work.

As far as I know, it is the first time that Halacha became the absolute foundation of the sum-total of the Jewish way of intellectual thought. Though there had been many previous efforts to explain the commandments of the Torah, no attempt had been made to clarify the philosophical foundations of the halachic system.

I believe that Rabbi Soloveitchik clarified the ambivalence expressed in the works of earlier scholars, even Orthodox ones, in their attempt to explain the philosophy of Halacha. It seems to me that the legality, dryness and the "far-fetched" minutiae of the law embarrassed some of them. They felt more comfortable with the prophets and their ethical message than with the halachic system; although they fully supported its authority.

[14] Philadelphia: Jewish Publication Society, 1983.
[15] NY: Seth Press, 1986.

Rabbi Soloveitchik succeeded in restoring the Halacha to its full philosophical glory.

SECULAR THOUGHT AS AN INTERPRETATION OF JUDAISM?

What is of great importance is that Rabbi Soloveitchik was able to infuse ideas based on general philosophy into his philosophy of Halacha. In both works referred to here, we find traces of Neo-Kantian epistemology (the theory of the methods or grounds of knowledge) and metaphysics as developed by several major, secular philosophers.

Student: I suppose that this is something with which not all traditional Jews would be comfortable. The use of non-Jewish sources to explain Judaism could be risky. One can no longer easily differentiate between authentic Judaism and secular thought.

LC: That is true. But for Rabbi Soloveitchik and others, such as Rabbi Kook, this was not a problem. They would never agree that Judaism depends on secular insights. They would ultimately claim that many profound thoughts coming from the secular world are God given. Their function is to explain, up until that point, undiscovered dimensions of Judaism. Their perspective was probably that these various outside philosophies possessed a religious intent.

Student: What do you mean?

LC: They would possibly see a manifestation of divine intervention, or emanation within the philosophical schools of thought in the secular world. These thoughts could find their niche within a religious philosophy in the Torah.

Don't forget that according to most Jewish philosophers, nothing can ever come about without God's constant intervention and will. Jewish philosophers need to ask themselves why there are secular philosophies in the world. They must have a religious value. Ultimately, their response will be that they should facilitate the understanding of the Torah and its application to life.

Student: So the Rabbis would claim that all literature is capable of contributing to Torah knowledge?

WORLD LITERATURE IS A COMMENTARY ON THE TORAH

LC: Not just that. They might also argue that all literature is somehow a commentary on the Torah, although its authors did not have any such intentions in mind when they wrote their works. After all, all literature and philosophy deal with a common issue: practical or metaphysical encounter with this world.Since the Torah can be viewed as God's anthropology of man and His encounter with life, there is a common ground. I admit that this attitude carries serious problems, but it is worthwhile taking note of such an ideology. It was Rabbi Kook, in particular, who constantly emphasized the all encompassing quality of the Torah.[16] According to him, even

---

[16] *Orot Ha'emunah* (Jerusalem: Mosad HaRav Kook, 1985) and *Arpalei Toma* (Jerusalem: Rabbi Zvi Yehudah Kook Institute, 1983).

dimensions of false ideologies such as idol worship or scientific theories (such as the theory of evolution once refined by the monotheistic world view) would lead to a better understanding of the Torah and its application.

THE APPLICATION OF HALACHA CHANGES PRECISELY BECAUSE THE TORAH DOES NOT CHANGE

Student: Okay, but let us come back to the halachic question of change.

LC: Here we encounter a most fascinating but equally dangerous situation. The possibility, or rather the necessity, of changing Halacha is a delicate issue. We have to be extremely careful how we argue in favor of change. The chance that we may fall into semantics is great. Let me therefore clarify this: since the Torah does not change, the application of Halacha *must* change. Expressed differently, the application of Halacha changes precisely because the Torah can never change.

Student: I am not sure I follow you.

LC: Let me put it this way: Halacha is the application of Torah to specific circumstances. Taking into account that circumstances constantly change, different halachic rulings have to be applied which relate to the new circumstances. The theology behind this, I believe, is clear. Since God created Torah, time and space as one, unseverable link, they must co-exist. Since changes take place within time and space, the Torah is only applicable to these new circumstances, when new applications to these changes are an integral part of its nature.

There is a statement by Maimonides which throws some light on this phenomenon: "God knew that the judgments of the

law will always require an extension in some cases and cur-
tailment in others, according to the variety of places, events
and circumstances. He, therefore, cautioned against such
increase and diminution and commanded, 'Do not add to it or
subtract from it'"(*Devarim* 13:1).

Constant changes would, in all probability, disturb the
whole system of the law and would lead people to believe that
the law is not of divine origin.

At the same time, however, permission is given to the wise
men of every generation—namely the *Beth Din HaGadol*
(Rabbinical High Court)—to take precautions with the aim of
consolidating the ordinances of the law. This is achieved by
innovation of the regulations, in order to repair breaches. In the
same manner, they have the power, temporarily, to dispense
with some religious acts prescribed in the law, or to allow that
which is forbidden, if exceptional circumstances and events
require it. Through this method the law will remain perpetually
the same, yet at the same time, will admit at all times and under
all circumstances such temporary modifications as are indispensable.[17]

Student: This is quite a statement. I am not sure that I fully
understand its implications.

LC: Maimonides is saying that Halacha can and does change.
And change needs to take place because the Torah's integrity,
as the word of God, needs to be preserved. Its practical implications are a subject of scholarly debate; not to be elaborated
on here. But what is clear is that there is enough flexibility
within the law to respond to completely different circumstances

---

[17] Maimonides, *Guide for the Perplexed*, 3:41.

without losing its own integrity. In fact, the changes *affirm* its integrity.

Student: Could you give me an example by way of illustration?

TEACHING TORAH TO WOMEN IS TO TEACH THEM FOLLY?

LC: Let's have a look at a topic of great contemporary interest, where some major changes have already taken place and which, in the eyes of some scholars, requires further adjustment.[18] The topic in question is the status of women within traditional Judaism; in particular, their involvement in Torah learning.

I do not have to tell you that the study of Torah sources has always been a primary concern within Judaism. Studying the great works of its classical sources, however, was always confined to men. Women were more or less excluded from this crucial activity. Moreover, some disturbing observations have been made about the study of Torah by women.

Maimonides summarized the law by saying: "Women are not commanded to study Torah, though if they do, they receive reward for their voluntary act. A father should not teach his daughter Torah and if he taught her the Oral Law, it was as if he had taught her folly."[19] Maimonides bases himself on a similar statement in the Talmud.[20]

---

[18] For example see: Emanuel Rackman, *Modern Halakhah for our Time* (NJ: Ktav, 1995) chapter 6. Also see Joel B. Wolowelsky, *Women, Jewish Law and Modernity* (NY: Ktav, 1997) and Eliezer Berkovits, *Jewish Women in Time and Torah* (NY: Ktav, 1990).
[19] Maimonides, *Mishne Torah, Talmud Torah* 1:13.
[20] *Sotah* 21b.

Student: "Taught her folly"? That is a most disturbing statement!

LC: As it stands, this is true. But there is also substantial evidence that suggests that from very early on, quite a few women studied Torah. Women seem to have been present at lectures and at least one woman, by the name of Beruria, was a halachic authority in her own right.[21]

In the Middle Ages, a Christian contemporary of Maimonides wrote: "A Jew however poor, if he has ten sons, will put them all to letters, not for gain as the Christians do, but for understanding God's law—and not only his sons, but his daughters too."[22]

Early authorities such as *Sefer Chasidim* noted that the exemption of women from study does not apply to the laws pertaining to them, for if they were not taught the law, how could they observe it?[23] But other authorities retained the narrow reading of the law.[24]

Most surprising, however, is the fact that one of the greatest sages of the last century, Rabbi Yisrael Meir HaKohen, known as the Chafetz Chaim, suggested that these talmudic rulings, exempting women from Torah study referred to specific circumstances, and were no longer applicable. The talmudic rulings spoke about a climate which no longer exists. In the days of the Talmud, young women lived in intensely focused communities, completely devoted to the highest standards of

[21] *Pesachim* 62b.
[22] Quoted in Paul Johnson, *A History of the Jews* (London, Weidenfeld and Nicolson, 1987) p. 193.
[23] *Sefer Chasidim*, p. 313.
[24] For a further discussion of this see Susan Handelman, "Women and the Study of Torah in the Thought of the Lubavitcher Rebbe" in *Jewish Legal Writings by Women*, Micah D. Halpern and Chana Safrai eds. (Jerusalem: Urim Publications, 1998) pp. 147–81, especially note 5 on pp. 151–2.

Judaism. The ancestral traditions were strong. Young women learned about Judaism by simply observing what was done and said at home. Formal classes and lectures on Judaism were unnecessary. In the modern world, however, Jewish families became dispersed as a result of massive upheavals, caused by huge waves of immigration from one continent to another and by brutal assaults by the Nazis and the Communists in Europe. This led, among other things, to the separation of women from their families and the subsequent loss of religious commitment.

THE CASE OF THE *BETH YAACOV* REVOLUTION

Moreover, many Jewish girls were receiving secular education, which if not counterbalanced by proper Jewish education, would result in further estrangement from Jewish religious life. So, it became not only permissible to give young women high level classes on Judaism, but it also transformed into a religious obligation.[25]

The powerful impact of this halachic ruling by one of the leading sages of his time was not long in coming. A network of day schools, called *Beth Yaacov*, was created throughout Eastern Europe. Its director was Sarah Schnirer, a member of the ultra-Orthodox group of Belzer *chassidim*. It instructed thousands of Jewish girls with the finest Jewish education available. This school system has grown beyond even the founders' wildest imagination. This is a clear illustration of halachic practice "changing" to accommodate altered circumstances. Since circumstances had radically changed, other halachic rulings had to be invoked. Thus, the new halachic ruling required young women to have a proper religious education. Since this was no longer achieved automatically

---

[25] Rabbi Yisrael Meir HaKohen, *Likutei Halachot* to *Sotah* 21a.

through the home, other measures had to be adopted to guarantee their education.

Maimonides had already stated that new halachic emergency measurements had to be applied "to bring the masses back to religion or save them from being corrupted." He went even further, by making use of an analogy: "Just as a physician may amputate a man's hand or foot to save his life, so too, the [Jewish] court may occasionally instruct to disobey some of the commandments so that the commandments as a whole may be preserved."[26]

Student: In other words, this emergency rule is in itself a halachic requirement!

THE PROHIBITION OF APPLYING THE WRONG HALACHA

LC: Exactly! This is the Halacha on which Rabbi Yisrael Meir HaKohen based himself when he gave his ruling. Halacha has to preserve the integrity of the Torah as the religious constitution of the people of Israel. What is crucial to realize is that if one would now invoke the original ruling, which stated that it is folly to teach Torah to women, it would be a violation of Halacha.

Student: But how could there have been a time when it would be folly to teach young women Torah? Excuse me for saying this, but it sounds absurd!

LC: Seemingly, there was a time, such as in the period of the Talmud, when many girls did not receive the education necessary for them to understand the Torah and its oral traditions,

---

[26] *Mishne Torah, Mamrim,* 2:4.

with its many minutiae. Still, their devotion towards Judaism was such that there was no need for such formal education.

I admit that this may sound completely incredulous to our ears, but that does not detract from the fact that the social and educational conditions of thousands of years ago were drastically different from ours today.[27]

Again, let us not forget that there were many exceptions to this rule. In many homes, girls did receive a proper Jewish education and became experts. But let us return to the general principle that circumstances change therefore necessitating the application of their "new" halachic directives. This definitely does not imply that scholars are of the opinion that, whenever circumstances change, we should relax the application of Torah commandments, at all levels. Sometimes the Rabbis were, and still are, of the opinion that it would be better to be more restrictive, so as to preserve Jewish continuity.

Student: I suppose that there are possible differences among these scholars as to when to be more flexible or restrictive.

TO GO OR NOT TO GO TO *BETH YAACOV*

LC: You remind me of a story which is told about one of the great sages of some generations ago. I think it was Rabbi Chaim Soloveitchik, the grandfather of Rabbi Joseph Ber Soloveitchik, about whom we spoke before, who was once asked why he was so permissive in allowing so many sick people to eat on *Yom Kippur*. He replied characteristically: "I am not more permissive with the laws of *Yom Kippur*, I am just

---

[27] For a full discussion of this see Eliezer Berkovits, *Jewish Women in Time and Torah* (NJ:Ktav, 1990).

stricter with the laws concerning *pikuach nefesh* (saving somebody's life)!"

It is obviously true that there are differences between scholars over when to be more flexible or more restrictive. One can even see this in the case of women's education. While it can be said with certainty that most Orthodox communities are greatly in favor of *Beth Yaacov* education for their daughters, there are still small groups within the ultra-Orthodox world who do not permit their girls to go to *Beth Yaacov* schools, and feel that their education at home is more than sufficient for their needs. They would argue that this new ruling would not serve to strengthen the integrity of the Torah. On the contrary, they believe that it is the very change in circumstances that necessitates the counterbalancing force of education at home.

Student: Perhaps they would argue that these schools may be beneficial to most Orthodox girls, but not theirs.

LC: That, too, is possible and I do not believe that one should reject their attitude altogether. Perhaps it is true that while being beneficial in some communities, it is just a compromise in others. Things are never black or white in this world. But, whatever the case, we have definitely witnessed here a major change of halachic application within the overwhelming majority of traditional Jewish communities.

Student: Are similar changes taking places in other areas of Halacha?

LC: There are some scholars who have suggested other major changes.

Student: Could you give a more controversial example, which is yet to be accepted by a majority of rabbinical scholars?

THE CONVERSION CRISIS

LC: Let us consider the issue of conversion. Presently, as you may know, a major debate is taking place in the State of Israel concerning the possibility of allowing Conservative and Reform Rabbis to confirm conversions. Here we touch on the fundamental aspects of Judaism. In accordance with the Halacha, as understood by traditional, i.e., Orthodox Judaism, conversion is only acceptable when there is *kabbalat hamitzvot*, the acceptance of the commandments of the Torah by the non-Jewish candidate for conversion. Once the rabbinical court has been convinced that he or she will keep all these commandments, they will permit this person to convert. The Reform and Conservative movements, however, do not require the acceptance of all the commandments. They are of the opinion that the candidate should only be required to accept certain commandments. This reflects their belief that not all the commandments are binding, since they are of the opinion that some of them are man made. Only those laws, which are of clear divine origin, are obligatory.

Conservative thinkers argue that many *mitzvot* apply, while Reform leaders feel that only a minority of these commandments require implementation. Some Reform leaders, indeed, would argue that each person should choose for him or herself which of the commandments to observe.

The background to this issue is far more complex than I have indicated. It is not only that the Orthodox claim that all the commandments stated in the Torah are of divine origin and are, therefore, obligatory.

There are also great differences between the Orthodox, Reform and Conservative movements regarding the authority of the Oral Law. Since the Orthodox consider the Oral Law also to be inspired by God, they demand that the non-Jewish candidate should also live a Torah life as understood by the Oral Law and as explained by the Orthodox Rabbis. The Conservative and Reform movements, however, have a very different interpretation of the Oral Law. To them it is not binding as it is with the Orthodox, because they feel that much of this Oral Law is not authentic, or believe that there is greater flexibility and leniency to which the Orthodox would object.

To return to our topic of conversion, it is quite clear why these movements bitterly disagree about accepting or not accepting certain non-Jews. Since Orthodox Judaism believes that one can only speak about the legality of a conversion when the candidate has fully accepted all the commandments, as understood by the oral tradition, it means that a Conservative or Reform conversion will not be accepted by Orthodox Jews. Thus, there are many people who are Jewish by the Conservative or Reform rabbinate's standards, but not by the Orthodox. By Orthodox standards, these people would not be allowed to marry a Jew in an Orthodox setting, because their conversion would not be considered valid. They could, however, marry a Jew according to Conservative or Reform criteria.

If left unchecked, this situation will ultimately result in a total breakdown of the unity of the Jewish people. Slowly, these three movements will grow apart and stop marrying each other, since in each case, more and more people will not be Jewish by the standards of the other party. The same may be true between the Conservative and Reform communities. Some Conservative Rabbis are of the opinion that Reform conversions are not valid by Conservative standards.

Student: If I understand you well, we would be confronted with three Jewish people, if not more: Orthodox, Conservative and Reform.

THE DANGER OF THREE JEWISH PEOPLES

LC: It is very possible that we will be confronted by even more sub-groups, since there are differences of opinion even within each of these movements. Many authorities within the Orthodox world still declare that there is nothing that can be done.

Halachically, one cannot convert people who do not declare that they are going to observe all the commandments. Since this is a matter of principle, which, according to Orthodox interpretation, is immutable (since it is considered to be the will of God), the Orthodox will state that, however much they regret the possibility of having three or even more Jewish peoples, there is no alternative but to learn to live with this new situation.

This has enormous ramifications. Take, for example, the situation of the many Russian immigrants in Israel. It is clear that tens of thousands of them are not Jewish, not even by Conservative or Reform standards. Since they are now Israelis, they are, however, part of Israeli society. So, one day their children will date Israeli girls or boys who are Jewish by birth and marry them. This will create an epidemic of mixed marriages and could cause enormous problems for the Israeli-Jewish society.

Student: I understand, but one could still not ask the Orthodox to accept these people as converts, knowing that most of them will not obey the rules of Halacha. For Orthodox Jews to say anything else would be inconsistent.

LC: That is true, unless you are prepared to take another factor into account.

Student: And that is?

LC: That there is still another halachic principle at work, which throws a completely new light on this matter: the obligation to ensure the unity of the Jewish people.

Student: You'd better explain.

THE HALACHIC DEMAND TO STAY ONE NATION

LC: According to some authorities there is a halachic require-ment to ensure that we stay unified as one people.[28]
  The reasoning is that the Jewish nation could easily disinte-grate if that unity is violated. The existence of three or more different major sub-groups will create such enormous problems that the Jewish people may disappear altogether.

Student: But would everybody agree with this grim assess-ment? Would it really be the end of the Jews?

A HALACHIC CONFLICT OF INTEREST

LC: I suppose that many Orthodox Jews would not agree, but once we accept this assessment to be true, we will be con-fronted with a conflict of interest within the Halacha. On the one hand, we have a law, which states that one cannot convert

---

[28] See Eliezer Berkovits, "Conversion According to Halacha," in his *Crisis and Faith* (NY: Sanhedrin Press, 1976) p. 122.

non-Jews who are not willing to observe all the command-ments. On the other hand, there is a halachic requirement to make sure that we stay *one* people, which will only be achieved if we find a way to convert all these people in "some" Ortho-dox fashion, even in the knowledge that they will not observe the commandments.

Now it is quite clear that nearly everybody claims that the existence of the Jewish people is crucial and, beyond any doubt, our greatest concern and duty. In that case, authorities argue that we must find a halachic compromise to the conflict between the Orthodox, Conservative and Reform communities when discussing the issue of conversion. If we do not, nothing will be left of the Jewish people.

Student: What would that entail?

LC: It would entail us converting as many non-Jews who are living in the State of Israel as possible, despite the fact they will not keep the laws of the Torah, as understood by the Halacha. They would have to undergo all the external require-ments of the Halacha, such as immersion in a ritual bath and, for men, circumcision: all this in accordance with Orthodox practice by an Orthodox rabbinate.[29]

This may sound paradoxical, but according to some opin-ions, the Halacha requires that the demand of an absolute commitment to Jewish law will have to be compromised for the sake of unity and the survival of the Jewish people. In other words, once the unity of the Jewish people is at stake, another halachic ruling concerning conversion may have to operate. That is, at least, what some scholars argue.

---

[29] See Rabbi Benzion Meir Hai Uziel, *Mishpatei Uziel*, Resp. 18 and 20.

DIVINE PROMISE?

Student: But how will that work? Besides which, do we not have some kind of divine promise that we will always survive?[30] What is there to worry about?

LC: It is true that some argue that we have such a promise. However, one could say that the divine promise is ensured because Halacha includes rules, such as the one I just mentioned.

Student: I thought that this was a promise, regardless of whether we observe any halachic requirement.

LC: I do not think so. But, whatever the interpretation may be, the national existence of the Jewish people is definitely the concern of Halacha.

Student: But where is it written that it is our halachic imperative to keep the Jewish people alive?

LC: Nowhere. That is, nowhere in the codex of Jewish law. It is one of the unwritten laws of Judaism. We may even argue that it is part of the Oral Law and was never put into writing because it was so obvious.

Student: That is all very nice, but at least there should be some indication of such a far-reaching halachic requirement! Is there no precedent anywhere?

---

[30] For example see Amos 9:8.

THE CASE OF ESTHER

LC: We could argue that there is. It is to be found in the book of Esther. One of the questions the Talmud addresses is the issue of how Esther could have married Achashverosh, the non-Jewish King in the Purim story. This was, after all, a grave violation of Torah law. The Halacha clearly states that it is forbidden to marry a non-Jew.

Student: Perhaps she was allowed to marry Achashverosh because she had no choice?

LC: But she should have then offered her life as a martyr—in accordance with the halachic requirement. Only through such drastic action could she have avoided intercourse with Achashverosh, which was a forbidden sexual act.[31]
    The question then arises as to how Esther knew that, in her particular case, such an act would be permissible? Or did she violate the Halacha?

Student: Indeed. In that case the question is appropriate!

ESTHER WAS PERMITTED TO MARRY ACHASHVEROSH

LC: The answer is that Esther was definitely permitted to marry Achashverosh. One reason given by the Talmud is that she was "*karka olam,*" which means that she was completely passive when Achashverosh took her as his wife. The Talmud seems to be of the opinion that her complete non-participation in the sexual act was the reason she did not have to take her own life or fight Achashverosh even until death. Another

---

[31] *Sanhedrin* 74a.

reason given, which is of crucial importance to us is that by marrying Achashverosh, she could protect the Jewish people from Haman. (It seems that Esther knew when she became Achashverosh's wife that antisemitism would ultimately show its ugly head.) The sages state: "Esther is different, she saved all of Israel." It was seemingly their belief that Esther was of the opinion that *all* Jews would have been murdered, leaving no survivors.

In such an extreme case, one is permitted, and probably even obligated, to violate all the laws of the Torah, even those prohibitions for which one "normally" should give one's life rather than violate.[32] Only in this way could one secure the continuity of the people of Israel.

Here we see how one "major" halachic requirement, i.e., "the need for national survival," overrides all others. In accordance to those who liken the current situation concerning the conversion crisis to the destruction of Israel, the halachic directive, as revealed in the story of Esther, is clear and persuasive.

Student: In other words, since the Jewish people may quite well vanish from the globe, in allowing the development of three or more Jewish nations, we are halachically forced to find a solution to the conversion crisis. And this has to be done in such a way that a chasm within the Jewish people will not occur.

LC: Yes! This would mean that halachically we would be obligated to convert people knowing that they will not observe all the commandments.

---

[32] See *Noda BiYehuda* of Rabbi Ezekiel ben Yehudah Landau (1713–1793, Chief Rabbi of Prague) Resp. *Mahadura Tanina*, 161.

Anything less would violate Halacha as previously argued above. If we held the "stricter" view, which states that we could only convert people who kept all the commandments, we would be transgressing Jewish law. Again, this is the opinion expressed by only a few authorities.

Student: Obviously, such a ruling has enormous consequences, since it touches on the very existence of the Jewish people. It would turn the conversion debate on its head.

THE ACTUAL SITUATION?

LC: It already has. But we should never forget that the question of whether or not we should apply such a novel halachic directive, will depend on how we see the actual situation of the Jewish nation. Will we or will we not vanish once we actually split into three or more different Jewish nations? It is my impression that the Orthodox camp seems to feel that we will survive, while the view which I have just explained suggests that we have never before been faced with such a dangerous situation and that we are not even allowed to take this risk.

Student: This would be a further example where we perhaps should "change" the Halacha so as to preserve the integrity of the Torah, in this case the halachic need to ensure that the Jewish people survives.

THE HALACHA IS NOT CHANGED OR ABOLISHED

LC: But remember according to those authorities that call for such steps, no Halacha would be changed or abolished. Their argument is that the circumstances have changed, requiring the implementation of another halachic ruling. I might add that such a view is definitely not accepted by the rabbinical establishment as the formula to solve this conversion crisis. At least not yet. It is still considered a radical view within Orthodoxy.

Student: Could several other halachic issues also be solved, based on the above principle?

LC: According to some authorities this is indeed the case. The main issue is how to decide whether a situation has changed to the extent that it justifies the application of another halachic rule. There is also the issue of how one differentiates between a statement in the Talmud, that is a halachic "given" and a circumstantial Halacha, which is subject to change.

Student: Could you give me an example?

DO WOMEN REALLY WANT TO MARRY ANYBODY?

LC: Certainly. The Talmud states that women prefer to be married to somebody they do not love rather than live on their own.[33]

Is this a halachic statement about the psychological make-up of most women in any century, or is this statement a sociological observation referring solely to the women who lived in the days of the Talmud, and is, thus, not a halachic "given"? Considering such matters carries with it far reaching ramifications in the determination of halachic rulings.

Student: Such as?

---

[33] See *Ketubot* 75a and *Kiddushin* 79a.

LC: Could a woman claim in court that if she would have known that her husband was so poor, she would not have married him? If we would be of the opinion that nearly all women in any generation would marry anyone, because they prefer this to being on their own, the court may not accept this belated claim of hers. This argument could thus not be used to free her from such a marriage.

Here we are working on the assumption that this psychological insight is an unconditional fact concerning the essential nature of nearly all women in all generations. As such, it is understood as a halachic "given" which is not open to change. If, however, we understand this to be a sociological statement limited to the women in talmudic times, it may be understood as no longer applying to women today. The court would then have to acknowledge her statement as reasonable grounds for divorce.

Student: This example opens up a wide range of possibilities.

LC: Potentially, the consequences are enormous, and not without danger. How are we to decide if a talmudic rule is an integral part of the halachic system or is circumstantially based? And certainly, there are other cases where halachic changes could take place on the basis of similar criteria.

Student: Before we continue, let me return to the conversion crisis. What do you think needs to happen in order to find a solution to this serious problem, if we do not follow the "new" halachic approach you just mentioned?

ANOTHER SOLUTION TO THE CONVERSION CRISIS

LC: If one wants to find a way to allow conversions with the guarantee that the candidates will observe all the *mitzvot*, it could work as follows: the Orthodox could reach a compromise with the Reform and the Conservative movements, while at the same time continuing to deny that they are legitimate representations of Judaism.

Student: How would that work?

LC: Simply to make the State of Israel recognize Reform and Conservative as full-fledged religious movements, giving them all the financial support, allowing their Rabbis to officiate at different occasions, such as marriages, *bar mitzvot* and perhaps at some other religious ceremonies. But all this would be under the clear condition that Reform and Conservative Rabbis will not involve themselves in conversion and divorce. These matters should be left solely in the hands of the Orthodox rabbinate. In addition, the Orthodox rabbinate will approve marriages by Conservative or Reform Rabbis only in accordance with the Orthodox understanding of Halacha.

Student: Why should Reform and Conservative Rabbis be permitted to officiate at marriages, and not at divorces?

MARRIAGE YES, DIVORCE NO

LC: There is a clear difference. Firstly, according to Halacha, the validity of a marriage is not dependent on the presence of a Rabbi. It depends on two witnesses. Once they have seen that these people have agreed to marry and have gone through the appropriate ceremony, they are married, even when no Rabbi has officiated. Any Jewish person can marry a couple. Everything depends on the proper evidence of the witnesses. They have to be able to testify that they saw these two people getting married. The only condition is that both witnesses must be kosher, i.e., that they are people who are fully committed to Jewish law, in other words people who are fully religious by Orthodox standards.[34]

The person marrying the couple does not require specialist knowledge. It is a simple affair, needing only some basic knowledge regarding the ceremony. When a Reform Rabbi officiates at a wedding where the witnesses are fully religious Jews, some Orthodox authorities believe that the marriage is valid, since all depends on the witnesses. But when the witnesses are not fully observant, the marriage is invalid. Consequently, the couple would be living together as husband and wife, but would be unmarried according to Jewish law. Yet, although Jewish law definitely does not allow such a relationship, no drastic result would develop. A child born from such a union is a full and normal member of the Jewish community. The reason is that such a relationship is not adulterous according to Jewish law. The definition of adultery, *arayot* in Hebrew, is different from the one given by some secular systems and religions.

The most well known example in Jewish law of adultery is the case in which a married woman has sexual relations with a man who is not her husband. However, Jewish law does not consider the union of two people, who live together as husband and wife, as adulterous when they are single. The reason according to Halacha could be because they would have been able to get married in accordance with Jewish law if they had

---

[34] For a different view see Eliezer Berkovits, *Not in Heaven: The Function of Halakha* (NY: Ktav, 1983) pp. 94–95.

decided to do so. It frequently happens that such a couple has an Orthodox marriage at a later stage in their lives. In other words, such a relationship, although forbidden, does not damage the Jewish people's normal growth and functioning. Their child could later marry any other Jew and everything would be in order. This is especially true since the parents could later decide to comply with the halachic marriage ceremony.

Student: So you are really saying that many couples married by a Reform or Conservative Rabbi have the status of a non-marriage (when there are no kosher witnesses) and are no better than the couple who just lives together as husband and wife?

LC: In accordance with the opinions I referred to before, the marriage is indeed invalid once the witnesses are not religious. Yet, since the couple *could* have been married in a valid ceremony in accordance with Jewish law, there is really no problem as far as the unity of the Jewish people is concerned. So, such a "marriage," endorsed by a Reform or Conservative Rabbi, would not be overly problematic. With regards to the marriage officiated by a Reform or Conservative Rabbi in the presence of religious witnesses, the marriage is also valid, according to some Orthodox authorities. In such cases, the validity of the marriage is not in question; no Halacha having been violated, which would make it forbidden.

Student: So, what about divorce?

LC: That is a completely different story. To validate a halachic divorce requires that those who officiate at the time—the Rabbis, or the rabbinical court—must be "divorce experts" and

Orthodox. The witnesses must also be Orthodox. If they are not, then, even when a divorce ceremony has taken place, Jewish law states that the couple is not divorced. But this time there are crucial consequences. For example: if the woman who now thinks that she is divorced because she went through a divorce ceremony in a non-Orthodox court, would marry another Jewish man, they would be living in violation of Orthodox Halacha. Their relationship would be seen as adulterous.

Student: Why?

THE PROBLEM OF ADULTERY

LC: Because the first marriage was never annulled. She is still married to her first husband. And since a woman according to Jewish law can only be married to one man at a time, her relationship with the second man is absolutely forbidden. In cases like this, we must ensure that only an Orthodox rabbinate will officiate at the time of the divorce. Otherwise, it was as if the divorce never took place. Again, I should stress that the halachic conditions for a divorce are very complex and only people who are experts in this field are able to determine and confirm a divorce.

Student: To summarize: a divorce performed by a Reform or Conservative Rabbi would be invalid in the eyes of the Orthodox, and therefore the couple is not divorced, and thus the second marriage would be adulterous.

LC: Precisely! Moreover, this time it would have severe repercussions on the Jewish people. A child born from the second couple would be considered to be a *mamzer*, a child who would be severely limited in the choice of his or her marriage candidates (See *Devarim* 23:3). This would be a major liability as far as the normal growth and life of the Jewish nation is concerned. It could also lead to a substantial increase of forbidden marriages (which can never be rectified), as well as being a major setback for the child.

Student: I wonder why such a law exists altogether. Is it not a grave injustice to make the child pay the price for the mistake of his or her parents? With regards to conversion, why should the Orthodox be the only ones to perform a conversion? How would that work?

ONLY THE ORTHODOX WILL CONVERT

LC: I have dealt with the question concerning the *mamzer* in one of my other books called *Between Silence and Speech*,[35] but let me address your main concern. A conversion by a Reform or Conservative Rabbi, as we have already observed, has no validity in the eyes of the Orthodox.

This is because of the assumption that there was no commitment on the part of the would-be convert to fully observe Jewish law. Those converted by a Reform or Conservative Rabbi are not considered Jewish; they cannot marry a Jew, and if they did, it would be, in the eyes of the Orthodox, a mixed marriage.

So we are back to square one: a deep division within the Jewish nation. To prevent this, the Orthodox must have a monopoly on conversion, and only conversions by Orthodox standards should be accepted.

---

[35] Nathan Lopes Cardozo, *Between Silence and Speech: Essays on Jewish Thought* (NJ: Jason Aronson, 1995) chapter 4.

Student: But why would the Conservative and Reform leaders ever agree?

LC: Rabbis who suggested this "deal" would argue that this is the fairest solution, in which both parties would benefit and the unity of the Jewish people will not be threatened. All converts will only be accepted by Orthodox standards, which means that they will all be able to marry a Jew by birth. This would greatly increase the possibility of retaining one united nation, something for which all parties involved should strive. (I should add that this solution would not work for those Gentiles who have in the past been converted by the standards of the Reform and Conservative movements and who are not planning on living a fully committed life.)

A ONE WAY ROAD

Student: But what would the Reform and Conservative really gain by this? Your suggestion basically gives all power to the Orthodox!

LC: Definitely not! As I stated before, the Reform and Conservative movements will be fully recognized by the Israeli State, something which, up until now, has not been the case. They will receive governmental financial help, like the Orthodox. They will be able to officiate formally in marriages and other religious rites. This would be a major breakthrough and a tremendous accomplishment for the Reform and Conservative movements in Israel.

Student: I still do not see why these movements would agree to such a compromise.

LC: Let me make another observation. The Reform and Conservative movements will have to understand that even when Orthodox Jews would like to change the law concerning conversion, they would not be able to do so, because they do not have the power to do so, as a result of their own belief.

Student: Why not?

A COMMON DENOMINATOR

LC: Because they believe that this law and its Orthodox interpretation is God-given and thus beyond questioning. The Orthodox believe that they only have permission to convert people once the rabbinical court is convinced that the candidate will live in full accordance with Halacha, as understood by Orthodox authorities. Anything else would be a violation of God's word. This is a fundamental belief of the Orthodox world. To ask them to uproot this principle would be asking them to deny their own beliefs. This would be totally unethical and completely unjustified. The Orthodox world is unable to be flexible because it feels that it does not have the authority to do so.

By contrast, the Conservative and Reform movements *can* be flexible. They will always agree that a conversion done by the Orthodox is valid and will not challenge its legality. If they believe that a partial commitment to Halacha is already sufficient in converting somebody, they will definitely agree that a full commitment will be more than sufficient.

Student: In other words, while the Reform and Conservative movements will definitely agree that somebody converted by Orthodox standards is Jewish, Orthodoxy is unable to do the same in return. It would be impossible for them to agree to a Reform or Conservative conversion. After all, the conditions of Reform and Conservative are not more, but rather, less demanding. So the only kind of conversion which has the approval of all three movements is the Orthodox one. That is their common denominator.

LC: And therefore Reform and Conservative leaders should agree to the demand to have conversions only by Orthodox standards. The proof of their claim of genuine interest in the unity of the Jewish people lies in the issue of conversion.

Student: That makes sense. I wonder why, though, they would not go along with this suggestion!

LC: I suggest you ask that question to some Reform and Conservative leaders. I have put this question to many of their leaders and never received an answer.

In all honesty, I sometimes wonder how sincere they are when they state that they really want unity. Moreover, we are confronted with serious revisionism of Jewish history. When Reform and Conservative leaders maintain that it is Orthodoxy which creates disunity between Jews because they do not accept conversions, which were done by the Reform and Conservative movements, they are not being truthful.

Student: Why?

LC: For nearly two thousand years there was only one standard for conversions: the Orthodox one. It were these two movements which changed the rules, not the Orthodox! It reminds me of the story of a member of an old, well-established family by the name of Rosenblum, who decided to change his name to

Jones. He then accused the family of creating disunity because they were not prepared to call themselves Jones as well!

Student: Good point.

LC: To be honest, I should mention that many Orthodox leaders would not agree on the compromise which I just mentioned before. They believe that such a deal, in which the Reform and Conservative will be fully recognized by the Israeli State, is unacceptable.

Student: Why is that?

LC: Because any compromise is to them a recognition of these movements. But there is a different way of looking at this, which compounds the problem and requires our serious consideration.

Student: Let's hear.

LC: If we think this through once more, then the "deal" which which we spoke about should really be very attractive to the Orthodox. They could have a monopoly on the most crucial issues related to Jewish identity, as discussed. In addition, one can argue that it would give the Orthodox a much better image in the eyes of many Israelis and Jews all over the world. It would show a kind of flexibility which people would greatly admire. The lack of flexibility is often taken as a sign of weakness. The refusal of the Orthodox to compromise creates, in the eyes of many, a great amount of irreparable damage. There are no overtures to reconciliation, there is no attempt at mutual understanding. Instead, accusations fly back and forth on an emotional level and everything gets undermined.

Student: Indeed.

"BUT"

LC: It is no doubt true that much would be gained if those with different religious outlooks were able to find a way to work together and forget about their differences. There is one "but." All this would be true if Judaism belonged to that category which also includes matters like politics, economics or science. But it does not! However important unity may be, we are speaking here about religious matters, and according to many, unity, as such, is not the priority.

Student: Why not?

LC: Let us take some examples from Jewish history. Avraham, as we all know, was surrounded by a value system steeped in idol worship and sexual immorality.

Would it not have been more beneficial for him if he would have made a compromise with that world, instead of taking such an extreme stand in condemning it in every way possible? No doubt, he and many prophets after him created considerable emotional upheaval when they spoke out on so many crucial issues. Many most probably viewed them to be extremists.

Student: While it is true that they all dismissed the values of their societies uncompromisingly, did they have any real choice?

LC: I can well imagine that Avraham's neighbors must have told him that he was shattering the unity of his people and that he would be more successful if he showed a little bit more flexibility. We could say the same thing about Moshe, Shmuel and Yirmiyahu. They all refused to go along with the so-called values of their day. For them, unity was never a priority. It was their commitment to truth, which was considered crucial.

Student: I have difficulty in following you.

CARDINAL NEWMAN

LC: Let us look at a case from outside world Jewry, that of the famous Cardinal John Henry Newman in the nineteenth century. Perhaps you remember him from your history lessons in school. Newman had a very prominent position in the Anglican Church, but after much contemplation, joined the Catholic Church and became one of its most famous cardinals, Catholicism making more sense to him. At the time, his move was the subject of intensive debate. Many people asked whether it would not have been wiser for him to stay in the Anglican Church. From the perspective of bridging the gap between the churches, the answer would obviously have been in the affirmative. He would have been far more influential had he stayed preaching in his Anglican Church in Oxford. He would have been viewed as an authoritative Anglican who had a strong tendency to Rome. The Anglican Church would not have been able to ignore him. But, the moment he became a Catholic, the Anglican Church ostracized him.

Student: So, why did he not stay in the Anglican Church?

CONSCIENCE IS THE LAST WORD

LC: This is precisely my point. The reason he left the Anglican Church altogether is that he could not prioritize reconciliation over his conscience.

Student: What do you mean?

LC: One chooses in favor of a belief because one affirms it to be true, and consequently, other beliefs to be untrue.

Cardinal Newman felt that he could not stay within the Anglican Church because he could not agree with its theology. True, it would have been far more beneficial if he had stayed in the Anglican Church, but his conscience would not permit him to do so. He had to decide between truth and untruth. At that moment, such a noble cause as reconciliation was insignificant.

Now, regarding Judaism and Jews, I agree that matters are more complex, but the principle is fundamentally the same. Jewish identity cannot be determined simply on the basis of what is less detrimental to our unity. This is an instance where one's conscience decides. For Orthodox Judaism such conscience will depend on God's will as expressed in the traditional understanding of Halacha. Orthodox Judaism knows very well that it might create unity for a while by being more flexible, but it would not be able to hold on to such a position for very long, since its motivation for flexibility would violate its conscience, which is determined by its commitment to Halacha.

Student: Some Orthodox Jews would therefore feel that they could not even agree on the compromise of which you spoke.

LC: That is true. They feel that they cannot even suggest that the State of Israel should recognize the Conservative and Reform movements. To them, these movements do not represent Judaism. In fact, they claim that these movements are un-, or perhaps even, anti-Jewish. One may or may not agree with such a point of view, but we have to admit that this is not a reflection of weakness but of principle. In that case we should respect those Orthodox for their opinion.

Student: According to this view, there is no way to compromise.

TWO WAYS TO COMPROMISE

LC: Correct. There is indeed no compromise unless we return to our earlier observation and determine that the Halacha of "survival" is more important than the condition of absolute commitment to Halacha by the non-Jewish candidate.

Student: In other words, there are really two ways to deal with the conversion crisis. The first one is to apply the Halacha for survival in the form of a compromise concerning the actual condition for conversion. In that case, Orthodox conversions would take place, even when the candidates will clearly not observe all the commandments.

The second way is to make a deal between the Orthodox, Reform and Conservative, by which the last two movements will be recognized by the State of Israel so that their Rabbis enjoy the right to officiate at religious ceremonies, such as marriage, on the condition that the Orthodox would have overall authority on matters like divorce and conversion.

LC: Of course, don't forget that the second option is still preferable to the Orthodox establishment than the first. Practically speaking, I would have to add that if Orthodoxy does not support these options, it may find itself confronting a far worse situation.

Student: Such as?

LC: Such as the Israeli State recognizing the Reform and Conservative movements in a way that allows their Rabbis to officiate not only at marriages, but also to have authority in matters of divorce and conversion. The ensuing chaos could have detrimental effects.

TO SAVE THE SITUATION

Student: It seems you are implying that through compromise, the Orthodox could avert this explosive situation, while at the same time maintaining their ultimate authority in crucial matters such as conversion and divorce. But if they delay in doing this, the Reform and Conservative movements will be recognized by the legislature of the State of Israel and even have authority over divorce and conversion. All will be lost.

LC: There is a good chance that this will happen; there are indeed many voices in Israel that demand such a move. The State will be forced to take this step and the situation will rapidly deteriorate.

Student: I see your point. It is a serious situation.

LC: It is indeed. Orthodoxy should thus ask itself, again, if it would not be required by Halacha to compromise in this way.

If the answer is affirmative, their personal conscience would dictate such a step. I must admit that I myself feel uneasy about all this.

Student: So why would you suggest that Orthodoxy carefully contemplate this possibility?

WINSTON CHURCHILL AND DEMOCRACY

LC: Because life is full of choices that we would prefer not to make. It reminds me of Winston Churchill's observation. He stated that democracy would be the worst form of government, if not for other forms of government being even more disastrous. I should, however, add that for the religious person, the problem of conversion is clearly God's problem. If He permits Reform and Conservative to exist, He will also have to solve the problem they create. We are not God nor should we try to take His place. Once we have done whatever is possible within the framework of the Halacha, it is no longer our responsibility.

Student: Rabbi Cardozo, you have given me a lot to think about. Sometimes, I feel that you contradict yourself, while at other moments it seems that what you say is absolutely consistent. So let us end here and continue tomorrow.

LC: Very well, but let me conclude by quoting the philosopher Alfred North Whitehead: "In formal logic, a contradiction is the signal of defeat, but in the evolution of real knowledge, it marks a first step in progress towards victory.

This is one of the great reasons for the utmost toleration of variety of opinion."[36] This may not be applicable at all in my case, but it does make me feel better.

---

[36] A.N. Whitehead, *Science and the Modern World* (NY, 1925) p. 12.

DAY TWO

The Charleston and Ice Cream; Man Is a Deep Sea Fish; Swimming Across the Channel; The Curse of Blatant Music; To Have Your Fling; Road-Hogging; The Elderly Are Becoming Immature; *Bekiso, Bekoso, Beka'aso, uBesachako*; A Decline in Religious Consciousness and the World to Come; The Power of Talmud Torah; Playing Bridge; The Assassination of Yitzchak Rabin *z"l*; A Creation *Sui Generis*; Carl Gustaf Jung and the Archetype; The Land Of Israel Is Only a Means; Israel As an Idol; The Terror of Moshe; The Two Tablets Are Base Pottery; The Religious Need to Destroy the Western Wall; The Torah Does Not Need Land; Is Zion Not Israel?; Orthodoxy's Greatest Challenge; The Need For Self-Critique; The Ten Commandments Are Only One Word; The Flood of Noach; The Lack of "*Menschlichkeit*" Is Worse Than Idol Worship; Religious Jews Have to Set an Example; A New Curriculum for *Yeshivot*; Re-education; Back to the Middle Ages?; Religious Parties and the Coercive Power of the State; The Status Quo and Discos; Bar-Ilan Street and CNN; Rabbi Shlomo Zalman Auerbach *z"l* and the Shabbat Car; Settling Accounts; How Secular Are the Secular?; Rabbi Aryeh Levin *z"l*; Television and Radio; The Trouble with Universities; The Danger of Inspiration; The Danger of Sociology; The Failure of a "Survival" Philosophy; The Goal of Music Is to Make the Musical Instrument Survive?; To Learn from *Sephardim*; Is Black More Beautiful?; Jews Only Play the Violin

THE CHARLESTON AND ICE CREAM

Student: Good morning. Here is my first dislocated question, which is unrelated to the theme of our last discussion, on the first day. I would like to know what induces many people in the West to do such strange things as rolling around Europe in a barrel, dancing the Charleston for more than 30 hours so as to break a record, hanging on poles for days after days, or taking part in contests to see who can eat the most ice creams!

LC (Lopes Cardozo): Total boredom!

Student: What is boredom?

MAN IS A DEEP SEA FISH

LC: Boredom occurs when we realize our needs too quickly. Instant gratification is the name of the game. The feeling of previous unfulfillment fades and we immediately start looking for new needs to satisfy. This need seems generic. We are like deep-sea fish, needing atmospheric pressure, without which we are lost. Since Western man is able to satisfy all his wishes without too much effort, he starts looking for absurd manifestations to satiate his need for pressure. This is not totally negative, however.

Student: What do you mean?

LC: Take the case of the fast walker. Walking is, in itself, a constructive form of exercise. But what then occurs is that some Tom, Dick or Harry creates contests, with monetary prizes as an incentive, to see who can walk the fastest. I really enjoy seeing these men run, especially when I do not have to do so myself! But I have to admit that it is something of a tragedy!

Student: Why?

LC: Because those who walk the fastest see the least! Instead of enjoying the beauty of nature, they run through it. And because they exhaust themselves to the limit, they are oblivious to things around them. They should pay a penalty for such apathy! Instead, we reward them at the finishing line with the very flowers they did not see on the road, and in many cases, with great sums of money for their "achievement!"

SWIMMING ACROSS THE CHANNEL

I remember when I was younger, a British fellow suddenly felt the need to organize a swimming contest crossing the Channel between England and France. Suddenly, the people running the Calais-Dover ferry service found that more and more of its former passengers were overboard!

THE CURSE OF BLATANT MUSIC

All that would not be objectionable if these people did not disturb others in the process. The trouble begins when these thoroughly bored people impinge on their environment in the most unimaginable way. This is especially true when it is indifference to their environment that prompts them. Today, this has become a particular problem since technological advancement has enabled people to corrupt the rest of mankind's natural environment. When my parents used to take my brother and me to the beach or to a beautiful forest, it was quiet and relaxing. We would dismantle our folding chairs and enjoy the silence, or hear the rush of the sea or the blowing of the wind. It was wonderful. But today you set up your folding chair in search of tranquility, only to hear the blaring of a nearby CD or car radio. You look up and meet the gaze of some fellow a few yards away, who just decided to turn his music on high on his portable radio. If you ask him to lower the volume of his CD, he will tell you that this is not a private park or beach and he can do whatever he likes! That he is disturbing many people is of no significance to him. This is *his* prerogative and that is all there is to it. If you curtail his liberty, you are denying *his* right to enjoy himself in any way he sees fit!

There is no defense against such an attitude. Many people are victims of such insensitivity. To our great sorrow, technology has afforded people this possibility. If you ask the parents of this fellow to tell him to lower his radio, they will tell you that it also disturbs them, but they can't do anything about it. Youth has to have its fling! I have never understood that phrase.

Student: Why not?

TO HAVE YOUR FLING

LC: "To have your fling" should mean to prove yourself, by utilizing your inner potential. Real maturity is surely caring about the happiness of others. Someone who has not yet learned this is denying him or herself one of the most beautiful human characteristics. He acts in the way he does because he happens to have parents, or educators, who believe that having a fling would be beneficial to his development. I find such a view peculiar, because these same people conscientiously and obsessively cut the grass and bushes in their garden, knowing that, if unmaintained, they will grow wild. However, the application of this mindset to their children's education is not something that occurs to them. When they read in the papers about the wantonness of today's youth, they shake their heads in dismay.

Student: You make me laugh when I hear you say that.

ROAD HOGGING

LC: I also have to laugh, because it sounds so comical, but it is really very serious. I do not know about other countries, nor do I want to make comparisons! But in the country of my birth, the Netherlands, some of the youth discovered another marvelous way to express their boredom. They take their motor bikes and speed as fast as possible through the city. Once they discover a cafeteria, they give a demonstration of some sophisticated road hogging and get off their bikes. They drink their beer, while leaving their motors running. This seems to be their highest form of pleasure! That some elderly people get headaches, or cannot cope with so much noise and pollution, and are forced to leave this otherwise quiet cafeteria, is of no interest to these young men. It is their right, so why not?

Student: But why is this? Surely most young people still have respect for their parents or elderly people. I suppose that there were always children and young people who did not care about the elderly, but you are suggesting that this has now become a universal phenomenon.

LC: I believe that the grown ups are themselves to blame.

Student: How so?

THE ELDERLY ARE BECOMING IMMATURE

LC: The value of what we term as maturity has been undermined. In the "olden days" it was a privilege to be mature; it was something for which people would strive. It meant maturity of attitude, having experience on how to deal with life problems. It meant well-considered opinions. This is no longer the case. This is not due to the fact that our youth became more knowledgeable or experienced overnight, but because the older generation, those who were supposedly mature, suddenly showed signs of immaturity. They stopped being mature. The most prominent manifestation of this is in how older people use their free time. While in the past, people dedicated their spare time (when not working) to creative, communal or family projects, most of today's "mature" people spend their freedom in complete passivity. They watch television, go to a movie or spend their time in bed. Radio and television have reverted us back to our childhood. We listen and watch just as we did when we were young. It is perhaps at this point that the distinction between young and old has been obliterated.

There is a distinct difference between a father who is involved in a creative activity (even when it is only building a chicken or dollhouse), and a father sitting for hours in front of the television screen. The former is "mature," the latter has regressed back to his childhood. It is under these conditions that children see their elders. His or her father may be a professor at the university, but at home he reverts to being someone who is adopting a second childhood.

Do not misunderstand me, I am not saying that television has no value. Sometimes the television offers first class information. I am just saying that we are selling our firstborn right for a soup of lentils. Once our behavior matches that of our youngsters, all distinction fades. So we should not be surprised when, at the same time, our dignity is lowered in the eyes of our youngsters. The end result is that the immature child considers him or herself to be mature, while the "mature" adult fails to recognize his or her immaturity. The son recognizes that he does the same as his father: nothing! Based on the negative example set by his parent, the child embarks on his or her life. He clothes himself with the garments of maturity, which his father has rejected.

BEKISO, BEKOSO, BEKA'ASO, UBESACHAKO

The Talmud discusses this problem in Tractate *Eruvin* 65b, where it observes that a person's true character is revealed in how he spends his "play" time. The relevant passage says that a man can be tested in three ways: *bekiso*, *bekoso*, *ubeka'aso*; by his "pocket"—whether or not he or she is a miser or a spendthrift—"by his cup"—how he or she responds to the temptation of alcoholic excess—and by his temper—can he or she control himself when provoked. The Talmud adds another standard based on which a person may be tested—"*af besachako*"—also by his or her play—how he or she utilizes his or her leisure time.[37]

Student: How interesting!

A DECLINE IN RELIGIOUS CONSCIOUSNESS AND THE WORLD TO COME

LC: But there is really more to it. In my estimation, our problem also relates to the decline in religious consciousness, and specifically, to the lack of belief in an afterlife. In the past, the youth somehow had respect for the elderly because they were closer to death and therefore closer to the "truth." Somehow elderly people were "nearly there." A few more years, months or days and they would experience the "real thing." As such, the older person sat close to the "door," while the youngster had to wait. But this is no longer the attitude today. The elder is no longer regarded as somebody "nearly there," but as somebody who is "nearly *nowhere*." This, I believe, has entered in the collective consciousness of modern man. The older person has, thus, lost much of his grandeur while the younger people see him as having outlived his days. Only in a religious setting will man discern the privilege of maturity. This does not mean that all secularists fail to show respect for the elderly. It just means that they unconsciously borrow a religious value.

THE POWER OF TALMUD TORAH

Student: But to address the issue of boredom. What has Judaism done to counteract it?

---

[37] For an outstanding essay see Rabbi Dr. Norman Lamm, "A Jewish Ethic of Leisure," in *Faith and Doubt: Studies in Traditional Jewish Thought* (NY: Ktav) chapter VII, p. 187.

LC: One of the great things about Judaism is that it has found a solution to this problem in the form of encouraging young and old people to study Torah—perhaps the most effective response against boredom. Once having discovered the great joy to be found in learning Torah, a Jewish child will never, until the end of his days, experience boredom. The enjoyment of learning Torah is by that time, so imbued in his very essence, saving him from the curse of apathy. Obviously this is only true when Torah has been taught in such a way that one really enjoys it. This is a topic in itself, to which I have already alluded, when we discussed the importance of questioning, and the danger of people who are no longer perplexed.

PLAYING BRIDGE

Student: Allow me to interrupt if you will, but many elderly people tell me that playing bridge, when one is young is a great investment for old age. It keeps the mind alert and sharp and the memory in good condition. So why learn Torah?

LC: Entienne Bonnot once said that "a game is any unserious occupation designed for the relaxation of busy people and the distraction of idle ones; it is used to take people to whom we have nothing to say, off our hands, and sometimes even ourselves."[38]

I leave it to you to decide whether or not this statement is true.

---

[38] Abbe de Condillac, *Dict. de Synonymes, Oeuvres Philis* (1947–51) p. 3.

THE ASSASSINATION OF YITZCHAK RABIN *Z"L*

Student: Rabbi Cardozo, let me change topics. A few years ago, we witnessed the traumatic assassination of the late Prime Minister of the State of Israel, Yitzchak Rabin and a couple of years before that, the murder of innocent Arabs at the hand of Dr. Baruch Goldstein. These crimes were committed by "religious people." Is this not indicative of a failure within religion and the Jewish tradition?

LC: It proves the failure of Jewish education, not of the Jewish tradition.

Student: What is the difference?

LC: Let me try to explain.

A CREATION *SUI GENERIS* (BEYOND CLASSIFICATION)

Prior to further elaboration, we first need to realize something of great importance; something which I believe has not been fully understood by most people, and that is: the deeds of Baruch Goldstein and Yigal Amir robbed the State of Israel of its most precious possession: its innocence. The reason for the Jews' special pride in the establishment of the State does not just lie in its heroic wars or in the knowledge that now, after a nearly 2000 year exile, Jews have a piece of land of their own. It is also due to the belief that the State of Israel was distinct; reflecting a specific Jewish moral dimension with which conscious Jews—religious or not—could identify. The Jews aspired to create a model State, in which its people—survivors of a brutal Holocaust, claiming six million of its flock—would show the world that integrity and honesty can prevail in society. Israel was supposed to be a country which would achieve the impossible feat of combating all crime: a place where an individual could walk around freely late at night, and where there would be a feeling of brotherhood and deep emotional attachment between all its citizens; a state of one large family. As a result of the horrific deeds of Yigal Amir and Baruch Goldstein, this image has now been shattered. It will take a long time for the rift to heal, although I believe that, without denying terrorist attacks, Israel is still one of the safest places in the world.

Student: Although you have not yet answered my question, let me ask you this: do you really believe that most Jews saw Israel in that idealized light? Let us be honest, Israel was never completely free from crime and other moral upheavals.

LC: That is very true. Perhaps it was wishful thinking, to some degree, on a conscious or subconscious level, but most Jews were able to keep the dream alive, because crime was so sporadic that many of them were able to overlook the few isolated incidents. But to return to what I said before: this belief in innocence has been shattered, causing great trauma. It pulls the carpet of a great dream right under the feet of millions of Jews, and poses a profound challenge to their outlook. Let us indeed not forget that up until the assassination of Yitzchak Rabin *z"l* and the atrocities of Baruch Goldstein, the belief was that the sporadic crimes in the State of Israel were nothing more than birth pangs of the newly established State. Once normalization would set in, even these isolated incidents would somehow disappear. After all, which Jew could really contemplate killing a fellow Jew, a family member, or anybody else for that matter? All this was radically changed with the murder of Yitzchak Rabin. This crime cannot be labeled as an unfortunate, isolated incident, to be forgotten. It should be recognized that the assassination was a symptom of an underlying current in the fabric of society. It reveals a major and far-reaching flaw in the very essence of the State. In fact many people wonder if these crimes will not ultimately result in the destruction of the State.

Student: Why do you take it as far as that? Other States have continued to exist after the assassination of its leaders!

LC: This is also true. However, our whole raison d'être is rooted in the principle that life is the most precious gift a person possesses. The basis of our identity is formed through this knowledge. Rabin's assassination alongside Baruch Goldstein's crime has caused great disillusionment amongst those Jews who took the sanctity of life for granted. I am not suggesting that other nations do not value life as holy, but it is up to us to educate the world of the sanctity of life. It is in our blood! But now this mission has been violated by our own people.

Student: Do you really believe that most Jews are thinking on such a profound level?

CARL GUSTAF JUNG AND THE ARCHETYPE

LC: Not at all! What I am claiming is that on a subconscious level, even the most secular Jews carry this responsibility with them. It is a kind of inheritance which Carl Gustaf Jung would identify as an archetype, the subconscious of a primordial mental image which keeps recurring in a nation. We are the children of the first Jew, Avraham, who through his deeds and *weltanschauung*, embedded this concept of the holiness of human life into our psyche. His deeds and thoughts are the primordial stuff from which our personalities are formed, whether we like it or not! I think that deep down many Jews and Israelis felt that these murders were a form of collective assassination, rendering us all guilty of having allowed them to happen at all! It signaled that we somehow lost our most precious common characteristic: to see life as the holiest possession we have and to never sink to the level of murder!

Student: Okay, let's assume that I agree with you. But let's return to my original questions: how can it be that religious Jews were responsible for these crimes?

LC: I beg you to listen carefully, since I could easily be misunderstood. I am convinced that Yigal Amir and Baruch Goldstein would never have dreamed of taking any life, even that of a harmless insect. In conversation, you would have found them polite and courteous people who would go out of their way to be helpful to others. I believe, however, that they and others like them have a complete and most dangerous understanding of the meaning of Judaism and its ideology. They sincerely believed that Jewish law unequivocally forbids, under *all* circumstances, *any* concession of *any* part of the land of Israel to other nations. Not even for the sake of peace! They would even be able to quote sources within the Jewish tradition to support their claim. I am well aware of these sources. What these people and their friends did not understand, however, was that you cannot read a text out of context. There are many other issues at stake which were completely overlooked, and which, as often happens in the halachic system, would override such a radical view.

Student: For example?

THE LAND OF ISRAEL IS ONLY A MEANS

LC: Well, most important is the fact that the Land of Israel is only a means to something else and not a goal in itself. This land was inherited by the Jews so that they would be able to develop themselves into a "light unto the nations" as the *Tanach* tells us so poetically. The land is the physical spring-board from which the Jews must operate to bring the light of moral Monotheism to the world. The land should function as a spiritual center from where this light is sent into the world, as a kind of a "nuclear" powerhouse, from where Jews take their energy to serve the rest of mankind in its search of a real, moral life. What happened, however, was something totally different: some religious people transformed the land into the ultimate goal of Judaism. In fact, they turned the land into an idol! And that is exactly what Judaism has been fighting against for thousands of years. The attempt to make a means into an end results in *Avoda Zarah*, idol worship!

ISRAEL AS AN IDOL

Student: So Zionism can lead to idol worship?

LC: Yes, as can anything. This is the tragedy. Decent people fell prey to a new "idol." In their misguided belief that protection of their idol was a compulsory requirement of authentic Judaism, Yigal Amir and Baruch Goldstein planned the ultimate expression of this belief: the murder of Arabs and assassination of the Prime Minister. In their eyes, Yitzchak Rabin was violating the land, and therefore the law. Yigal Amir was fully aware that he could be killed by Prime Minister Rabin's security guards, but he was prepared to pay any price, even that of his life! Do not misunderstand me. I am not advocating the concession of land. I cannot be the judge of that. Perhaps Yitzchak Rabin was completely mistaken in his methods to bring about a peace agreement. It is foremost an issue of security, which only the army can determine. (In this case, there were major differences of opinion between Premier Rabin, himself a career soldier, and other generals in the Israeli army.) It is also most relevant to stress that cities like Jerusalem or Hevron, which Yitzchak Rabin was (perhaps) prepared to relinquish (at least partially), are of utmost importance to the soul, and therefore to the very existence, of the Jewish State. I should also add that there are several halachic rulings, which make it far from easy to relinquish land. I fully understand that these rulings were of major consideration to Yigal Amir. Also, I understand Baruch Goldstein's sincere concern for the safety of his fellow Jews. But, in accordance to Jewish law, such commitment or concern could never *ever* justify their deeds.

Student: Did this tragedy occur simply because religious texts were misinterpreted out of context?

LC: Frankly, I believe that, to some extent, these tragic acts are the result of secular Zionism in its extreme. Some of the Zionist leaders of the days preceding and following the establishment of the State viewed the creation of the State to be the ultimate value and goal of their lives. To them nothing else counted. They had completely rejected the traditional foundations of Judaism out of which Zionism had clearly grown. So, they sublimated Zionism into an ultimate ideology to which everything else had to pay deference. Instead of creating a Zionism which would promote the revival of Judaism, sending its moral message to all mankind, it became self-contained and in many ways very narrow-minded. Subsequently, this attitude was adopted by some religious Jews, who supplemented this way of thinking with religious texts taken out of context, which ultimately resulted in extreme religious nationalism, to which we have now been witness. It is most disturbing that people hold the venerable Rabbi Avraham Yitzchak Kook responsible for this attitude. Careful reading of his works prove otherwise.

Student: So you condemn secular Zionists for giving impetus to the deeds of Yigal Amir and Baruch Goldstein?

LC: Definitely not. I am speaking of its *leaders* who were unaware that as a result of their love of the land, the wrong message was being conveyed to many young Israelis. But let us not forget that there were several people in the Zionist movement who opposed this kind of nationalism. People like Martin Buber and Achad Ha'am, who definitely did not belong to the Orthodox camp, constantly emphasized that Zionism should be a spiritual movement and not just a nationalistic one. I should also make it clear that many religious Zionists were, and are, among the more moderate groups that do *not* subscribe to this extreme nationalistic attitude.

Again, what confronts us here is the problem of seeing Israel as an ultimate value and consequently making it the object of idolization. One should, after all, never forget that anything is capable of being idolized, even something deeply religious.

Student: You surprise me. How could such a thing be possible?

THE TERROR OF MOSHE

LC: Well, we have a clear precedent right in the Torah. At the very end of *Devarim* (34:12), the Torah tells us of Moshe's death and goes on to praise him for the great signs and wonders, and for the "terror" which he displayed before all of Israel. Rashi, our famous French commentator, makes a most shocking observation regarding this passage: he states that the "terror" which Moshe demonstrated in front of the children of Israel came across in the breaking of the tablets after the tragedy of the golden calf. In addition, Rashi continues, God thanked him for this act: "And the opinion of the Holy One Blessed be He was in agreement with him: [And He said to Moshe] 'May your strength be firm for having broken them!'"[39]

Student: Wait a moment! Are you are saying that God actually agreed with Moshe's radical response of destroying the tablets on which the Ten Commandments were written?

LC: Yes, indeed! Neither should we forget that these "Ten Commandments" were written, according to Jewish tradition, by God Himself. His own "fingers" had actually engraved the letters on the tablet.[40]

God writing His own text is something completely unprecedented in the whole of *Tanach*, yet now He thanks Moshe for smashing these very words and letters!

Student: This seems quite incredible to me. How are we supposed to understand it?

THE TWO TABLETS ARE BASE POTTERY

LC: I will tell you. One of the great rabbinical thinkers and commentators of the past century, Rabbi Meir Simcha

[39] Rashi, *Devarim* 34:12.
[40] *Shemot* 24:12.

HaKohen of Dvinsk (1843–1926), author of one the most intellectual commentaries on the Torah written in that era, called *Meshech Chochma*, explains this incident as follows: After realizing that the Jews had created the golden calf, Moshe became terribly afraid that the Israelites would also create an idol out of the tablets. They were written by the hand of God Himself and were therefore liable to become the object of idolatry, the very deed that is vociferously condemned in one of the Ten Commandments. What Moshe wanted to show is that the tablets were only "base pottery," having no intrinsic holiness. Only God is holy, not the tablets. Not the creation. Nothing.

Student: Not even the Temple?

LC: Not even the Temple! In the words of Rabbi Meir Simcha HaKohen: "Do not imagine that the Temple and the Tabernacle are intrinsically holy. Far be it! The Almighty dwells amidst His children and if they transgress His covenant these structures become divested of all their holiness. Violent men came and profaned the Temple; Titus entered the Holy of Holies together with a harlot and no harm befell them, since its holiness had lapsed!"[41]

Student: I still cannot believe my ears.

LC: The Rabbi from Dvinsk makes it very clear: the land of Israel is not intrinsically holy, it is only conditionally holy depending on how man uses it as a means to worship God and help his fellow man. That is what went wrong. When people see an intrinsic holiness in the land itself, and therefore start

[41] Commentary on *Shemot* 32:19. See also *Shabbat* 87a.

worshipping it, this can lead to the most dangerous scenarios, as we have seen.

THE RELIGIOUS NEED TO DESTROY THE WESTERN WALL

Professor Yeshayahu Leibowitz *z"l*, one of the most controversial Orthodox thinkers in modern Israel, once called on the Israeli authorities to knock down the Western wall, in the fear that people would start worshipping it. While I do not agree with such a radical suggestion, or for that matter with other radical opinions of his, I *do* believe that there is some truth to this observation. Let me add a detail which may come as a surprise, even to religious Jews. Jews do not have a "native" land, in the normal sense of the word. Israel, as a people, has a covenant with God, which is expressed in a mission. Let us not forget that the Torah was deliberately *not* given in Israel to make that point clear. It was given in the desert, i.e., "nowhere land," to impress upon us that ultimately, Judaism is not entirely dependent on the Land of Israel.

Student: What do you mean?

THE TORAH DOES NOT NEED LAND

LC: In the biblical account of their sojourn in the wilderness, the Israelites were told to place the ark, the visible symbol of the divine Presence and covenant, in the tabernacle. It was forbidden to remove the poles that were used to carry it: "The poles shall be in the rings of the ark, they shall not be taken out"(*Shemot* 25:15). Even after Canaan (the Land of Israel) was conquered and the empire of King David and King Solomon established, the poles had to permanently stay in their place. Even after the Temple, in which the Ark was to be permanently lodged, had been erected, the poles—symbols of God's controlling hand—were still not to be removed (*Melachim* 1, 8:8). This means that Israel was indeed in possession of the land, but the Jews were not *bound* to it. Israel was ready in anticipation to take up the Ark and begin their wanderings anew. In other words, there was no concession to the "gods of space" as some philosophers would call it.

Let me explain. Zion is not so much our native land as it is our promised land. The bond between Israel and the Jews, despite all dispersions and separations, is consistent throughout the whole *Tanach*. The destiny of Israel begins with Zion. At the very beginning, God summoned Avraham to Zion. Zion was also the place where God took the children of Israel, after their exit from Egypt. It is also the land where the final fulfillment of the messianic age will take place. But between the starting point and the finishing line lies the great mystery of Israel's existence: the task of influencing mankind through its adherence to the moral code. The Jewish people's mission is to live in Israel, but its message must extend farther beyond the borders of the physical domain of Israel. Consequently there is a role to be played by the people of Israel in Exile. The dispersion came not only as a judgment upon Israel, as some of the sages stated, but also to influence the Gentile world and sanctify God's name universally.[42]

Student: If all this is true, then what you said earlier about the idolization of the land is even more pertinent. What can be done to repair the situation, especially since many Israelis hold the Jewish tradition responsible for the acts of Yigal Amir and Baruch Goldstein?

---

[42] See *Pesachim* 87b: "The Holy One blessed be He scattered Israel over the earth so that proselytes might be added to them."

ORTHODOXY'S GREATEST CHALLENGE

LC: This is indeed a most serious problem, which demands unequivocal attention from the religious leadership. I believe it will be the leadership's greatest challenge. Only a "tour de force" of major proportions will change the direction in which the wind is blowing at the moment. Clear and honest thinking will be a *sine qua non*.

Student: What do you mean?

THE NEED FOR SELF-CRITIQUE

LC: Firstly, it will be necessary to do some honest soul-searching on the part of the Orthodox establishment and its leadership. Sincere self-critique. Self-righteousness, which can sometimes be a problem in certain religious groups, is unconstructive. Only penetrating self-criticism is beneficial. Sincere soul-searching has always been a pillar of authentic Judaism; it being a sign of strength, and not of weakness. That is what Orthodoxy needs today. More than anything else, it has to ask itself: where did we go wrong? And how can we change?

Student: So you admit that Orthodoxy is somehow responsible for this crime, and not just the individual who happened to be identified with Orthodoxy?

LC: Absolutely! We should not use this excuse and deceive ourselves. We, the Orthodox, are all guilty! There are many Orthodox Jews, like myself, who feel that we failed to give our students the kind of Jewish education which would

automatically preclude such acts. Perhaps we were too occupied in teaching our students about the holiness of Shabbat,
kashrut and other important rituals, while focusing insuffi-
ciently on matters which relate to the holiness of life itself!

Student: But perhaps these rituals are more important in the
eyes of Judaism than the laws pertaining to the relationships
between man and his fellow man? The blame in that case lies
within the Jewish tradition itself!

THE TEN COMMANDMENTS ARE ONLY ONE WORD

LC: Definitely not. Let me refer you to a remarkable observation of one of the great sages of our days, Rabbi Yitzchak
Hutner *z"l*. In his work *Pachad Yitzchak*[43] he quotes a famous
statement by Rashi on *Shemot* 20:8 that the Ten Commandments were all said, *"bedibur echad,"* in a single utterance or
word.

This means that the Ten Commandments were not pro-
nounced by God, in progression, but were relayed simultaneously, in some mysterious way. Only after that, were they
explained separately. Rabbi Hutner asks: Why? What was the
purpose? His answer is symptomatic for Judaism.

God wanted to make it clear that all these commandments
were all equally important: one cannot claim that the observance of the fourth commandment, the Shabbat, supercedes the
fifth commandment, for example, the law of honoring one's
parents. There is no order of importance! Only after this was
made clear, was it possible for God to state every commandment separately in later instances.

---

[43] *Shavuot* VIII.

116

Student: That is a powerful observation!

LC: It is. Though I should add that it seems that on a *national* basis, the interpersonal laws between man and man may be more "important" than the laws between man and God. Certainly, there is a tendency within the Jewish tradition to support this stance.

Student: This sounds slightly heretical.

THE FLOOD OF NOACH

LC: If we examine the story of the flood in chapter six of the Book of *Bereishit*, verse 11 states, "And the earth was corrupt before God and the earth was filled with violence." Rashi comments that the meaning of this is that the generation of the flood was immersed in sexual immorality and idol worship. It could not have been worse. In Jewish law, these are two crimes for which a person must even forfeit his life in order to avoid committing—even under duress. Indeed, these are two laws for which one is demanded to give up one's life and die as a martyr.[44]

Verse 13 continues: "And God said to Noach: 'The end of life has come before Me, for the earth is filled with violence on account of them, and so behold, I am about to destroy them with the earth.'" Rashi here makes a rather strange comment: "The decree [of the flood] was sealed because of robbery."

In other words: it was not the heinous crimes of sexual immorality and idol worship which sealed mankind's punishment, but robbery!

---

[44] *Sanhedrin* 74a.

This is most surprising; especially in concurrence with the Jewish tradition that believes that even God is bound by His own laws, and will have to judge man accordingly.[45]

While the Halacha requires the death penalty for idol worship and sexual immorality,[46] robbery is more of a minor transgression (with the exception of kidnapping), which requires monetary compensation and perhaps a fine. Nowhere does it demand the death penalty (*Shemot* 21:37 and 22:8)!

Yet Rashi insists that the death of possibly millions of people in the days of the flood were *not* a result of crimes demanding the death penalty, such as immorality and idol worship (although they transgressed each one of them), but because of a "minor" transgression, namely robbery, which in halachic terms requires only monetary compensation.

Student: This means, in other words, that God punished these people for the wrong reason!

THE LACK OF "*MENSCHLICHKEIT*" IS WORSE THAN IDOL WORSHIP

LC: That seems to be the case. The aforementioned Rabbi Simcha Meir of Dvinsk, in his work, *Meshech Chochma* (*Shemot* 14:24), states that matters pertaining to courtesy and civil behavior, such as strife, slanderous talk and robbery, require minor punishments in the Torah. However, the Rabbi of Dvinsk continues by classifying that this is only true when *individuals* are violating these precepts. When the population as a whole is involved in transgressing the laws of courtesy and civil behavior, then the Jewish tradition reneges and declares

---

[45] Jerusalem Talmud, *Rosh Hashana* 1:3a.
[46] *Sanhedrin*, ibid.

that this is much worse than when the community is involved in idol worship and sexual immorality! The reason for this is that when everyone in a society is guilty of idol worship and sexual immorality, people start to believe that such practices are permitted and normal. Idol worship is definitely a terrible crime. But, as is true in the case of two people in a mutually consenting sexual relationship, which is forbidden, nobody is hurt as a result.

Both these actions are religious transgressions against God, rather than transgressions against society (even though they have indirect ramifications on that society). But when the society *en masse* transgresses the laws of civil behavior and courtesy, then the functioning of society is uprooted and normal life becomes impossible! So a "major" crime (such as sexual immorality and idol worship) becomes a "minor" transgression when committed by society as a whole. But when a "minor" transgression such as robbery becomes the standard of the whole society, then it is worse than idol worship and sexual immorality and is consequently seen as a "major" sin! Nobody can claim that they do not know better. This is the reason why Rashi states that robbery was the immediate cause of God bringing the flood and not idol worship or sexual immorality.[47]

Student: This seems to prove that when speaking of national behavior, courtesy is more important than those laws which regulate the relationship with the divine.

---

[47] For another similar example see *Torah Temima* on *Devarim* 22:25–26.

LC: In fact, Rabbi Simcha Meir also writes that today, when so many Jews violate the Sabbath, "God will postpone His judgment," since this is their habit to do so, based on ignorance.[48]

However, when our society starts misbehaving toward each other, we are immediately liable for punishment. Why? Because of the immediate danger of such violations! This approach also contains another significant element. God informs us that He can forgive humanity when they transgress those laws which regulate the relationship between man and Himself, but He cannot forgive someone for his transgressions towards his fellow man.

Student: Why?

LC: Because in the first case, man offended God. In such matters, God can decide if He should forgive them or not. But in the case where man violated those commandments which affect his fellow man, God informs us that He has no right to forgive us for such violations. After all, our fellow man is affected. In that case it is the hurt person who must forgive us. This is, by the way, the reason why *Yom Kippur* does not absolve us from such transgressions. Only those violations of the commandments between man and God are absolved, with prayers of supplication. Violations, on the other hand, against our fellow man, oblige us to ask forgiveness from them and only after that from God!

Student: The implications of this are far-reaching.

---

[48] *Meshech Chochma*, ibid.

LC: It is this exact point that we have to hammer home clearly to our students. Religious education must dedicate more time and attention to these important principles. Do not misunderstand me. I am not implying that laws regarding the observance of Shabbat, *kashrut* and family purity are of secondary importance. They provide the foundation of the Jewish tradition and as such are indispensable. But, their full potential will never be realized unless they are observed within the broader dimensions of the laws between man and man. Neither am I suggesting that things are any better in the non-religious camp. In fact, it has recently been brought to my attention that there has been a noted increase in violence in the Israeli secular school system. What I am arguing is that Orthodox Jews should be distinctive *because* they are religious Jews. They should be an example to all others. They should know better. What does it otherwise mean to be religious? Let us be honest, the secular community does not claim that it has a supreme way of living, but we the Orthodox do! The secularists have no pretensions in matters such as these. At least they are honest in their attitude. But we, the Orthodox, do claim to have a "holier" way of living, therefore rendering us more vulnerable if we fail to live up to our ideals.

Student: Rabbi Cardozo, forgive me, but are you not a little too critical of the Orthodox world?

RELIGIOUS JEWS HAVE TO SET AN EXAMPLE

LC: Maybe I am, but understand my point. I am, as I told you before, somebody who was not reared in a religious environment. Because of my awareness of the differences between secular society's perception of morality and the exalted, ethical message of Judaism, I came to appreciate the beauty of

Judaism. I am also well aware of the unbelievable kindness, charity and good deeds which flourish in the Orthodox world. I would even venture to claim that such a level of concern exists in no other society. Just think of the city of Jerusalem. The number of organizations and people who are involved in programs of kindness and charity is mind boggling. In fact it is totally astonishing. Yet, this is exactly my problem! It is because of this that I am so deeply disappointed with Orthodoxy's failure in behaving consistently with its own ideology. When I see how capable the Orthodox communities are in the way that they exceed the normal boundaries of helping people, I feel deep frustration that they do not apply a consistent level of conscientiousness in other areas.

Student: So, what can be done?

LC: After serious soul-searching, I believe that religious teaching should be restructured in such a way that far more time will be devoted to the study of Jewish texts, which deal with the holiness of life, ethics and moral conduct.

Student: Are you suggesting that our religious schools and *yeshivot* should change their study curriculum?

A NEW CURRICULUM FOR *YESHIVOT*

LC: Yes. There should be some real changes which give students the opportunity to deal with issues such as ethics on a more profound level. One should not forget that there used to be a much greater emphasis in *yeshivot* on these matters. *Mussar*, a kind of study program on human ethics, was initiated by the great sage Rabbi Yisrael Salanter *z"l*, in the nineteenth century. It engendered remarkable sensitivity in people.

Refinement was visible within people, which served to demonstrate what man was really capable of in his personal conduct. I should also mention that a completely different and more common philosophy, that of chassidism, started by the Baal Shem Tov, Rabbi Israel ben Eliezer (1700-1760), had similar outstanding results. Even those who opposed the specific *mussar* or the chassidic approaches (and there were even some Rabbis who did) agreed that there should be great emphasis placed on human ethical conduct. They simply disagreed about the methods through which this lofty ideal was to be attained.

In this vein, there is a tremendous need to start teaching in earnest *Chumash*, the Five Books of Moshe, in *yeshivot*. The learning of *Chumash* has considerably decreased in many such learning institutions. It seems that many educators forgot that teaching and studying the five books in depth, with the commentaries of great Rabbis throughout the ages, is one of the most inspiring experiences one can possibly have. Besides this, I believe there is a need to start having proper, extensive classes on *Hashkafa*, the Jewish world outlook. These kind of studies are indispensable. They provide us with warmth, music and outstanding beauty found at the core of the Jewish way of life. What I am saying is that it is time, once more, to bring this part of Jewish teaching to the forefront of our educational system, making it central in our study program. Let us be clear about one thing: ethics cannot be taught solely through the intellect. It is not mere academics. It is a way of transforming our entire personality, penetrating deep into the inner parts of our heart. That is what *mussar* and chassidism are really all about!

RE-EDUCATION

Student: It sounds like you are suggesting that there is a need for a radical change in approach to the education system.

LC: Definitely. Neither is there anything wrong or shameful about that. Throughout Jewish history, the sages have looked for new methods to educate the Jewish people, parents and children alike.[49] Every generation needs new ways to relate to the great ethical principles of Judaism. How would the Jewish tradition have otherwise made such a profound impact on Western civilization?

BACK TO THE MIDDLE AGES?

Student: To return to my original question: what can be done with all those who are irreligious or even anti-religious? We secularists shiver when we think of impending religious legislation in Israel, which will deny us our basic freedom. Back to the Middle Ages!

RELIGIOUS PARTIES AND THE COERCIVE POWER OF THE STATE

LC: I can see only one path. The Orthodox leadership should ask itself whether the religious parties should continue in their attempt to use the coercive powers of the State as a means of enforcing halachic observance. For years, it has been taken for granted that since Israel is a Jewish State, it is both right and necessary to use the secular arm of government to enforce

---

[49] See Bava Batra 21a.

halachic norms, in as many areas as possible. But the question now is whether, under today's totally new circumstances, this is still the best strategy for the enhancement of Judaism and the preservation of the Jewish character of the State. More and more religious people wonder if the kind of religious legislation, which was perhaps necessary in the days when the State showed more socialist leanings, is still the best way to proceed, bearing in mind the present political structure which strives to model itself on the Western democratic tradition. The truth is that social conditions have changed so drastically that little is gained by the preservation of some—though not all—of the religious legislation.

Student: Once more you surprise me with your observations! Please give me an example of earlier religious legislation in Israel that would no longer be viable.

THE STATUS QUO AND DISCOS

LC: Take the case of the status quo concerning places of entertainment, which until recently, kept movie theaters closed on Shabbat. At the time, the strategy was a ploy to keep youngsters from prematurely leaving the Shabbat table. But today, this is more or less completely obsolete, for the closure of these places no longer keeps the youngsters at home. This reasoning has lost all connection with reality. Movies are no longer the only major form of entertainment, while discos (which are not part of the old status quo) proliferate undisturbed. By the religious halachic standards, discos are far more objectionable, especially in light of the accompanying alcohol abuse and sexual indulgence. It is no longer the choice between the movie and the Shabbat table, but between the movie and the disco. What the religious leaders should also realize is that there is little benefit in closing down the cinemas and other places of entertainment when they are unable to be substituted with a religious uplifting experience, which would restore the beauty of Shabbat in the eyes of these young people.

BAR-ILAN STREET AND CNN

Student: That's all very nice, but take the recent case, which made headlines on CNN and was seen by millions of non-Jews around the globe. They all witnessed the spectacle of Jews fighting with each other over whether or not to close Bar-Ilan Street (one of Jerusalem's main roads) to traffic on Shabbat. Is this not embarrassing? Is this the fate of the people once called a "light unto the nations"?

LC: I believe that most people do not really understand the issue at stake. The truth is that all this touches on much broader issues. Although I would, of course, prefer if Jews would not drive on Shabbat, I really doubt that these demonstrations (against Shabbat violation) are the right strategy to keep the State more Jewish. The late and saintly Chief Rabbi of Jerusalem, Pesach Zvi Frank *z"l*, who definitely belonged to the old guard of rabbinic personalities, pointed out that when the question of Shabbat road closing in predominantly religious neighborhoods in Jerusalem first arose, in the early years of the State, the problem was not so much a Shabbat-religious issue, but was of a social nature. The issue is not one of Shabbat violation (for there will be no fewer cars on the street as a result of one or more roads being closed), but is one which touches on the needs of different people.

Student: In that case, what do you suggest as a solution?

LC: I would like to make the point that I see no reason why Bar-Ilan Street needs to stay open to normal traffic on Shabbat. My reason is that it is an interpersonal issue. Since many religious Jews live on the Bar-Ilan Street and are subsequently disturbed on their day of rest by the noise of the cars, it is only fair that it should be closed. Let us also not forget that there are quite a few non-religious people who also complain about all the noise! The cars of non-religious people could indeed take another route; it is a matter of common courtesy.

I remember when I was living in the Netherlands, we would never wash our cars or hang out the washing on a Sunday. This was so as not to offend the sensibilities of our Christian neighbors. Just as a side point, I would state from a halachic perspective, that it would be more correct to leave the road open.

Student: Why?

LC: Just think about it. Every time a car has to take a diversionary route, the car will consume more petrol, the brake lights will be used more frequently—all of which will only increase the driver's violation of the Shabbat. From that point of view, it would be better to keep this main road open. It would cause less Shabbat violation!

Student: I never thought of it like that!

RABBI SHLOMO ZALMAN AUERBACH *Z"L* AND THE SHABBAT CAR

LC: Let me tell you something about the world renowned halachic authority Rabbi Shlomo Zalman Auerbach *z"l* and the famous *Tanach* teacher Nechama Leibowitz *z"l*. She once sent one of her students to Rabbi Auerbach *z"l* with the following halachic question. Every Shabbat morning she would walk to the synagogue. But she was often stopped by people who would pass by in their cars and say "Shabbat Shalom" to her (she was widely known in non-religious circles) or would ask her which road to take to reach their destination. Apparently, she did not know what to do. Should she answer these people and show them the way or should she be silent, knowing that she would otherwise be helping these people to violate the Shabbat?

The venerable Sage responded by saying that she should say "Shabbat Shalom," since there is a halachic requirement to be friendly towards fellow Jews and moreover she should tell them how to take the fastest road to their destination so that they would not violate the Shabbat even more.[50]

Student: This is most inspiring but let us be honest. The controversy over Bar-Ilan Street is getting out of control. Nobody is on the level that you just described!

SETTLING ACCOUNTS

LC: Let me broaden the focus of our conversation to address a much greater problem, which we, in the Orthodox world, will have to acknowledge. The constantly increasing volume of anti-religious rhetoric in Israel is a warning that the ground rules and strategies, respecting the symbiosis between the Jewish tradition and the secular Israeli society are radically shifting. Today, the religious parties have substantial political power, which is ever increasing. What really worries me is the

---

[50] Told to the author by Rabbi David Shapiro of Boston who heard this story from a student of Nechama Leibowitz, *z"l*.

question of how long this will last. There is a good possibility that we are at the helm of a backlash, which could be so severe that it could cause the complete eradication of all the "religious" laws of the State, threatening its very premise. The way in which the Bar-Ilan controversy has been handled by the Israeli High Court could very well be a foretaste of this backlash. As the political realities change, the notion of "settling accounts" is evolving, as a reaction to the demands of the religious parties. It may be true that these changes will never take place, but in my humble opinion it is something the religious establishment in Israel will have to carefully consider, so that it is prepared, in the event that they come about.

Student: Is it not already too late?

HOW SECULAR ARE THE SECULAR?

LC: No, it is not. Not yet. But we, the religious, have to work fast, and above all, with a lot of wisdom. There are several ways through which a major change can be accomplished. The most important issue is to rebuild the image of Judaism in the eyes of the secular population. This we can do only by finding a common language with those who are not religious; a common denominator upon which the Orthodox and the secular can agree. We should realize that a large percentage of secular Israelis is not as secular as some of us like to believe, and that it will be possible to utilize that knowledge with great wisdom and "diplomacy."

Student: What do you mean? How does one create a "common language"? Does something like that really exist in Israel?

LC: It is exactly what I mentioned before: Jewish ethics! All of us, Orthodox or irreligious, agree that we will not survive without proper human behavior. As I indicated before: in the Jewish tradition we speak of the *mitzvot ben Adam lechavero*, the commandments concerning man relating to his fellow man. These commandments are the key to our problem. We must show our fellow Jews, in every way possible, the Jewish tradition's approach to human relations. My own studies have shown me that the Jewish tradition has the most remarkable and developed moral message of all known ethical systems. We must invest in this system and make people aware of it.

Student: How?

LC: By simply using every resource which is available to us. First of all, we must make sure that these values are taught in every school. This means that it has to be adapted as a major part of the school curriculum. It will have to be taught by people who have been well educated in the fields of Jewish Ethics. We may have to create special programs to educate the teachers. Programs need to be developed which will introduce these great principles in ways which will inspire our young people. We should bring examples from day to day life and show how the Torah would like us to behave towards our fellow man.

RABBI ARYEH LEVIN *Z"L*

Take the personality of Rabbi Aryeh Levin *z"l*, a famous *tzaddik* (righteous person) who lived during the days of the establishment of the modern State of Israel. He was a Rabbi of the "old school" with a long black coat and white beard. There are numerous unforgettable stories about him. The love, which this man showed to his fellow Jew, especially to non-religious Jews, was legendary. Most impressive are those stories which relate his involvement, care and worries for Jewish prisoners at the hand of the instigators of the British Mandate. He used to visit them regularly, especially on Shabbat, and even managed to enter the women's prison, where Jewish girls were jailed. While these men and women were completely secular and had no religious affiliation whatsoever, he spoke to them as if they were his own sons and daughters. He gave them encouragement and told them about their families and went to the British High Commissioner to plead for them. These qualities, combined with the unique radiance emanating from his face and his humble personality, were etched in the memory of these Jewish inmates. Even years after they had established families in Israel, they would see him and ask for his blessings. Although they themselves were barely involved in Jewish religious life, they had a certain respect for the Jewish tradition, thanks to Rabbi Levin, *z"l*. Even today one comes across people who were transfixed by his deeds of kindness.

A book on his life is called simply *A Tzaddik in our Time*.[51] This work should be on the curriculum of every school, religious or not. There are stories about other Rabbis and *tzadikim* which would, no doubt, make a deep impression on the secular Jewish community. My personal experience shows me that they are more impressive and effective than the most inspiring discourses.

---

[51] Simcha Raz, *A Tzaddik in Our Time* (Jerusalem: Feldheim, 1972).

It reminds me of a story about Avraham, which appeared in Rabbi Leo Jung's book, *Heirloom*.[52] The story sounds midrashic, although I have not found a source for it in the classical midrashic texts. I have told this story to numerous people, who walked away with a tremendous pride to be a grandchild of our forefather Avraham.

The story is as follows: "The house or tent of Avraham was situated on top of a hill. There were doors in all directions, so that the weary traveler, seeking its famed hospitality, might find its way without undue delay. One morning, Avraham found an old man struggling painfully up the hill. In accordance with his way Avraham rushed out of his house to meet the stranger. He helped him to reach his house on top. Additionally, he bathed his feet and offered him food and drink. The old man was profoundly grateful and when he was sufficiently relaxed, Avraham said to him: 'Now that you are happy, let us say grace to God.' The stranger looked to him without comprehension and said: 'What is God? Who is God?' 'Well,' said Avraham, 'He is the Creator of the world. He is the Father of all human beings. He is the Provider of everything we enjoy.' Said the old man: 'I know nothing about that God. I worship fire.' Avraham tried to explain to this man about God, but failed. He tried over and over again, but without any success. Slowly Avraham lost his patience and said: 'You wicked man. I cannot have a man in my house who does not acknowledge God, so leave.' The man left, deeply hurt and more lonely than ever. That night God appeared to Avraham in a dream and said: 'Avraham, I have suffered this foolish man for seventy years and you cannot have patience with him for a few hours!'"

Rabbi Jung adds: "That dream changed the course of Avraham's life. Through that dream, he truly found God, he became

---

[52] Leo Jung, *Sermons, Lectures and Studies* (NY: Feldheim, 1961) p. 32.

closer to Him. That dream has been the promise and the challenge and the whole purpose of Jewish history." I would add that this dream made Avraham into *Avraham Avinu*—"Our Father"—and transformed him into a new human being. And so Judaism began.

Student: Well, it says a lot about tolerance! A much needed ingredient in our days!

LC: Not just that. This is the whole foundation of tolerance: God is saying to humankind: "I have to have patience with millions of foolish people who do not, or cannot, believe in My existence and you (that is we) cannot even live with one of them for a few hours!"

Student: How stimulating! What else would you recommend to achieve this goal?

TELEVISION AND RADIO

LC: Despite my earlier reservations, we should use television and radio as a medium. We should create movies with a strong moral Jewish message. I would suggest creating advertisements which "merchandise" morality, using the great ethical slogans of our sages. Let us create a nationwide outreach program in every city and settlement. Let us have seminars around the country on *mitzvot ben adam lechavero*, the laws governing man and his fellow man. Let us have special courses in the universities on these subjects. And let it be well understood that these seminars should not preach, but try to teach through dialogue.

Student: Do you really believe that this could unify the Jews? Don't the universities already have courses on Jewish law, philosophy and subjects related to Jewish ethics?

THE TROUBLE WITH UNIVERSITIES

LC: True, but this is not what I have in mind. I am talking about classes which *inspire*, which make people feel uplifted, in which their very being is deeply touched. This is one of the great problems of our universities today. They offer every kind of course, but not one on how to be a "mensch" (a decent human being). Analytical and academic studies, however important and necessary, will not produce better people unless a great amount of love for the subject, as well as for fellow man, is clearly integrated and displayed. I am not talking about love of the intellect, but a profound love, which will be able to relay the message of what it means to be "a mensch." Lecturers of courses in Judaism do not educate their students on the practical application of ethical knowledge. Professors usually limit their involvement with their students to the cerebral state. Their analysis of the Jewish sources is often dry and cold; a kind of dissection of a dead corpse, instead of highlighting the living experience!

This is also a huge problem in the secular (and perhaps also in some religious) primary and secondary schools in Israel. Judaism is treated as an old fashioned tradition, to which our forefathers fell victim. Many schools study *Tanach* like Spinoza did—only to conclude how primitive our forefathers really must have been. No doubt this is the best way to ensure the termination of the Jewish People. If you are uninspired by the Jewish tradition, in the belief that it is outdated and primitive, you walk on dangerous ground. I know there are exceptions to the rule. There are some professors who do indeed

134

teach with passion and love for Judaism, but this is definitely not the general rule in many of our Israeli universities.

THE DANGER OF INSPIRATION?

Student: This may be true, but I think you are touching on a major problem. Whenever I hear the word "inspirational," I feel we fall into the pit of a "feel-good experience." Such experiences have been characterized as "vibrating on a mountain"—after which people tend to descend, and return to "business as usual." The people who had this elevating experience relapse into their own secular and materialistic ways.

I understand the same is true of groups who get involved in Kabbalah, but do not translate anything of what they learn into day-to-day life. Typically, they remain "*luftmenschen*," people who hover in the air, as it were, feeling that they have accomplished their "spiritual" duty.

LC: There is definitely truth in what you say, but I would still argue that a *modus vivendi* could be found. I believe that being on the mountain, even for a short period, has positive results. Some kind of good feeling is retained, which may motivate people to look for spirituality, without losing the ground under their feet. Moreover, I believe that Judaism has an "anti-feel good experience" device, built in to its very nature.

Student: What is that?

LC: Learning with intellectual depth while conforming to halachic requirements.

Student: Wait a moment, you just said that you oppose this type of approach, because you feel it often results in "dissecting a dead corpse!"

LC: Then I have not been sufficiently clear. What I mean to say is that intellectual understanding and learning do not exclude the possibility of being inspirational. I know from my own experience that the two are mutually compatible. A deeply practical talmudic debate with all its halachic ramifications can also be inspirational. It all depends on how the teacher and the pupil approach the text. The text has to come "alive" and the question must constantly be asked: what is the text saying to *us*? How is it relevant to *our* lives? In other words, it is a question of perspective.

THE DANGER OF SOCIOLOGY

There is another point, which I feel needs further clarification. One of the biggest problems today is the tendency to use a sociological approach to understand our society. The most frequently asked questions regarding Jews and Judaism are whether the Jews should be defined as a race, a people, a religion, a cultural entity, a historic group, or a linguistic unit? This implies that the only important question concerning Judaism and Jewish life is to which sociological category do we belong! I do not wish to minimize the importance and validity of sociology, but I think that there are more significant questions than sociological ones, such as: what do we Jews stand for? How are we defined morally and spiritually? This is far more important than the sociological distinctions between people or religious groups.

Who are we? Masses of protoplasm, sophisticated robots, tool-making machines?

It is high time that we woke up and asked what is the meaning of our communal and individual existence? The Jewish community today throughout the world is more obsessed about whether we are a cultural group than with the spiritual quality of life, the nature of good and evil, love and hatred, and how to handle envy and jealousy. Little concern is shown for the intimate spiritual needs of the individual's soul. The danger is that many people see the ultimate worth of a human in his or her usefulness to others. But a person needs to know that he or she is accepted as a value in him or herself. Even the most secular person rebels against being used as a means to an end, or as being subservient to other men. So too, the rich want to be loved for their own sake, for their essence and not for their possessions.

Student: But is it not true that Judaism sees itself as a collective religion? There is constant emphasis on the group and community.

LC: There is a certain truth to that, since it is only through the group that the individual is able to understand his or her own personal significance.

THE FAILURE OF A "SURVIVAL" PHILOSOPHY

I sometimes get the impression that people see the Jewish way of living as a kind of communal behavior system. The argument is something along these lines: the Jewish customs and laws have been indispensable as bonds of unity and forces of survival. Because we have kept these laws and customs alive for thousands of years and we prayed the same prayers and recited identical portions of the Torah in all our synagogues, we feel closely linked to each other and therefore we stayed alive throughout the centuries.

Student: Well, is this definition not correct? Is this not exactly what happened?

LC: Definitely not! What would you say if someone argued that one of the most powerful customs through which Jews survived was that of standing on their heads each morning for half an hour and then hanging from a tree for another half an hour? Could one not argue that the Jewish people have been able to survive because millions of Jews, over the last 4,000 years, throughout the world, have carefully, habitually performed these customs?

Student: It certainly would be outrageous. There must a deeper meaning to all this, a significance beyond the simple, sociological acts of behavior.

THE GOAL OF MUSIC IS TO MAKE THE MUSICAL INSTRUMENT SURVIVE?

LC: Jewish survival does not depend on external forms of conduct. It has to possess an inner life, otherwise it could not provide the force which has enabled us to continue for 4,000 years. The Jewish tradition cannot be viewed just as an instrument of Jewish survival. It would be tantamount to arguing that the main purpose of music is to ensure the continual survival of musical instruments!

What some Jewish spiritual, educational programs seem to miss is the emphasis on proper learning, or *"lernen"* as the Ashkenazi world would call it. *"Man darf steigen in lernen"* they say in Yiddish: one has to be elevated through one's

138

learning. This is achieved through practical application of
study, thus becoming transformed by it.

TO LEARN FROM *SEPHARDIM*

I am biased in this matter because I am a Sephardi Jew, from a
Spanish-Portuguese background, but I would argue that the
Ashkenazi communities should adopt some of the Sephardi
customs. This would help them overcome some of their
problems of lack of inspiration and spirituality.

Student: Such as?

IS BLACK MORE BEAUTIFUL?

LC: Examples include greater participation in the synagogue
service, such as communal singing, trying to build stronger
bonds within families. There is a certain undefined religious
warmth within the Sephardi world which, in a very different
way, is found in the German and Chassidic worlds.

Let me add another point here about the Sephardi world,
which may be of some help. Historically, *Sephardim* have
dressed in much more "optimistic" ways than other Jews, and
specifically those from Eastern Europe. The Ashkenazi community has often worn black, and many of their descendants do
so until today. The time has perhaps come to embrace the
Sephardi "custom" of "many colors."

Do not misunderstand me: I fully understand why the Ashkenazi community dressed the way it did. First of all: it lived in
countries with little sun, requiring heavy and warm dress. But
there is also a psychological dimension to it, which is that East
European Jewry constantly encountered antisemitism and
poverty. This harbored a more pessimistic outlook on life.

It was Rabbi Dr. H.J. Zimmels, who in his seminal work, *Ashkenazim and Sephardim: their Relations, Differences, and Problems as Reflected in the Rabbinical Responsa,* made me aware of this.[53] Chapter nine in this book gives a great number of examples and historical references to this phenomenon.

The question which needs to be asked is as follows: would it not be worthwhile for the Ashkenazi community to adopt a more Sephardi outlook on life? One of the reasons I emphasize this is that on more than one occasion, I have heard that Orthodox Jews create a depressingly negative impression based solely on the way they dress.

Thank God, many Jews today, including those who are living in Israel and America, no longer encounter the kind of antisemitism which their grandparents in Eastern Europe experienced. We have, on the whole (despite all different forms of existing antisemitism), much more comfortable and pleasant lives. Perhaps we should express that in the way we dress, if only so as to make a more "optimistic" impression on our children and secular fellow Jews!

JEWS ONLY PLAY THE VIOLIN

I am reminded of a comment made by a journalist on the Israeli radio that deeply impressed me. He said that it is interesting to note that most violinists of world repute were Jews, while this is not true of pianists.

He explained it the following way: a violin is an instrument, which allows escape. You can run away with it. You just take it under your arm and run. That has been the condition under which Jews have lived for many centuries. With a piano,

---

[53] Dr. H.J. Zimmels, *Ashkenazim and Sephardim* (London: Marla Publications, 1976).

however, one cannot escape. Consequently, Jews did not invest in the art of playing the piano as they did with the violin! A violin is a *galuth* (diaspora) instrument!

Student: Quite an observation!

LC: It is! Now that we have our own country and the general state of Jews has improved drastically, we are now able to play the piano! We no longer live under conditions which require us to specialize in the violin.

Student: On this optimistic note, let us call it a day and continue our conversation tomorrow.

DAY THREE

The Problem of Coercion; "Greater Is He Who Is Commanded..."; *Sine Qua Non*; Gentle Persuasion; A *Sefer Torah* for Yitzchak Rabin and Slamming the Door; Outreach for Academics; Modern Orthodoxy; The Stigma of the *Charedi*; Great Sages and the Academic and Secular World; Rabbis and the Humanities; Light Years Apart; Pluralism between the Orthodox; Why Not Reform and Conservative?; To Play Chess; How "Car-Like" Is a Steering Wheel?; Is Israel in California?; No Longer Only *Kashrut* and Marriage; Shalom; "*Vat Is Dis Luff* the Strangers?"; Car Honking and El-Al Planes; Business Ethics; Orthodoxy Makes the Same Mistake As Reform?; Sport Is War Minus Shooting; Women's Soccer Won't Go; Sisyphus and Vacation; *Chumrot*, Stringencies?; *Kappores Shloggen*; To Drink Wine; The Trouble with Black Shoes; Sexual Abstinence; The Religious Obligation To Enjoy Life; The Swiss Mountains and Rabbi Samson Rafael Hirsch; The Obligation to Eat from the Trees of the Garden of Eden; There Is No Pleasure Which Is Forbidden; Judaism Versus Christianity; Christianity and Halacha; What Is the Nature of Man?; God's Experiment at Sinai Failed?; The Holocaust Proves Christianity Right?; The Danger of Justifying Sin; Judaism Is a Little Too Optimistic; God's Realistic Acceptance of Human Limitations; The Captive Woman; Judaism Is the Art of Surpassing Civilization; Are Christians Evil People?; The Christian Paradox; The Problem Concerning God; Judaism Versus the Greco-Oriental Religions; Is God in the Sun and in the Rain?; Monotheism, Pantheism and Deism; *Deus Absconditus*; Rabbi Shneur Zalman of Liady and the Deists; Chacham David Nieto and Spinoza; Chacham Zvi; *Natura Naturans* and Not *Natura Naturata*; Is Nature Part of God?; The Illusion;

There Is Meaning to Illusion; Plato's *Phaedon*; Other-Worldly?; The Denial of Morality; The Danger of Being Too Spiritual; The Promise of Escape; The West and Its Hedonistic Pleasures; Has God Feet and Does He Get Angry?; God Has Personality; Did Anybody Ever See an Atom?; Judaism Never Objected to Ascribing Human Qualities to God; Why Is God Jealous? He Is Outright Emotional!; Depersonalization Leads to Demoralization; Spinoza's Pantheism Is Idol Worship

THE PROBLEM OF COERCION

Student: Good morning. We spoke yesterday about the relig-
ious-secular clash. I thought about it last night, and was
wondering if you are willing to elaborate on this issue. Is it
really true that there is a large and growing secular community
in Israel? You initially indicated that Israelis are less secular
than the stereotype suggests. You also affirmed that Israelis
should perhaps abolish religious laws which were passed in the
Knesset. I understand your point, but I see clearly why the
religious parties would not agree. They would no doubt argue
that without these laws, Israel would lose its Jewish character
and its essence would dissipate.

LC (Lopes Cardozo): Oh yes, I see that point as well. I also
believe that there needs to be a *minimal* amount of religious
legislation.

Student: Why do you say that there should only be a minimal
amount?

LC: Because there is strong evidence that aspects of Judaism
for which there is no legislation are still, by and large, observed
by the vast majority of Israeli Jews. This is even true for those
whose commitment to Judaism is quite minimal. Take the

almost complete silence on *Yom Kippur*, even in the streets of
Tel Aviv and Haifa. Consider the celebration of *bar* and
bat-mitzva, the desire to be married by a Rabbi, the celebration
of *Pesach* and *Chanuka* and the lighting of Shabbat candles.
These and many other forms of Judaism are still completely or
partially observed by the less or non-religious communities.

"GREATER IS HE WHO IS COMMANDED..."

Student: Why is that?

LC: I think it is connected with a great psychological law laid
down by Rabbi Chanina in the Talmud: "Greater is he who is
commanded and performs than he who is not commanded and
performs."[54] It is human nature to react negatively to what is
perceived as external coercion. Non-religious Jews want to
take part in Jewish tradition, but they object to any kind of
pressure. In this case, it is better to use the approach of
non-coercion in order to allow people to find their way to
Judaism.

Student: Are you, as an Orthodox Jew, really suggesting that
Israel should abolish religious legislation, in order to facilitate
people's greater participation in Judaism? I am afraid that
many of your own colleagues will oppose you and accuse you
of being unrealistic and naive!

---

[54] *Bava Kama* 87a.

SINE QUA NON

LC: I am sure they will. But I am not suggesting that we remove *all* religious legislation. As I said, I do not believe that Israel could survive without some of it. Religious legislation must remain *sine qua non*, enabling religious people to function without hindrance in the workplace, and in society at large, as well as retaining laws that secure the right of their children to attend religious schools. In other words, religious legislation remains vital, but the raison d'être should no longer be the concern for the souls of our fellow Jews. Rather it should be limited to providing what is required for religious Jews to participate in Israeli society. Legislation should guarantee that religious Jews will never be faced with the necessity of working on Shabbat. It should also make sure that observant Jews can eat in the cafeterias of public institutions or the Israeli army. There is also need of some legislation concerning marriage and divorce, as we discussed before. This is necessary in ensuring unity. But besides the above examples, it should do no more than guarantee Orthodoxy's democratic rights. If matters drastically change (and they could, as I mentioned before), religious schools may become so costly that most families will no longer be able to afford the fees.

Student: So what is it that you want?

GENTLE PERSUASION

LC: I want religious legislation to continue in order to protect the rights of religious Israelis, but I do not want it to have any theocratic (form of government by God or priestly order) ambitions. That would be counter-productive and, if anything, make the State increasingly secular. Educating toward Judaism can only be taught through gentle persuasion, not through legislation.

Student: To return to your earlier statement that Israelis are still interested in Judaism: how do you know that this is true?

LC: I think this was clear, for example, at the time of the Rabin assassination. Why were Israelis so terribly upset? Why has there been such unprecedented outpouring of grief over the past months and years, even from those who opposed Prime Minister Rabin's policies? It was, and is, most unusual, even for an event of this magnitude. People were literally walking around crying. There is no end to the number of people who visit the scene of the crime in Tel Aviv or the graveside of Yitzchak Rabin. People have not ceased speaking about it months and even years later. I believe that the reason behind all this is a deep Jewish sensitivity. We cannot tolerate the violation of something which has always kept us together: Jewish ethics! It is precisely this matter that provides us with the key to our problem: Jewish ethics. What people do not realize is that their protest and outrage against the assassination of Prime Minister Rabin is nothing else but a manifestation of being deeply rooted in Judaism. We saw a similar phenomenon when President Kennedy was assassinated. America, however secular, is, deep down, a religious country in which similar biblical/Jewish values play a decisive role.

Student: So, you are saying that those who now hold the Jewish tradition responsible for this act, are in fact doing so in the name of Judaism?

A *SEFER TORAH* FOR YITZCHAK RABIN AND SLAMMING THE DOOR

LC: Exactly! The tragedy is that they do not realize it. This is because they lack even a small particle of Jewish knowledge. Nevertheless, their whole being has been profoundly effected by Judaism. Take another remarkable phenomenon. Members of the Knesset, Israel's parliament, and many of those who work in its offices, have decided to employ a scribe to write a *sefer Torah*, a scroll of the Torah, in memory of Yitzchak Rabin. This is a religious act, the last of the 613 Commandments, in accordance with the code of Maimonides. What is most astounding about this is the fact that it reflects a most strange paradox: those who have called for the writing of this scroll are the very people who hold Judaism responsible for the assassination! It is like the case where somebody storms out of his house after a major quarrel, slams the door, but ends up inside!

Student: Remarkable! But let us return to your original idea of starting a nationwide outreach program. This is an enormous undertaking, perhaps the largest Israel could ever achieve. Your suggestion entails reaching out to millions of people through every kind of possible program. It needs tens of thousands of people to get actively involved. It requires thousands of teachers, and schools to teach the teachers. How would this ever work? How would it be funded?

OUTREACH FOR ACADEMICS

LC: Before answering that, I would like to focus on those who are among the most respected segments of Israeli society: the academics. They are important because they play a crucial role in the future of the Israeli State. They will shape its character for many years to come. So, if we want to make sure that the State stays Jewish, we will have to focus on them. What is so worrisome is the fact that this group is mostly secular and thus difficult to influence. Many of them, too, belong to left-wing political parties, a common phenomenon among academics worldwide.

Student: So how can you influence them?

LC: Here, I believe, lies a most important task for what people call "Modern Orthodoxy."

Student: Who are the Modern Orthodox and what is this important task?

MODERN ORTHODOXY

LC: It is not easy to provide you with a precise definition. In general, one could say that Modern Orthodoxy is a movement that consists of a large number of Orthodox Jews, including many professionals and academics. They believe that religious Jews should interact with the outside world, while at the same time adhering to Jewish values, without any halachic compromise. Typical members of this community are graduates of Yeshiva University in New York, which may be seen as the school which stands at the center of this ideological platform.

Student: And you believe that they could have some influence on the secular academic community in Israel?

LC: Yes. The dialogue could only take place with learned Orthodox Jews who possess expert secular knowledge, enabling them to find a common language with Israeli academics. This, I believe, can also be achieved by those people who are often affiliated with the Young Israel communities in the United States, an Orthodox organization of Jewish communities throughout much of the English-speaking world in the USA, alongside graduates of Yeshiva University, Bar-Ilan etc. As I indicated before, these communities comprise all types of professionals—lawyers, accountants, scientists and physicians. Their ranks also include academicians of world stature. We will have to include them in our venture. This group is small, but we will have to find a way to make sure that they become a major force in Israel.

Student: Are you saying that the so-called ultra-Orthodox *charedi* community is not able to have that kind of influence on the academic world?

THE STIGMA OF THE *CHAREDI*

LC: Let us first of all be very careful with the word *charedi*. It is used "in and out of season." *Charedi* literally means "devout." I would like to stress that there are many people who belong to the Modern Orthodox camp, who are *charedi*, because they are most anxious to live a completely religious life. To my great regret, the word has now become stigmatized, indicating a certain group, with connotations of religious fanatics, as perceived by the media. I hope I am able to say that I am also *charedi*, in the true sense of the word, or at least aspire to be one day. But now that the word *charedi* is associated with that group of Orthodox Jews who have little contact with the academic and modern world, I have to admit that it would be far from easy to initiate a dialogue between them and the secular Israeli academic world.

I once watched a TV debate between a famous and once very secular Israeli figure, who had become religious and joined the *charedi* community, and a completely secular professor of archeology. The *charedi* person tried to prove that archeology was completely unreliable and false. The professor wiped the floor with him and showed in the most clear terms that his opponent did not know what he was talking about. Indeed, the religious person made himself appear completely ludicrous, but instead of recognizing his inferiority of knowledge in that area, he continued making the most outrageous statements, which only served to underline his foolishness in front of hundreds of thousands of Israeli viewers.

This was a travesty of the first order. But it is far from true that all *charedi* people are exactly the same in that respect. It is my belief that it is almost always beneficial when the academic world meets, however sporadically, with the *charedi* world. Though infrequent, and perhaps paradoxically, there are some professors and scientists who are part of the *charedi* world.

There is a lot of overlapping between Modern Orthodoxy and *charedi* Jews. Many *charedim* are Americans or Europeans. Among them are some remarkable individuals who are quite able to hold their own in an intellectual conversation with secular academics. It should also be mentioned that some of the greatest sages of our century, who were *charedi* Jews, are known to have had extensive knowledge of secular subjects, and were able to have highly intellectual discussions with the members of the secular community.

Students: Could you give me some examples?

GREAT SAGES AND THE ACADEMIC AND SECULAR WORLD

LC: Once more, I should mention the late Rabbi Shlomo Zalman Auerbach *z"l*, a halachic authority of world renown, of this past generation. He was an expert on electricity and other scientific matters, and was especially known for his knowledge of medicine. His rulings on problems related to medical ethics are famous. I have read that several professors in the medical field said that he was a great expert of the current knowledge in their fields. His grasp of the issues was profound and his clarity phenomenal. I should also mention one of the great American sages, Rabbi Yaakov Kaminetsky *z"l*, one of the most brilliant minds of our days. As well as being the dean of *yeshivot*, he advised tens of thousands of people who came to him from every walk of life, and was able to speak with them on any topic.

Rabbi Avraham Yitzchak Kook *z"l*, the Chief Rabbi of Palestine just before the State of Israel was established, should also be noted here. In many ways he was even more remarkable, because he did not deal so much with the scientific communities as with the humanities. He never studied at university, but he must have read a great deal of secular works. It seems that he read extensively from general philosophy, including that which was of a non-religious and often anti-religious nature. He is known to have written one of the best critiques on Spinoza![55]

But I should remind you of the fact that he was a Rabbi of the "Old School" attending *chaderim* and *yeshivot*. He used to walk around with a *shtreimel*, the old-fashioned fur hat chassidic Jews used to wear in Poland and other European countries.

---

[55] Rabbi Avraham Yitzchak Kook, *Ekvei HaTzon*, pp. 130–41.

He belonged to the "Old Yishuv," the earliest group of religious settlers who made *aliyah* in the 18th and 19th centuries,
well before the modern State of Israel was established. He was
also a featured speaker at the opening of Hebrew University.
He was, without doubt, one of the greatest and most original
religious thinkers of his day. Today, he is also quoted with
great respect by non-religious scholars. In summary, we would
do well not to stereotype *charedi* as a group of people who do
not, in any way, relate to the secular world. It is really far more
complicated.

Student: Why do you consider the study of humanities by
Rabbis even more remarkable than the study of science? Does
it not have a similar value to Rabbis studying science?

RABBIS AND THE HUMANITIES

LC: No, I believe there is a difference. When Rabbis study the
exact sciences, they basically do not take a risk as far as their
belief system is concerned. At least from a Jewish point of
view, physics is religiously neutral. Or almost. Even evolution
theories pose no great threat. They do not challenge religious
belief. In contrast, the humanities are often non-religious, or
even anti religious. We have Atheism, Pantheism and perhaps
problematic exercises such as Bible criticism, which challenges
the divinity of Torah and other biblical works. Most Rabbis,
even those who have a tremendous knowledge of Talmud and
other Jewish classical works, have little or no knowledge of
these matters, and are often unable to respond when confronted
with these theories. Rabbi Kook and others were able to rise to
this intellectual threat, and even refuted those secularists who
believed that they had won the day. These, however, were
exceptional cases.

Student: You do not deny then that, by contrast, most *charedi*-educated people are distanced from the secular world.

LIGHT YEARS APART

LC: It cannot be denied that, in general, both communities are light years apart from each other. To be fair, I should emphasize that many of us could learn a lot from these "ultra-Orthodox" Jews. Their commitment to Judaism is most impressive. It is time to remove the element of suspicion and skepticism from the term "ultra-Orthodox."

PLURALISM BETWEEN THE ORTHODOX

Let me make another point. Different groups within Orthodox Judaism often argue that their interpretation of Judaism is the most authentic one, and that the others should "*see the light*," and return to their correct understanding and practice of the Jewish tradition. We see this occurring not only within the *charedi* community, but also among the Modern Orthodox, the Chassidic and the sephardic Orthodox world. I believe that this is a great error. What all these groups should understand is that Judaism can easily incorporate diverse portrayals of its tradition, so long as they agree with the foundations upon which Judaism stands. Beyond that basis, however, Judaism is a multi-colored tradition which encourages as many interpretations as possible.

One of the great chassidic Rabbis from the Gerer dynasty was once asked why he did not agree with the Satmar Rebbe, Rabbi Joel Teitelbaum *z"l* (a twentieth century Jewish authority), regarding his attitude towards Zionism. Unlike the Gerer Rebbe, the latter was known to be an outspoken opponent of

Zionism, who saw this movement as a threat to Jewish survival! Rabbi Teitelbaum felt that Zionism would ultimately
secularize all Jews and the Jewish homeland. The Gerer Rebbe
responded that if the Satmar Rebbe would not have been such a
strong opponent to Zionism, he, the Gerer Rebbe, would have
been. In other words, he was of the opinion that *somebody*
should oppose Zionism forcefully, because of its secularism.
Since the Satmar Rebbe had already taken that task, he, the
Gerer Rebbe, could present a more favorable portrayal of its
positive aspects. This, I believe, is significant. Only through
such an approach will it be possible to find a balance. It seems
that rabbinic authorities were very aware of this dialectic.
These Rabbis believed in a pluralistic approach within Orthodox Judaism so as to give expression to the totality of the
Jewish tradition. I would argue that this should also apply to
the attitude to the *charedi* and Modern Orthodox world. They
are both needed, since they are, in some ways complementary.
They need each other, so as to allow for a full appreciation of
Judaism.

WHY NOT REFORM AND CONSERVATIVE?

Student: So what about Reform and Conservative Judaism?
Are they not included in this pluralistic bracket of Judaism?

LC: No doubt the Orthodox would respond by arguing that this
is impossible, as these two movements deny certain fundamental tenets of belief that are crucial to Judaism. Once one
denies them, one can no longer speak of authentic Judaism.

This clearly includes Orthodoxy's belief in *"Torah min Ha-shamayim,"* the divinity of the written Torah and the authenticity of the oral, talmudic tradition.[56] As discussed earlier, the written Torah is, to the Orthodox, the "word-by-word" account of God's will, spoken to and written by Moshe. *How* this revelation took place is a matter of much philosophical debate, but the fact that it *did* take place, is, as far as Orthodoxy is concerned, a principle crucial to the corpus of Judaism. And that is exactly what mainstream Conservative and, even more so Reform, ideologies have abandoned. This means that they have changed the ground rules, the rock bottom foundations of Judaism. Once removed, it is debatable whether one can still speak of Judaism. I should add that there are even secular thinkers who have made this point.

Student: So you are saying that authentic Judaism is only Orthodox Judaism, and that Reform and Conservative Judaism could not make a claim to this title?

LC: This is definitely true for Orthodoxy. But let us not forget that we are getting involved in semantics which only obscures that which we are trying to understand.

Student: I am not sure I understand what you are saying.

---

[56] For a comprehensive overview see the author's *The Written and Oral Torah* (NJ: Jason Aronson, 1998).

TO PLAY CHESS

LC: Some time ago, a secular Israeli journalist made the point that although he is completely secular, he would not be prepared to see Reform officially classified as Judaism.[57] His argument may sound simplistic, but it is basically correct. Let me restate his point a bit more eloquently.

As with other products of human culture, it is really history that provides us with working definitions of man made reality. Once we change the meaning of these definitions, we become confused since we are violating their philological understanding.

Consequently, words and definitions can lose their meaning. Take the word "car." This word is only meaningful when we identify it in a way in which we have traditionally understood it. Now there may be many different models of cars, but all of them will still be identified with this word as long as they fulfill certain *fundamental* conditions which are essential to the word "car." Once these basic conditions are no longer fulfilled, we can no longer speak of a "car."

Take another example: what is chess? We have to say that it is the game which tradition has identified by the name "chess." No one would allow the playing of chess by the rules of draughts. True, the latter may be a more interesting game, but it is not chess. Even if there were many new enthusiasts of the game, they cannot complain that the International Chess Competition will not accept them. Why? Because the International Chess Federation is an organization that includes only those who play chess as it has been defined historically and agreed upon.

---

[57] David Navon, *Yediot Achronot*, February 5, 1998.

So it is with "Judaism." The definition of this word historically includes the belief that the written Torah, as we have always known it, was revealed and given, word by word, by God to Moshe and the Jewish people. Moreover, it includes an oral tradition, whose foundations are rooted in the same revelational experience. Once this is accepted, one can argue about nearly anything else within the Jewish tradition. But one cannot deny these principles without making the word "Judaism" meaningless

Without doubt, pluralism definitely exists within Judaism, accompanied by disagreement about many of its principles of belief. However the belief in the divinity of the Torah and some of its basic oral traditions is fundamental.

Student: So is there nothing Jewish about Reform and mainstream Conservative "Judaism"?

HOW "CAR-LIKE" IS A STEERING WHEEL?

LC: That is not what I am saying. There are many Jewish dimensions to these movements. What I am saying is that it is impossible to fully call them "Judaism," since it would defy the very meaning of this term. How long could one still call a car a car?

It is only legitimate to call a steering wheel a gear, or a tire "car-like," if the basic requirements of what is meant by that term is fulfilled. Moreover, the more items you have like these, the closer the object described will be to being car-like. It will get very close to being a car, but it will never be a car until it has fulfilled all the fundamental requirements of an automobile. So too with the Reform or mainstream Conservative movements. They are very Jewish and some manifestations of these movements may get very close to Judaism, but it is difficult to see them as a *full* representation of Judaism.

IS ISRAEL IN CALIFORNIA?

In order to be accepted by the Orthodox, the Conservative and Reform movements will have to agree that for thousands of years the Orthodox interpretation of the divinity of the Torah has been the only accepted definition of Judaism. Let me illustrate my point. What would happen if some people came tomorrow and told us that the State of Israel is not built on soil of land in the Middle East, since the real biblical land of Israel is probably in California—would we accept that; would the Reform movement accept that?

Student: It would be outrageous!

LC: But why? Could you really prove that the Israel of today is located on the very soil of the Holy Land?

Student: I suppose not.

LC: Exactly. We believe that the State of Israel is built on the soil of the Holy Land because *tradition* has told us that the Holy Land used to be on this spot on the shore of the Mediterranean. Once we start to doubt this, everything falls apart and it would signify the end of the State of Israel. We cannot even take the risk in *allowing* for such changes to our traditional definitions since too much is at stake. This is the reality behind the Orthodox argument in their definition of the word "Judaism."

Student: I see your point and have to think about this more. In the meantime, let us return to your suggestion to establish a nation-wide outreach program. Once more: how are we ever going to realize all this and how would it be financed?

NO LONGER ONLY *KASHRUT* AND MARRIAGE

LC: I have already conceded that it will take many years to realize this. Yet it is by far the greatest challenge confronting Orthodoxy. We will have to think ambitiously, and above all, look to the future. We will have to ask ourselves what will be in another 50 years? How Jewish will Israel be? What kind of a country will we leave behind for our grandchildren? There is a need for broad thinking, careful analysis and a lot of unprecedented creativity. There is no time to focus only on tomorrow. Our religious leadership can no longer afford to focus solely on matters, however important, related to *kashrut*, marriage and divorce. The time has come to ask the underlying questions and to provide guidance and superior answers.

As for finances, perhaps I am a little naive, but I believe that if we mapped out a major plan, we will be able to find sponsors. Jews around the world are very worried about the future of Israel. They are aware that things are not going well for Israel. While they see Israel as their child, they feel that the child does not always behave. A successful Israel is still their dream. Sometimes, people prefer to sponsor dreams than to give large amounts of money to facts that they can not change. If we change the image of Judaism, as I indicated before, we will find the finances as well. I admit, it won't be easy. I am just saying that we will have to try. We have no option.

Student: What kind of courses do you believe should be prominent in this nationwide outreach program?

SHALOM!

LC: We should not start with full courses, but, rather with educating people to say "shalom" to everyone they meet, even people they do not know. It engenders a completely different atmosphere when a fellow Jew, or a human being suddenly encounters a smile and a greeting from somebody he or she does not even know. It could change their mood and the world will suddenly look much more pleasant

"*VAT IS DIS LUFF* THE STRANGERS?"

I am reminded of a beautiful story, told by Rachel Naomi Remen, who is a physician, very involved with people stricken with cancer. One day a Holocaust survivor was brought to her retreat for cancer patients. This man, by the name of Yitzchak, was overwhelmed by all the love and hugging, which was part of the treatment. With a heavy accent, he asked: "*Vat is all dis, all dis* huggy huggy? *Vat is dis luff* the strangers? *Vat is dis*?" It was clear that he had never experienced much love besides that of his intimate family. Having lived in concentration camps, he was deeply disturbed by all this "new" love and felt most uncomfortable. It took some time, but he became more relaxed and open. One day, Dr. Remen came to see him and asked how he was doing. "Much better," he replied. He had spoken with God and asked Him what this love was all about.

"Ah, Rochele, I say to Him: 'God, is it okay to *luff* strangers?' And God says: 'Yitzchak, *vat is dis* strangers, you make strangers, I don't make strangers!'"[58]

---

[58] Rachel Naomi Remen, MD, *Kitchen Table Wisdom* (NY: Riverhead Books, 1996) p. 156.

Student: Great!

CAR HONKING AND EL-AL PLANES

LC: We have to teach people to have more patience, and not to start honking when somebody tries to get his or her car re-started in the middle of the street. To say "thank you" to the stewardess or to the waiter in a restaurant and give him or her a compliment. I am always very disturbed when I find myself in an El-Al plane (which I do frequently) and witness Orthodox Jews praying and "*making a minyan*" in a back aisle. In most cases they block off all passage coming from that side. People can't go to the washrooms and the stewardesses become frustrated because they can no longer continue serving the travelers. In all honesty, I believe it would be better to pray without a *minyan*, which indeed I once suggested. Isn't that better than giving yourself a bad name and consequently that of Judaism too? Making people aware of these matters could be done with a lot of humor and common sense. If you keep on telling people about proper, ethical behavior day after day, month after month, year after year, you will inevitably see some major changes in people's personal conduct. Let there be advertisements with a moral message.

Major companies should sponsor large advertising posters. But, remember, my point is to have all this embedded in Jewish tradition. There should not just be general statements about human behavior! Every item of human ethical behavior must be furbished with quotations and examples from our sources. Many quotations found in "*Pirkei Avot*," the Ethics of the Fathers, could lead us in the right direction.

After all, most human ethics are actually derived from the Jewish tradition. They may have been "secularized" over time, so that most people do not recognize their origins, but the truth is, that without Judaism, most of these principles would have been unheard of.

BUSINESS ETHICS

Student: What else would be in your program?

LC: I suggest we educate the great value of speaking the truth and the dangers of lying, and the problem of *Lashon Hara*, speaking evil about one's fellow man. Then there are business ethics, a major problem today.

Student: Is that not standard education in the Orthodox world?

LC: Officially it is, but again, one needs to be honest about this. For all sorts of reasons, certain Orthodox circles today have given a one-sided picture of Judaism: only *mitzvot ben adam leMakom*, between man and God, are adequately taught. That is dangerous.

Student: But why did this happen?

LC: Rabbi Joseph Ber Soloveitchik *z"l* of Boston, states that it is a much greater challenge to live by the ethical standards of Judaism, than by its ritual counterpart. "One who scrupulously fulfills the *Choshen Mishpat* [Judaism's code of ethical business legislation] would find it considerably difficult to become a millionaire, because of its restrictions on many popular money-making practices. There are some who, though stringent in ritual observance, are less than meticulous in human relations.

This, though inexcusable, may not be due to hypocrisy, but to the formidable standards of the *Choshen Mishpat* with its demands that we discipline our greed in recognition of the rights and feelings of others.

Even the *mitzva* of *tzedaka*, giving charity, requires a readiness to lessen one's hard earned equity for the sake of strangers, which is almost unnatural, and most find difficult to observe properly."[59]

ORTHODOXY MAKES THE SAME MISTAKE AS REFORM?

Student: This is quite understandable.

LC: I agree, but the trouble is that Orthodoxy should be careful not to fall victim to precisely that which it objects to within Reform Judaism. Reform is guilty of selecting *mitzvot* whenever it pleases her. It espouses a sort of casual Judaism.

Orthodoxy strongly objects to such an interpretation, and rightly so. I am raising only one question: isn't Orthodoxy doing exactly the same when it highlights the *mitzvot* between man and God more prominently than those between man and man?

Student: That is a good point. But there is one obvious difference. Orthodoxy would never *officially* abandon any *mitzvot* including those between man and man while Reform has *officially* discarded several *mitzvot*.

LC: True.

---

[59] Avraham R. Besdin, *Man of Faith in the Modern World: Reflections of the Rav* (NJ: Ktav, 1989) p. 153.

SPORT IS WAR MINUS SHOOTING

Student: Rabbi Cardozo, here is another dislocated question. We spoke before about swimming; what do you think of sport in general?

LC: Well, you know, somebody once said: sport is war minus shooting. There is a certain amount of truth in that. Sport has lost a lot of its original meaning and purpose, as a form of spiritual and physical relaxation. It has often turned into "war," because it became the subject of money and discord. Maimonides wrote that we are commanded to exercise so as to keep our bodies in good condition, since our bodies are given to us by God on loan and have to be carefully looked after.[60] Our bodies are not our own.

Seen from this perspective, sport is a *mitzva*, a divine imperative. The trouble is that we are inclined to think, when we watch a football game, that we are actually participating in it! I am always fascinated by the fact that tens of thousands of people are completely mesmerized when they see a ball being kicked around by twenty-two fellows. Do not misunderstand me. I don't deny the art behind soccer. There is more to soccer than meets the eye. As a Dutchman, I know what I am talking about. But it is not the sport itself which is so fascinating as much as the psychology behind it.

Student: What do you mean?

LC: I am increasingly inclined to think that the most important part of these games is the verbal bashing and screaming that takes place in the stands. The great thing about soccer is that

---

[60] *Mishne Torah, De'ot*, chapter 4.

twenty-two people run themselves crazy for our benefit. We sit in the stands, shaking our heads in approval or disapproval. In either case we play the "expert" who knows it all. We human beings need that. We play the wise old lord, while the shouting is nothing more than therapy. Many of us have to go to work everyday and be submissive to our employers. We can't tell them what we really think of them. So when we shout at the soccer player, telling him that he is a *schlemeel* and that he does not know how to handle the ball, we are really shouting at our boss. It brings tremendous relief. In other words, it is a moment when we can rid ourselves of our pent up frustration, abandoning the artificial courtesy which we are obliged to show at work.

WOMEN'S SOCCER WON'T GO

That is, by the way, the reason that women's soccer will probably never achieve mass popularity. Because there again, we need to be polite. Shouting and yelling is unbecoming when we see twenty-two ladies running after a ball.

Again, do not misunderstand me. Sport is an art and should be greatly encouraged. I am deeply impressed by some soccer players who seem to perform magic with the ball. Moreover, there are certain forms of sport which completely fascinate me precisely because I cannot decipher them.

Student: For example?

SISYPHUS AND VACATION

LC: Tobogganing and perhaps skiing. I agree that both sports are great. In my home country, the Netherlands, tobogganing is a very popular sport, and I myself indulged. But really, I can't make any sense of it.

Student: Why?

LC: Because there is something very bizarre about it. I cannot really understand how we are prepared to climb a mountain for more than a quarter of an hour, leaving us sweating and breathless, and then in a matter of a few seconds undo all this, by chasing down the same mountain! It is very discouraging. It reminds me of Sisyphus, the famous personality in Greek mythology, who was doomed to roll a heavy stone up a mountain. Every time he neared the peak, he slipped and had to start all over again. For us, this is winter sport: for Sisyphus it was torment. Sisyphus was doomed to do so as a punishment. We save money the whole year to be able to do the same! It seems that man is prepared to torment himself as long as he convinces himself that winter sport awaits him! I find this fascinating. Don't get me wrong. I too enjoy it, I look forward to sitting with my grandchildren and riding down the mountainside on a sledge at record-breaking speed, but it is beyond me why I do. It is probably connected with speed, and again, as we mentioned at the outset, a need for pressure. Perhaps we try to beat time, because we know that it is time which makes us mortal. In any event, it remains a puzzle.

CHUMROT, STRINGENCIES?

Student: Let me turn to another matter which greatly disturbs me: self-imposed *chumrot*, severities. From my understanding the religious are clearly living in days in which *chumrot* have become well established and accepted. Is this a sign of greater religiosity? Moreover, do you believe that it is healthy?

LC: I am sure that, for many people, it is an expression of a genuine desire to come closer to God. That can only be admired. It is understandable that living in an age of such great comfort and pleasure, people want to increase their religious commitment. More than that, I believe that each person should have his or her self-imposed *chumra*, that is to take a *mitzva* and be more particular and strict about ***that*** *mitzva* than what the letter of the law requires. From an educational perspective, this is healthy, but there is, no doubt, another side to the coin.

Student: A less favorable side?

LC: Precisely! One should be most careful not to use a *chumra* as an escape. What I mean to say is that there are people who use a *chumra* to conceal their lack of observance in other religious areas. This could no doubt happen, as I mentioned before, in a case where somebody is very particular about eating *glatt* kosher, but is not particular when it comes to business ethics. Or when somebody is more strict in matters related to the observance of Shabbat, but does not care about the feelings of his fellow man.

Asking for *glatt* kosher food while sitting in jail as a convicted felon, is tantamount to asking, after one has murdered both parents, for dispensation on the basis that one is an orphan. There may be some exceptions to this rule, but in most cases, such *chumrot* are used as a disguise.

Student: But this type of "escape" is not limited to *chumrot*. This may also happen with laws and very well established *minhagim* (customs).

LC: Very true. I have seen cases where people will *"shlog kappores"* on the eve of *Rosh Hashana* or *Yom Kippur*, yet also violate the law.

KAPPORES SHLOGGEN

Student: What do you mean? What is *"shlog kappores"*?

LC: Well, you know that there is a custom, mentioned by the Rema (Rabbi Moshe Isserles) in the *Shulchan Aruch*, the Code of Jewish Law (*Orach Chaim* 7), which states that one should take a live chicken (some use money as a substitute) and move it above one's head as a kind of symbolic atonement for one's sins throughout the previous year. This is done right before *Yom Kippur*. (It is somehow, although not identical, a reminder of the atonement-sacrifices in the Temple.)

The obvious intent in the Code is to do this very carefully so that the chicken does not get hurt or scared. After all, there is a law which states that it is absolutely forbidden to cause any unnecessary pain to an animal.

This prohibition is called *tza'ar ba'ale chayim*. Authorities believe that this law is a *D'oraita*—a biblical law—and not just a rabbinical decree.[61] What I have witnessed, however, is very sad. To help facilitate performance of this custom, some people brought these chickens to a central location in small plastic boxes, put them in the sun without providing any water and left them there for hours. After that, people came to *"shlog kappores"* with them, swinging these creatures around without any compassion.

---

[61] For a full discussion see Noah J. Cohen, *Tza'ar Ba'ale Hayim* (Jerusalem: Feldheim, 1976).

They believed that they had done a great *mitzva*, when in fact, they had only added another transgression to their list. They had done exactly the opposite of what they wanted to achieve. I consider such a matter to be an enormous tragedy because it is a manifestation of a much larger problem with which the religious community is sometimes confronted: the collapse of proper religious values and priorities. Again, it is a great pity, because it makes many irreligious people disillusioned with religion and religious people, besides the issue of causing pain to these creatures. By the way, I should mention that it is perhaps time that kosher consumers should no longer just look for *glatt* kosher, but also for "mercy *glatt*." Too many animals are raised under inhumane conditions (for example, the raising and feeding of geese for their livers and calves for veal). While it will be difficult to improve these conditions and meat may become too expensive, rabbinical authorities should seriously consider this possibility. When asked if he was a vegetarian for health reasons, Isaac Bashevis Singer replied, "Yes, for the chicken's health...."

But to return to "*kappores shlogen*," many *Sephardim* do not practice this custom. Perhaps this custom is unacceptable in these communities because of the problem of *tza'ar ba'ale chaim*. Other reasons are given by classical sources.

Student: How did the sages of Israel view stringencies in general?

TO DRINK WINE

LC: Firstly, one should be aware that even the Torah discusses the need for stringencies, but only in very special circumstances. In the Book of *Bamidbar* (chapter 6), for example, there is the case of the Nazirite, a person who voluntarily denies himself the enjoyment of wine and other alcoholic beverages, among other things. The Torah appears to encourage this self-abnegation in those who are in need of it, in order to get their priorities in order and to increase their religious commitment. However, the Talmud limits the time frame of such abstinence to no more than thirty days, and warns that such procedures may be counterproductive.[62] Interestingly, the text calls for an atonement offering by the Nazirite at the end of this period and commands him or her to drink wine (*Bamidbar* 6:21). The abstinence of wine requires atonement! It is clear from this statement that it is not the abstinence from wine or any other alcoholic drink which is considered to be the ideal. Rather, it is the drinking of wine in the right spirit and with the right intention that counts. To drink at the right time and for the right purpose and to stay in control, knowing one's limitations—this is the ideal. But to achieve that goal, one may first require a period of abstinence.

THE TROUBLE WITH BLACK SHOES

Let me show you another statement in the Talmud which relates to this issue. A story is told of a scholar by the name of Eliezer Ze'era who wore "black shoes" (which were uncommon in those days) as a sign of mourning for the destruction of Jerusalem.

The sages considered this to be an act of arrogance, since they believed that he was trying to show off by proving that he was more religious than anybody else. So they put him in jail![63]

---

[62] Jerusalem Talmud, *Nazir* 1:3.
[63] *Bava Kama* 59b.

On another occasion, we are told that a certain very "religious" person was not prepared to follow a lenient ruling of the sages and was nearly excommunicated![64] These stories speak volumes.

SEXUAL ABSTINENCE

Student: This brings me to my next question regarding Judaism's attitude towards sexual abstinence. I understand that Judaism's attitude toward sexuality is very different to that of Christianity, for example.

LC: The difference between Judaism and Christianity is a major issue and entails lengthy elaboration. But let me first answer your question. Judaism views sexuality in a positive light. It does not see sexuality as the manifestation of the evil inclination in man. God gave man sexual feelings and therefore they cannot be evil. They are neutral and depending on how man uses his sexuality, it could be positive or negative. This is also true regarding all other things from which man may derive enjoyment, such as eating and drinking. It all depends how man uses these inclinations. This is one of the great messages of Judaism: all feelings and desires, even the most physical, can be sanctified. There is a rabbinic observation which says that when husband and wife come together, the *Shechina*, the divine Presence, is between them! I have seen sincere Christians turn pale when they heard me quote this!

---

[64] *Bava Kama* 80b, 81a.

THE RELIGIOUS OBLIGATION TO ENJOY LIFE

Student: So Judaism wants man to enjoy life, even its physical aspects?

LC: Absolutely. The sages observed that if one does not enjoy the pleasures of the world while the Torah permits them, one will have to give account for that in exactly the same way as one would after having transgressed something, which is forbidden in the Torah.[65]

THE SWISS MOUNTAINS AND RABBI SAMSON RAFAEL HIRSCH

I am reminded of a story I once heard about the aforementioned nineteenth century sage, Rabbi Samson Rafael Hirsch, who decided, when he was a very old man, to go on vacation to Switzerland. His community was taken back by this decision since the Rabbi would never go on vacation. When he was asked about this sudden change of heart, he replied: "I am afraid that when I die, upon being summoned before the Heavenly Court, the Lord will ask me: 'Samson Rafael, did you see My beautiful mountains in Switzerland?' And I will not know what to answer!"

Student: Beautiful!

LC: I will let you in on a little secret! This is the reason why Adam and Chava did not "make it" in the Garden of Eden and ate from the "Tree!"

---

[65] Jerusalem Talmud, *Kiddushin* 48b.

Student: What do you mean?

THE OBLIGATION TO EAT FROM THE TREES OF THE GARDEN OF EDEN

LC: Well, if you look at the text in *Bereishit* (2:16–17), it says "And God gave the commandment to man: 'from every tree of the garden you may eat, but as for the tree of knowledge of good and bad, you must not eat of it, lest you shall die.'" We normally understand this verse the way I translated it: "From every tree you may eat..." But this is not what it says. The text says in Hebrew: "*achol tochel*" (the word "to eat" is repeated) which does not mean "you *may* eat" but "you *must* eat!" In other words, God says to man: I want you to eat and benefit so that you will have pleasure from all the trees in the garden. This is a *mitzva*: enjoy! But Adam and Chava understood these words as "you *may* eat." So they started their religious journey in life on the wrong foot. They believed that the first religious step through life started with a prohibition, but in reality it started with a positive commandment: Eat and Enjoy! The bottom line is this: if you do not know how to enjoy the God-given world, you will end up transgressing! And perhaps it is for this reason that God warns them: if you do not know how to enjoy this world, you will ultimately die by delving into those pleasures which you should stay away from![66]

THERE IS NO PLEASURE WHICH IS FORBIDDEN

Student: But still, you cannot deny that Judaism has many restrictions!

---

[66] Rabbi Meir Simcha of Dvinsk, *Meshech Chochma, Bereishit* 2:16.

LC: True, but not to the extent that a specific pleasure will altogether be forbidden. A careful look at the Jewish tradition shows that there is no pleasure that is completely denied to man. There is a most interesting passage in the Talmud about this. A woman by the name of Yalta, the wife of Rabbi Nachman said: "Whatever the Torah has forbidden to us, it also permitted us something similar. The Torah forbade the consumption of blood, yet it permitted the eating of liver (an organ which is so filled with blood that it can never be entirely emptied of its contents). The Torah forbade the eating of the flesh of the *chazir* (swine), but it permitted the eating of the brain of *shivuta*, a certain fish which tastes like the meat of the hog. The Torah forbade the eating of milk and meat together, but it permitted us to eat the udder of the cow even if it was cooked together with its milk content" (*Chullin* 109b). What the Torah *does* say, however, is that not *every* form of a specific pleasure is permitted, without certain limitations.

Student: In other words, the pleasure is not denied altogether, but is channeled in a different way.

LC: Correct! And it is not so difficult to see why. Pleasures are most enjoyable when they are indulged sporadically. If indulged on a continual basis, they lose their attraction, becoming bland and unattractive. Familiarity breeds contempt!

Student: But is that not a sign of weakness? It means that in principle anything is permitted, but only under certain conditions. How much of a real sacrifice is this? Does it not show much greater strength and commitment when something is altogether forbidden? The Catholic Church, for example, forbids its priests to have any sexual encounters.

LC: To forbid is always easy; to permit something, under certain circumstances, but with certain limitations imposed on it, is far more difficult to fulfill.

JUDAISM VERSUS CHRISTIANITY

Student: You previously indicated before that Judaism and Christianity do not see eye to eye with each other. What do you mean?

LC: That is a long story. Let me first of all make the point that today it is difficult to speak about Christianity as one homogenous religion. By now, Christianity exists of so many different "schools" that it becomes utterly impossible to generalize. So when I speak of Christianity in the next few minutes, be aware that I refer to *classical* Christianity as seen by the great Church fathers and by the Catholic Church, although it has started to change its views on many of its earlier conditions of belief as well. Having said that, I should mention that many people mistakenly believe that Christianity and Judaism, on the whole, agree on everything, aside from the issue of Jesus being the Messiah—Christianity affirming that he is, while Judaism refutes this and claims that he is *not*. People thus speak about the Judeo-Christian tradition, but I have very great doubts if such a tradition really exists.

Student: Nevertheless, they do have quite a few beliefs in common. There is the belief in one God and the authority of the *Tanach*.

LC: You are right, but even these beliefs are the source of considerable differences. But let us focus here on the issue you mentioned earlier: the attitude towards the physical world and abstinence.

Student: Fine.

LC: Let me ask you the following: what would you say is the great difference between the way in which Jews and Christians live their lives?

CHRISTIANITY AND HALACHA

Student: It seems to me that the great difference between the Jewish and Christian way of living is that Christianity has no Halacha (laws that govern all religious and social actions). There is no duty to live by the 613 commandments and all their minutiae, as there is in Judaism.

LC: Don't you think that this is a little strange? After all, classical Christianity also believes in the authority of *Tanach* as the word of God. So how was it able to circumvent the Halacha, the 613 commandments? They are clearly stated in *Tanach*, or, as the Christians call it, the Old Testament. Real Christians doubtlessly believe that the law was given at Sinai as much as Jews do. So why the lack of Halacha in Christianity?

Student: I don't think that this is really a problem. Only Jews are bound by the Sinai legislation. The Torah makes that very clear. Only the Jews, the Chosen people, were instructed to live by these laws. Christians are not bound by all this.

LC: I don't think it is as easy as that. Firstly, classical Christianity has always claimed that the Church replaced the Jews as the Chosen people; the early Church Fathers believing that Christians are the "new Israel." This is often called the replacement theology. So, the Christians should now be obligated to live by the law! Secondly, even those schools within Christianity who do not believe in this replacement theology do not believe that Jews have to live by the Halacha, even if they are still considered to be the Chosen people.

The most common reason given is that Jesus has basically "fulfilled" the entire corpus of law and that there is no longer a reason to keep the commandments. There are considerable issues at stake.

Student: Please proceed!

WHAT IS THE NATURE OF MAN?

LC: Here in fact, we touch on one of the most dramatic differences between Judaism and Christianity. Judaism and Christianity do not see eye to eye when discussing the nature of man.

Student: Why?

LC: Judaism has a far more optimistic view of man than has Christianity. While Christianity is clearly "sin oriented" and does not see much hope that man will ever be able to rise above the inevitability of sin, Judaism somehow believes that it is possible for man to cope with sin in a more positive way.

Student: Forgive me for interrupting you. But don't you think that it is wishful thinking to believe that man really will rise above sin? Even the stories in *Tanach* indicate that this is impossible. The Jews are constantly castigated for their sins. Righteousness has not been very prevalent throughout history!

LC: But if it is really impossible for man to be righteous, why does God keep on punishing His people for their failure in this area? What's the point? From another perspective, I might add that it is perhaps not so much the actual fulfillment of the Torah which is required, but the constant struggle to try to do so.

Student: I suppose you are right about that!

GOD'S EXPERIMENT AT SINAI FAILED?

LC: What Christianity is saying is the following: the reason why Halacha can no longer be at the center of worship is because it believes, so to speak, that God's experiment at Sinai failed! God "overestimated" man's moral and religious capabilities at Sinai. When He gave man the Torah, He believed that they would be able to live up to the challenge, but as history proves, they did not. According to Christianity, Jews have constantly failed to live up to the standards set in the Torah. God thus felt the need to replace the old covenant with a new one, one which would no longer make such heavy demands and would basically rely on salvation. That, Christians believe, is the New Testament!

Student: That makes a lot of sense. But what does Judaism have to say about this? After all, historically, Halacha has indeed fallen short of success!

LC: I am not so sure that one can argue that Halacha has not been successful. It may be true that Jews have often violated its commandments, but it has definitely created a strong bond between Jews throughout the ages and allowed them to survive the most dangerous conditions. Likewise, Halacha has allowed them to continue striving for a moral life. It should also be said that we know of generations upon generations who carefully observed every law and lived lives of great spiritual heights. Historically, as a people, Jews have seen the Halacha as their prime reason for existence. Even when they violated it, there was simultaneously an admission of violating the law of God, which paradoxically, created a strong feeling of unity and mission. Having said that, it is true that Jews have doubtlessly violated Halacha many times. The founders of Christianity saw this very clearly. They were clever people and deep thinkers and drew their conclusions. Non-Christians should not under-estimate Christianity, declaring it to be a simplistic religion. It is not.

Student: Wait a moment, whose side are you on?

LC: Don't worry. I am, of course, on the side of Judaism. Moreover, I believe that in this matter specifically, Christianity is completely mistaken.

Student: I am confused!

LC: Let me clarify my position. What I am saying is that although Christianity may be mistaken, this does not mean that it is foolish or simplistic. I can formulate this as a question so you will see what I am trying to say: which event in modern history would prove Christianity's point that man is basically a sinner and that Halacha is too demanding?

THE HOLOCAUST PROVES CHRISTIANITY RIGHT?

Student: I would say the Holocaust! The evil and cruelty inflicted in the concentration camps is beyond belief. It proved how evil man could really be and how incapable he is in overcoming his evil nature.

LC: So that would be a strong point for Christianity!

Student: Surely. The Holocaust demonstrated the validity of Christianity's analysis. Here were highly civilized German men and women who turned into beasts overnight!

LC: This is true, but let us ask one more question: how did they become so evil? How did they get away with it?

Student: What do you mean?

LC: Let me rephrase myself. Which is preferable: to overestimate or underestimate a person? Should we expect people to live by the highest moral standards, in the knowledge that only a few will actually succeed? Or shall we resign ourselves to the fact that each person is essentially a sinner, who is incapable of stopping him or herself in the face of temptation?

Student: I suppose it is better to tell someone that they are able to live by high moral standards.

LC: Why?

Student: Because then they will at least try to achieve these standards, even though they may never succeed in the endeavor. But if you tell a person from the outset that they are incapable, they won't even try. It's a recipe for disaster.

THE DANGER OF JUSTIFYING SIN

LC: Exactly. And that is, with all due respect, the failure of Christianity in the eyes of Judaism. It has taught millions of people over thousands of years that they are sinners, that they cannot help themselves. It has injected poison into millions of fine souls—a belief in the inevitability of sin. If you keep telling people for centuries that they are sinners, then they *will* become sinners, and behave accordingly. For any evil perpetrated, they will have a ready answer: you are right—it is evil, but I could not help myself. I am by nature a sinner, what can I do? Judaism has never had such an attitude.

Student: Your point is that since Christianity taught people for generations that they were sinners, they became so indoctrinated by this belief that they acted accordingly!

LC: Yes.

Student: That may be true, but surely Judaism asks the impossible when it requires strict adherence to the law, as you more or less admitted yourself.

JUDAISM IS A LITTLE TOO OPTIMISTIC

LC: It may be argued that Judaism is a little too optimistic regarding the individual's capacity to overcome evil, but it seems to me that it chose this optimism realizing that it would otherwise fall victim to a theology of despair. It is better to be over-optimistic, and cause people to be accountable for their deeds, than to be too pessimistic, which opens the door to the justification of evil. Christianity paved the road to the Holocaust since, for nearly two thousand years, it indoctrinated millions of people with the belief that they were sinners, weak and unable to overcome their bad inclinations. So, when they were confronted with the monstrous plans of Hitler, they succumbed, arguing that they were too weak to oppose the evil of Nazi racism and its military machine.

Student: That may also be true, but don't you think that Judaism did not know where to stop? After all, it makes such heavy demands on people that it seems to have lost sight of how much an individual is really capable of. Is this not just as dangerous as underestimating a person's potential? My impression is that there is a romanticized ideal of man in Judaism. He is considered to have the power to become some kind of an angel.

GOD'S REALISTIC ACCEPTANCE OF HUMAN LIMITATIONS

LC: I cannot agree with you. Despite my earlier observation, it seems to me that the law is the expression of God's realistic acceptance of the limitations of human beings. It is fascinating to note that all the laws of the Torah deal with human conditions; they being down-to-earth and pragmatic. There is no assumption of the ideal of living a sinless life.

On the contrary, it constantly discusses man's involvement in matters which could lead him to sin. "When you find yourself in a dispute with your neighbor...," "When a man kills his fellow man..." and so on. All these laws reflect the acceptance of man's corruptible nature. Do not kill, do not steal and many other prohibitions reveal a most realistic view of man.

This is also shown in famous talmudic statements such as: "The Torah speaks in the language of man,"[67] as well as "the Torah speaks in relationship to the evil instinct in man."[68]

Student: Could you provide me with an example where the Torah would have preferred a higher standard of morality, but "declined" because it would be difficult, if not impossible, for man to achieve such a moral standard?

THE CAPTIVE WOMAN

LC: One incredible, even disturbing, example occurs in *Devarim* (21:11–14) where we read about the case of a non-Jewish woman taken into captivity by the Jewish army. The Torah focuses on the strong desire of the Jewish soldier to have sexual relations with her. Under normal circumstances, Torah law would never allow such a thing. Here, however, since it takes place under unusual circumstances, in the heat of battle, in which people no longer act in a normal way, the Torah permits (under certain circumstances) such a sexual relationship!

The Talmud comments on this episode as follows: "The Torah speaks only in regard to man's evil inclination. If it did not allow this man to have a sexual relationship with this woman, he would take her illicitly, since his evil inclination would not be able to resist."[69]

However unusual and disturbing this case is, it does show a realistic understanding of the limits of man's nature. But even in cases when I would agree and admit that Judaism does include standards, which, at face value, can appear to be too

---

[67] *Sifre, Shelach* 122 and *Bava Metzia* 31b.
[68] *Kiddushin* 21b.
[69] *Kiddushin* 21b.

demanding, I would argue that there is a profound reason for this.

Student: What do you mean?

LC: Experience shows that whatever moral standard you set for man, he never tries to attain the plateau.

Student: Why not?

JUDAISM IS THE ART OF SURPASSING CIVILIZATION

LC: It is because man has a tendency to argue that he does not have to go "all the way."

If you tell someone that there is a need to be civilized, there is a tendency to reply that if he or she is only civilized up to 80%, it is enough. Judaism, however, claims that men must surpass regular civilized standards. He should strive to be a *tzaddik*, a righteous person, in the belief that he can do better than average! *Judaism is the art of surpassing civilization.* By making much higher demands, you will, at least, achieve fully civilized citizens!

ARE CHRISTIANS EVIL PEOPLE?

Student: To return to your earlier observations, are you not implying that Christians are, therefore, evil people?

LC: God forbid! Not at all. I am saying that many Christians are better than some of their beliefs.

Student: But then you are claiming that Christianity is a dangerous religion.

THE CHRISTIAN PARADOX

LC: What I mean is that there are dangerous dimensions within Christianity, such as the one I mentioned before, but I think that we are confronted here with a paradoxical phenomenon within Christianity. Nobody can deny that Christianity teaches kindness and good conduct. But it should be argued that this is despite its theology of despair. Christianity became embroiled in this philosophy of human failure, and seeing that it could lead to a great deal of evil, tries to diminish the damage by introducing a theology of good deeds. But it was never able to reconcile this with its theology of despair. That is the paradox.

Student: In that case, what has your earlier observations concerning abstinence to do with this theology of despair?

LC: Quite a lot. Classical Christianity does not believe that man will ever be able to sanctify the physical. This is completely consistent with its own theology. If man is basically evil, he will not be able to take on the physical world and sanctify it. It is totally beyond his capacity. From this follows that matters such as sexuality can never be sanctified. This is the reason why the Catholic Church could never permit its cardinals or priests to marry. Here again appears a paradox! Because of the theology of despair and the incapacity to sanctify the mundane, Catholicism somehow fell victim to a law far more restrictive than Halacha itself! (What is even more paradoxical is that the Church, which by necessity demands abstinence, depends upon the sins of others to supply it with the priests of tomorrow!)

Student: And you already observed that it is easier to say a conclusive *no* to something than to leave the door open!

LC: Good point! In Catholicism, the holy man is the one who *denies* himself as many physical pleasures as possible, whereas in Judaism, the holy man is one who *sanctifies* the physical, and as such, enjoys it. But there is really much more to it.

Student: Please continue.

THE PROBLEM CONCERNING GOD

LC: It brings us to the question of God and what we mean by that term. The first issue to realize is that the term "God" is used arbitrarily. It often stands for completely opposing entities used by different religious or quasi-religious ideologies. We may formulate a broad definition by stating that there are two opposing creeds which use the term God: monotheistic and the pantheistic.

The monotheistic creed is most known through Judaism which passed it on to Christianity and Islam. The pantheistic idea is mainly represented by the Greco-Oriental world, commonly identified today within certain forms of Buddhism, and possibly Yoga. A more sophisticated form of Pantheism is found in the philosophy of Spinoza.

Student: Could you elaborate on this?

JUDAISM VERSUS THE GRECO-ORIENTAL RELIGIONS

LC: The Judaic and the Greco-Oriental religions agree that one should affirm some Absolute Reality as the Ultimate. But they differ fundamentally on what that reality is. For the pantheistic "religions," it is a primal impersonal force: some kind of ineffable, immutable, impassive divine substance that pervades the universe or, more precisely, *is* the universe. This is the "all is God" philosophy which is identified with Spinoza. In his philosophy, we speak about immanence, the "indwelling" of God. However, this philosophy is already found in the Greco-Oriental world. In contrast, in Judaism, God is not only immanent, but also transcendent, which means that He surpasses the universe and is superior to it. Moreover, He is a Living Will and an active Being endowed with "personality," as such. This is dramatically different from the pantheistic notion in which God is seen as an impersonal force. For Judaism, He has created the world but cannot be identified with it without blasphemy. God is absolute, unqualified, transcending every phenomenon.

IS GOD IN THE SUN AND IN THE RAIN?

Student: So God is not in the sun, stars, rain or wind?

LC: According to most Jewish philosophers, that is indeed true, but I believe there is more to it. Your query touches on one of the great controversies in Judaism itself. There is a serious debate between those who believe that God is also in the stars and the wind and those who maintain that He is *not*.

Student: This is surely of fundamental significance.

MONOTHEISM, PANTHEISM AND DEISM

LC: Let us go back a step. There are actually three ways in which God has been understood by philosophers. One is through Monotheism, another through Pantheism and a third through Deism. As I already mentioned, Judaism believes that God is immanent and transcendent, i.e., He is inside the universe filling it with His spirit, but is also above and apart from it. Pantheists believe that God is only immanent, while Deism believes that God is only transcendent. Monotheism believes that God is both.

Student: So Deism is the belief that God is solely transcendent, i.e., that He is outside the world and that He has no concern with the world and its creatures?

DEUS ABSCONDITUS

LC: Indeed, Deism purports that God created the universe, but He does not govern it. In His relationship to nature, God is considered the Maker of a machine. Once created, the machine is left by itself, no longer needing the constant concern of its Creator. God is *Deus Absconditus*, the absentee God; sitting idle since the first Shabbat on the outside of His universe, observing its work.

Student: But this, I now understand, is not what Judaism is saying. But why not? It makes a lot of sense.

RABBI SHNEUR ZALMAN OF LIADY AND THE DEISTS

LC: Let me tell you about one of the great Jewish thinkers of the eighteenth century who dealt with this question. He was Rabbi Shneur Zalman of Liady, one of the most outstanding Chassidic–mystical thinkers we know of, the first Lubavitcher Rebbe. In his famous philosophical work *Tanya* he reveals one of the most inherent problems within Deism. Speaking of Deism he writes: "Here lies the answer to the heretics [the

Deists] and here is uncovered the error, in which they deny God's providence over particulars and the miracles and wonders as they are recorded in the Torah. Their false imagination leads them into the error, for they compare the work of God, Creator of heaven and earth, to the works of man and his artifices.

These foolish people compare the work of heaven and earth to a vessel which emerges from the hands of an artist. Once the vessel has been formed, it no longer requires its maker. Even when the maker has completed his work and goes about his own business, the vessel retains the form and appearance it had when it was formed. They are too blind to notice the important distinction between the works of man and his creations—in which something is made from something else, the form alone being changed from, say a piece of silver nugget into a silver vessel—and the creation of heaven and earth, which is the creation of 'something' out of 'nothingness.' The latter is an even greater marvel than the splitting of the Red Sea. For example, when the Lord caused a strong east wind to blow all through the night, the waters were divided to stand in a heap in the form of a wall. If God would stop the wind for but a moment, the waters no doubt, would have begun to flow in their normal, natural way and would no longer have stood upright like a wall. It follows that with regards to creation ex nihilo, which is a much greater marvel than the division of the Red Sea, it is certain that creation would revert to the state of nothingness and negation. Existence would come to an end if, God forbid, the power of the Creator were to be removed from it. It is essential, therefore, for the power of the Creator to be in His work constantly if it is to be kept in existence."[70]

---

[70] Rabbi Shneur Zalman of Liady (1714–1813), *Tanya Sha'ar HaYichud VeHaEmunah* (Vilna edition, 1930) chapter 2, pp. 153–4.

What this means is that Nature itself is "unnatural," contrary to the "nothingness" from where it emerged. The substance which keeps the "machine" (world) alive itself needs to be kept alive and that is as such "unnatural," needing the constant involvement of the Creator.

Student: That makes a lot of sense. But what has that to do with the question of whether God is present in the rain or wind?

LC: Obviously a lot. After all, how does God keep nature alive? Is this because it is part of Him, or because He created it as a separate entity?

Student: You'd better explain.

CHACHAM DAVID NIETO AND SPINOZA

LC: Let me tell you about a famous controversy which took place in the European Jewish community in the seventeenth century. In England, there lived a renowned Sephardi Sage by the name of David Nieto. He once gave a discourse at the famous Spanish Portuguese Synagogue in London which got him into a lot of trouble. So much so, that he was accused by his own synagogue members of being a pantheist, and therefore a Spinozist. Spinoza had just died. Nieto's discourse was intended to attack the Deists who were particularly active in England in those days. He thus felt the need to prove them wrong. But he did it so well that he was accused of Spinozism! This created so much trouble that rabbinical scholars of international fame had to intervene in his defense. He was nearly fired by his *parnasim* (community leaders) and was almost excommunicated.

Student: What happened?

LC: In this discourse he said that "nature" was a fairly new word and that in reality it was only another name for God. He actually said the following: "God and nature and nature and God are one and the same."[71]

Student: That is Spinozism, is it not?

LC: That is only true when you do not read any more of the sermon. The truth is that he continued to quote *Tehillim* 147:8—"He who covers the heavens with clouds, He who prepares rain for the earth, He who makes grass to grow upon the mountains." What he meant to say is that nature is another word for God's providence and that all nature is due to His action. He was not saying that God, as a Being, is equal to nature. He denied that nature was an independent entity, which is what the Deists were claiming. No, the reverse was true: the regular and ongoing providence of God is at the source of all that makes things exist.

CHACHAM ZVI

The members of Nieto's community did not in fact pay close enough attention to their spiritual leader's words and accused him of Spinozism. Zealously, they sent a query to Chacham Zvi Ashkenazi, Chief Rabbi of Amsterdam, an international authority, who then resided in Altona, to hear what he had to say about the matter. After careful study of David Nieto's discourse, Chacham Zvi responded that Nieto was perfectly

---

[71] David Nieto (1654–1728), *De la divina providencia* (London, 1704).

correct in his observations and that the community leaders had misconstrued his words.

Student: So for Rabbis Nieto and Ashkenazi, the basic difference between the Jewish view and Spinoza is that for the latter there is really no God, only nature, and God is only a synonym for nature. Whereas from a traditional Jewish viewpoint, there is in reality no nature. Nature is just another word for God's providence!

NATURA NATURANS AND NOT *NATURA NATURATA*

LC: Correct! In philosophical language the Jewish tradition would say: *natura naturans* and not *natura naturata*—Nature is part of "essence," but it is not the "essence" itself.

Student: But wait, does that mean that it is incorrect, and in fact heretical, to believe that things within nature are part of God?

IS NATURE PART OF GOD?

LC: Some Jewish thinkers have gone a step further. They actually believe that God is to be found in a drop of water. Rabbi Schneur Zalman of Liady was of that opinion. According to him, the universe is really only appearance and not reality.

This conflicts with our viewpoint that the universe *does* exist; but from God's point of view, as it were, there is no universe at all, only God Himself. His proof is a verse in the Torah: "Know this day and put it to your heart, that the Lord your God, He is God in heaven above and on the earth below, *there is none* [i.e., nothing else]" (*Devarim* 6:39).

So God is equal to nature but only in the sense that what we experience as nature is really only Him. Nature itself has no independent existence.[72] So, God is actually present in a drop of water, though from His perspective, the water is an illusion.

THE ILLUSION

This does not mean that Rabbi Schneur Zalman has Spinozistic leanings. For him, God is transcendent and immanent. Not so for Spinoza, who believes that God is only immanent. Secondly, the Rabbi believes that God created the world (or at least the illusion of the world) while Spinoza would disagree.

Student: Returning once more to our earlier conversation: what has this to do with Christianity's view of the world and man? Clearly Christianity also believes in immanence and transcendence!

LC: True, but there is still a clear difference between the Jewish view and that of Christianity.

Student: How so?

LC: There is an inherent problem in Pantheism. No longer is it the Pantheism of Spinoza, though it is related. Earlier Pantheists, among them thinkers in Far Eastern religions and perhaps some Greek philosophers such as Plato, maintained that since God (or better god with a small g) is equal to nature, one should deny the existence of nature and see it as an optical illusion. How, after all, can one confirm the actual existence of

---

[72] An excellent exposition of this view is offered by Rabbi Schneur Zalman's grandson, Menachem Mendel of Lubavitch in *Derech Mitzvotecha* (Poltova, 1911) in the chapter "Unity of God."

a physical substance when it is at the same time God? If so, it must be infinite and that must mean that it has no real existence in any physical form. So the universe and all it contains is unreal, a shifting flux of sensory deception. Only the absolute, the spiritual, which is beyond time and space is real. Life and history are, therefore, essentially meaningless and irrational. True knowledge consists of breaking through the veil of illusion of empirical life. One needs to look beyond this illusory world in order to obtain a glimpse of the unchanging reality that it hides. This is the way of salvation. It is this philosophy which was *partially* adopted by Christianity.

Student: But did Rabbi Zalman not make the same point?

THERE IS MEANING TO ILLUSION

LC: Definitely not. He did not say that the world is an illusion and *therefore* loses all meaning. He said that from God's point of view it does not really exist, but from our point of view it definitely *does*, and has a lot of meaning. In other words, the objective world may be an illusion, but it contains meaning since God created it and is thus of great importance. This is the difference between Pantheism and something which philosophers call Panentheism. Panentheism means: God is in all, but all is still less than the sum-total of God!

Student: I understand, but why do you say that Christianity only *partially* adopted the pantheistic view, which calls for the need to "break through the veil"?

LC: Christianity could obviously not accept this philosophy in its entirety, because it would be unable to agree that God and nature are one. In that sense, Christianity is monotheistic and not pantheistic. However Plato's philosophy, which states that the soul is incarcerated in the body, out of which it wants to break free, was adopted by Christianity. It was this outlook that became central to Christian ideology. Again, I must add that this is the view of classical Christianity, and was later rejected by several Christian thinkers.

Student: I am sorry, but what has this to do with your earlier observations?

PLATO'S *PHAEDON*

LC: Let me explain. In his book *Phaedon*, Plato maintains that the relationship between the body and soul may be likened to a man in prison; he wants to escape, in the pursuit of real freedom. Such freedom is considered to be the highest good. This really means that the physical is seen as an obstacle to the spiritual. This attitude was clearly adopted by Christianity when it denied the importance of the body. Its roots are found in Pantheism, which denied the significance of the totality of all physicality. The founders of Christianity may not have been consciously aware of this, but it is clearly there.

Student: Is this, as you commented before, the reason why Christianity denigrates the human body and matters like sexuality?

OTHER-WORLDLY

LC: Christianity, and to an even greater degree, the pantheistic religions, are clearly other-worldly. This explains the radical difference of outlook between Judaism and Christianity which we mentioned earlier. These two views of humanity are fundamentally irreconcilable. What one affirms, the other denies and vice-versa. For this reason I called Christianity the theology of despair, a conviction that man is inherently weak and incapable of living within the boundaries of Halacha. But now we can understand *why* man is considered to be weak. The root of this philosophy is the denial of the physical side of man and his individuality.

Student: I am sorry but I didn't follow you.

LC: From the pantheistic viewpoint, the world does not really exist. This means that the human being in its physical form is also an illusion. His body is part of the optical deception. From here it follows that the goal of life is to escape one's "physical" existence. Real man is not his body but his soul, which is part of God. This must lead to the devaluation of man as a human being.

Student: Why?

LC: Because by denying the physical side of man, you deny the "wholeness" of man. "Man" means soul *and* body. If there is no body, then there is no man. Apart from anything else, this outlook is dangerous.

Student: What is so dangerous about it?

THE DENIAL OF MORALITY

LC: It is dangerous because it inevitably leads to the denial of morality. If the physical side of man is denied, then you are also denying the importance of his deeds. As they are also part of the illusion, how important are they? Moreover, every involvement with the empirical world is an affirmation of that world. So when you start to take moral issues seriously, you hinder the possibility of self-liberation, since they tie the spirit down to the world of desire and action. From a pantheistic perspective, this is sin!

Student: Are you suggesting that these pantheistic religions are anti-moral and only add to the evil of the world?

LC: Not exactly. What I am saying is that this kind of Pantheism is "beyond good and evil." Ethics is only instrumental and useful in clearing the way for higher things. Obviously, no man can regard himself as detached from the world and free from craving, if he harbors hate, anger or envy. So the pantheistic view wants these negative emotions to be removed. But why? Because they stand in the way of the ultimate liberation. The goal is thus *not* ethical behavior, but the liberation of the soul from all bodily limitations, including the need to be moral! This means that if there were another way to secure this liberation, this philosophy would no longer see the need for moral behavior. In fact it would have to admit that if indecent behavior would be the key to this liberation, it would no doubt opt for that. That is the danger.

Student: And that stands in absolute opposition to Judaism?

THE DANGER OF BEING TOO SPIRITUAL

LC: Indeed. That kind of philosophy is an evasion from life and the world. Judaism, by contrast, focuses on life and on this world. For the Jew, the moral life, the life of personal concern and loving service, is not something to be abandoned at any stage in the individual's spiritual development. The more spiritually occupied a person is with this world, trying to elevate it, never escaping it, the more real he or she is. By this measure, we can claim that Pantheism, and to an extent, Christianity are more "spiritual" than Judaism. But this is precisely their mistake. No doubt one can become too materialistically inclined, as we see in the West. But it is just as dangerous to be overly spiritual. Western materialism denies the soul, Christianity, the body. Judaism represents a healthy balance.

Student: Why then are the Far Eastern religions, with their Pantheistic affiliations, so popular today? Should not the Jewish attitude of affirmation be far more attractive to people with a Western background? We see so many young Jews go to the Far East to learn with a guru and other religious leaders.

THE PROMISE OF ESCAPE

LC: This seems to me very understandable. It is the promise of escape from the world which is so attractive. The denial of moral issues, or at least the denial of its centrality in human existence, appeals to many people. One is able to live a high "spiritual" life, without too much morality attached to it. In this way, one is seemingly able to benefit from both worlds simultaneously.

Judaism cannot offer this option. There is no escape or shortcut from one's moral duties and their centrality to existence. It requires courage and perseverance. It seems that not all men, including Jews, are ready for this. This is also partially true as far as Christianity is concerned. Christianity, as we have seen, also has a tendency to deny, which as I explained, must lead to a decentralization of morality. For that reason, Christianity is much less world-focused than Judaism and much more spiritually "attractive" than Judaism. This fact also seems to play a large part in the popularity of Reform Judaism. While I do not want to claim that the builders of Reform Judaism were only looking for some means of escape from religious obligations, I *do* believe, however, that this is one of the more appealing features that Reform Judaism offers to its many followers. From an Orthodox standpoint it offers a religion of convenience.

THE WEST AND ITS HEDONISTIC PLEASURES

Student: But if this is the case, why has the West indulged itself in radical forms of hedonism and other material pleasures? While it may be true that many people have turned to the Far East for inspiration, the truth is that most people are hopelessly involved in the physical pleasures of the West, and have turned sexuality and food into substitute religions.

LC: This is a natural reaction. When the emphasis is misguidedly placed on the denial of the existence of our material world, and an abstinence from physical pleasures, a counter-reaction is provoked through an over-indulgence of the physical world. This is perhaps the great tragedy of Western society. It only knows about extremes, over-denial or over-involvement. It would have been saved much trouble and pain if it would have adopted the balanced view of Judaism.

Student: I am still not satisfied as far as your explanation of the Jewish view of God is concerned. Do you mind if we explore that a little more?

LC: Not at all. God is, after all, the most captivating "player" in history. His track record is both unusual and unprecedented!

HAS GOD FEET AND DOES HE GET ANGRY?

Student: I am greatly bothered by the notion of God's personality within Judaism. You mentioned this before when you made a distinction between Monotheism and Pantheism. Judaism speaks about God in terms that are so frighteningly physical, you get the feeling that it sometimes is transgressing the second law in the Ten Commandments: "Thou shall not make an image." In the *Tanach*, God has eyes, even feet, speaks, gets angry, and so forth. Why is there such an emphasis on all that? Why is there a need for this?

GOD HAS PERSONALITY

LC: This is an excellent question. Let us first understand that in the Jewish tradition, God is not an abstract idea, but a dynamic power. He is active in the here-and-now of our world. He is not a God-idea, but a Living God. For many people, this is the grossest anthropomorphism, and is viewed as being scandalous. Obviously, God is completely abstract and all such definitions are inapplicable and misleading.

But if that is the case, why, you ask, are there so many misleading terms used to describe Him?

There is a very good reason for that. We have to talk about Him in such terms so that we become aware of how He plays an "active" role in our lives. The only way we are able to do this is by speaking about Him in terms which are comprehensible to us. We have two options: either stop speaking about Him altogether, since no description will do Him justice—in which case utter silence would be preferable—or to speak about Him in terms which really fall completely short of what one could say about Him, but which at least gives us the opportunity of "staying in touch" with Him.

Student: I am still not sure I understand you. Perhaps you could elaborate.

LC: Things have to stay relational to us. We can only understand matters as far as our minds are able to grasp them. Since our minds are limited, we are only able to understand something in a confined format. This means that we are never able to get the "whole" picture. So we have to speak about God in human terms since this is the only language we comprehend. Obviously there is a danger here. But as long as we know that we are using only metaphors and are therefore not attempting a description, we can keep things in perspective. After all, we do that in so many other departments of human knowledge.

Student: For example?

DID ANYBODY EVER SEE AN ATOM?

LC: When we draw an atom on the blackboard, we do not claim that we know how an atom actually looks. In previous years, nobody has ever claimed to have seen an atom. But because we needed to visualize an atom, we created a model. The model is obviously not "authentic." It is only a picture, a metaphor. And that is true about so many scientific facts which we are unable to see.

JUDAISM NEVER OBJECTED TO ASCRIBING HUMAN QUALITIES TO GOD

What is important to remember is that Judaism never objected to ascribing human qualities to God, but only in ascribing absolute, divine qualities to man. Yet attempting to express what one means by the term, God, is very much like trying to represent a three dimensional reality on a flat surface.

Student: That is a nice way of expressing it.

LC: What we have to realize is that God can never be *expressed*, only *addressed*. One experiences God, yet one cannot know Him objectively.

WHY IS GOD JEALOUS? HE IS OUTRIGHT EMOTIONAL!

Student: But why are there such disturbing terms such as God being angry or jealous? In the biblical stories, He appears to be pathetic and outright emotional.

DEPERSONALIZATION LEADS TO DEMORALIZATION

LC: There is a very profound reason for that. Every other way of describing God will invariably lead to the depersonalization of man, and therefore to his demoralization.

Student: I am again lost!

LC: Our Western world is built on a Greek concept that our feelings are purely subjective and, therefore, not real. They do not really count. They are biased. Man is only his body, and that itself is only a mechanism. Emotions are just optical illusions which are not to be taken seriously.

It is this kind of attitude against which Judaism strongly protests. If one entirely denies or ignores the emotional life of man, you basically destroy him, creating a major breakdown in morality. After all, if emotions are not to be taken seriously, why should I be concerned about the feelings of my fellow man? *So, by giving God, metaphorically speaking, emotions, we elevate these emotions to a supreme state of importance.* If God has such emotions they must be real and serious, not something that can be denied. On the contrary, they become the foundation of morality.

Student: In other words, Judaism was prepared to take the risk of making God an "emotional" Being for the sake of making sure that morality would never be curtailed or even slightly diminished.

SPINOZA'S PANTHEISM IS IDOL WORSHIP

LC: Correct! But simultaneously, Judaism goes out of its way to emphasize the wholly otherness of God. He is the Creator ex nihilo. He is totally transcendent. He constantly does things which are totally "impossible" and defy definition. His role as Creator is crucial; it is a warning against Pantheism.

Nature is not self-sufficient; it is the result of God's creation. Spinoza's *"Deus sive natura"* (God is equal to nature) leads to the worship of the world and the violation of its Commandment: "You shall not make an image." The Jewish concept of God precludes idol worship of the universe, as perceived by Spinoza. From a Jewish perspective, Pantheism is idol worship.

Student: Let us end our discussion for today.

LC: Very well, we shall meet again tomorrow.

DAY FOUR

Idolatry Is the Absolutization of the Relative; Dostoevsky's Raw Youth; Science As *Avoda Zara*; Is God an Idol?; Belief in God?; "Electricity Just Is"; Sir Francis Crick's Fingers; Schumacher's Visit to Leningrad; Aristotle's Slenderest Knowledge; The Problem Concerning "Life"; To Knock a Dog Unconscious; Evolution; Is a Dog a Barking Plant?; The Mysterious Car; Max Planck; Immanuel Kant's Stars; An Ontological Presupposition; Belief *That* and Belief *In*; Rabbi Moshe Cordovero; But Does He Encounter Us?; God Can Get Lost; *Mysterium Tremendum ad Fascinas*; The Problem of Evil; Divine Displeasure; Iyov and M. Scott Peck; C.S. Lewis and the Extension of Pain; Money Can Be Divided, Lashes Cannot; One Death?; Why Have a Universe Altogether?; John Hick; No Right Action; From *Tzarah* to *Zohar*; Edwyn Bevan's Dog; Only Disaster?; Esoteric Subconsciousness; Afterlife; Can God Do the Impossible?; Can God Create a Married Bachelor?; Bribble, Brabble, Brubble; Bending Paper; Pascal

Student: Yesterday we spoke about Spinoza's idol worship. I wonder what this term means in Judaism. I gather from what you said that it is not confined to the worship of sticks and stones.

LC (Lopes Cardozo): For most Jewish religious thinkers, idolatry is the root of all wrongdoing and moral evil. Maimonides, in particular, stresses this point. The question we need to address is: what is it that turns something into an idol?

Student: Wait, are you saying that nothing, as such, is an idol, but that anything can become one?

IDOLATRY IS THE ABSOLUTIZATION OF THE RELATIVE

LC: That is an astute observation. Idolatry is the absolutization of the relative; it is absolute devotion paid to anything other than God, who is the only true Absolute. Moreover, as you indicated with your question, the object of idol worship may be a receptacle of good, but since it is not God, it is necessarily a good that is only partial and relative.

This is clearly suggested by a statement in the *Mishna*: "The [Jewish] elders in Rome were asked: 'If God has no pleasure in an idol, why does He not make an end to it?' To which they replied: 'If men worshipped a thing of which the world has no need, He would bring an end to it, but since they worship the sun, moon, stars and planets, shall God destroy the world because of fools?'"[73]

Student: In other words, idolatry transforms an object into an absolute value, thereby destroying the partial good within it and turning it into an evil.

LC: Precisely, and Judaism thus speaks about idols as vanities and demons, since they become the source of corruption, chaos, violence and perversion in human life. This, by the way, is the reason why Gentiles are also forbidden to have any association with idol worship.[74]

Student: This suggests that idol worship is still prevalent in our day and age.

DOSTOEVSKY'S RAW YOUTH

LC: It certainly is. Dostoevsky argues that contemporary life is immersed in idolatry, to an appalling degree. In his book, *A Raw Youth*, he writes: "It is impossible to be a man and not to bow down to something. Such a man could not bear the burden of himself. If he rejects God, then he bows to an idol...fashioned of wood or of gold or of thought...."

Having rejected genuine religion, many people today who experience a vacuum in their lives, replace the void with an influx of legions of "gods," demanding absolute worship. You find this already in the Romantics, in Nietzsche, in the worship of sex, the dark forces of instinct. It was expressed most clearly

---

[73] *Mishna, Avoda Zarah* 4:7.
[74] *Mishne Torah, Melachim* 9:1.

in the Nazi philosophy of "blood and soil." Today, idol worship has become, if anything, a greater problem because it is concealed behind many highly valued items. In more primitive epochs, idolatry was clearly visible; its adherents would, for example, declare openly that nature is god. Today, we have a whole series of highly valued items which have ultimately become gods, but are disguised in more sophisticated ways.

Student: For example?

LC: Race, nation, empire, class, state or party, science. Even the church and the synagogue have become gods. All of them are most valuable, but once absolutized into idols, they become corrupt and demonic. We already spoke about this before when we discussed the possibility of the land of Israel becoming an idol.

SCIENCE AS *AVODA ZARA*

Student: You claim that science could also become an idol?

LC: Yes, I do. And for very good reasons! When "scientific truth"—which is no more than the accurate reporting and use of what happens under specified conditions—is held to be the ultimate truth, i.e., a "be all and end all," then we have idolatry.

Student: But even if this were so, what is so bad about that? Science is still science. Even when some people idolize it, it does not detract from its power and crucial significance in today's world.

LC: Without arguing against its obvious importance, I would still claim that it could become very dangerous and destructive, even self-destructive.

Student: How?

LC: Because it could only lead to an uncontrollable situation whereby we would be unable to prevent man from treating mankind as all other scientific material, to be manipulated or expended with as science may dictate. Men would be turned into guinea pigs, and if we objected on moral grounds, the response would be: Why not? If this is required for scientific progress, no "sentimental" obstacles should stand in the way! The horrible experiences which we Jews and, alas, many other human beings suffered during the Holocaust, is a clear example. German scientists—in the name of scientific research and enlightenment—tortured people in ways in which even the word monstrous would be an understatement in describing them.

IS GOD AN IDOL?

Student: I see your point, but why did you say that even the church or the synagogue could become idols? Is this not a contradiction in terms?

LC: Oddly enough, it is not. Pagan idolaters worship their gods directly and shamelessly. They do not know of a real higher authority. But in the West, with our long-lasting monotheistic traditions, we cannot just turn our false absolutes into gods. We have taken idol worship a step further. We try to turn God into a progenitor of idols, by making Him the sanctifier and protector of the idols we really love. God has become our Promoter of our physical desires, interests and ideals.[75]

They are all the more dangerous on that account. For example, in promoting programs to which we are devoted, we often absolutize them to the point of being oblivious to everything else. This is really a form of self-idolatry, since it is self-projected. This can happen to the individual as well as to communities or mass movements. Communism was a good example of this. At the end of the day, the big question remains: is our way of life God-centered or self-centered? Egocentricity is a sin, theocentricity is a *mitzva*. It is for this reason, by the way, that Rabbis called Adam an *apikores* (heretic) once he ate from the tree. The tree became an absolutized value, therefore rendering man incapable of keeping away from it.[76]

BELIEF IN GOD?

Student: This is most interesting, but let me change the topic slightly and ask you what is obviously on the minds of many secularists: why believe in God at all? It is all very nice what you just said about God, but who says that He actually exists? I don't have to tell you that there are a whole series of reasons why we should not believe in His existence. First of all, there is the problem of existing evil.

Secondly, it can be asked whether or not belief in God is just wishful thinking, as Freud indicated. People seek comfort in holding on to Somebody or Something larger and more powerful than themselves.[77]

---

[75] See Eric Fromm, *To Have or To Be* (Abacus, 1976).

[76] *Sanhedrin* 38b.

[77] See Sigmund Freud, *Totem and Taboo* (1913); *The Future of an Illusion* (1927); *Moses and Monotheism* (1939).

LC: You are touching on many topics simultaneously. Each needs a lot of attention and careful consideration. Let's start at the beginning.

Student: So let me first ask why I should believe in this God, even without all the problems. I am aware that there are so-called proofs for the existence of God, but is it not true, that most, if not all of them, have been undermined by different philosophers?

LC: That is absolutely true, but that does not mean that there are no arguments or reasons why the existence of God has to be taken very seriously.

Student: Give me one example.

"ELECTRICITY JUST IS"

LC: In fact it relates to what I just said concerning science. Let me quote a statement by the renowned "discoverer" of electricity, Thomas Edison. A lady once asked him: "what is electricity?" "Madame," he answered, "electricity is! Use it!" Perhaps this is the best argument ever stated in favor of the existence of God!

Student: I do not understand what this has to do with the existence of God.

SIR FRANCIS CRICK'S FINGERS

LC: It has a lot to do with it. What Edison was trying to say to the lady is this: we have no idea why things are the way they are. Neither do we have a clue as to how to explain them. In other words, everything—whether it is of a physical or spiritual nature—is really a complete mystery, about which we have not the slightest idea. But in the meantime, use it!

The historian of modern science, Professor Avraham Pais, related that when James Watson and Francis Crick discovered DNA, Pais had remarked to Crick that scientists might soon know all that was needed to know about creation. Crick responded by holding up his hand: "See these five fingers? If you think I have the faintest clue why I have five and only five fingers, you are badly mistaken."[78]

Student: Are you saying that all our scientific insights and knowledge are meaningless?

LC: Oh no, I don't mean that at all. In fact, I made this point already earlier in our discussion when we spoke about science becoming an idol. What I am saying is that science does not help us when it comes to the ultimate questions as to why things are the way they are. More simply stated: science tells us *how* and *why* things work, in the *utilitarian* sense of the word, but not in the *existential* sense of the word.

Student: You had better explain yourself.

SCHUMACHER'S VISIT TO LENINGRAD

LC: Let me endeavor to explain what I mean. Please interrupt me whenever you wish. You see, there was something which was once called "philosophical maps." There is a story told by

[78] Avraham Pais, *A Tale of Two Continents: A Physicist's Life in a Turbulent World* (Princeton: Princeton University Press, 1997) p. 337

the philosopher E.F. Schumacher about his visit to Leningrad. At one point he found himself standing right in front of some huge churches, but when he looked at his tourist map, they were not there! When he asked somebody about this, the answer he was given was: "In the USSR, we do not show churches on our maps!"

Student: In other words, they denied the existence of the churches?

LC: Right. And with it the concept of religion. Schumacher then comments: "It occurred to me that this was not the first time I had been given a map which failed to show many things that I most cared about and that seemed to me to be of the greatest possible importance to the conduct of my life."[79]

Everything with which our forefathers were occupied is considered by many philosophers and modern people to be irrational or superstitious. Oh yes, they have to be treated with respect, after all they could not help their backwardness. But the rationalists, writes Schumacher, had a principle: if in doubt, leave it out.

Student: What do you mean?

LC: These philosophers were of the opinion that real knowledge designed for real life is only composed of that which could be proven.

Student: Is this not a healthy approach? Why should we try to eliminate doubt, when there is no way of removing it?

---

[79] E.F. Schumacher, *A Guide for the Perplexed* (Harper and Row, 1978) p. 1.

ARISTOTLE'S SLENDEREST KNOWLEDGE

LC: I think the reason is obvious. First of all, everything is open to doubt. Secondly, is not the unprovable part of life, i.e., where I may have to take a risk and possibly err, not of the highest importance? In other words: is it not true that when I do not want to consider any element of doubt, I lose out on the most important, subtle, and rewarding things in life?

Aristotle once said: "The slenderest knowledge that may be obtained of the highest things is more desirable than the most certain knowledge obtained of lesser things."[80] In other words: higher things cannot be known with the same degree of certainty as can the lesser things, in which case it would be a very great loss indeed if knowledge were limited to things beyond the possibility of doubt.

Student: I can see that, but what has this to do with our discussion?

LC: Rather a lot, I think. Here we should introduce the quality of human amazement. To stand in wonder at the ultimate mystery of existence. We have lost the art of amazement because we have convinced ourselves that everything can and will be rationalized, even lofty things. For many people, everything has a link to science, believing that science will answer all our questions. But the truth is the reverse: the more we know scientifically, the more we realize how little we know, in the existential sense of the word.

---

[80] Quoted by Thomas Aquinas, *Summa Theologica*, 1:1.5, addendum 1.

Student: You better be more specific. Your statements are too abstract for me to follow.

LC: Let me give an example: our ancestors used to divide the world into four levels: mineral, plant, animal and human. In the olden days, they used to start with the highest and finish with the lowest. Today we seem to do the reverse.

Student: Why?

THE PROBLEM CONCERNING "LIFE"

LC: Because we are deeply influenced by the concept of evolution, i.e., with the theory that life started with the simplest form of matter and progressed towards human life; which, for the time being, is the last link in the chain. For the purpose of our discussion it is unimportant where we start. What is important is that we realize that when we start at a lower level, like the mineral kingdom, we can find an increase in qualities or powers as we move to the higher levels. No one has difficulty in recognizing the astonishing and mysterious differences between a plant that is alive and one that has died and thus fallen to the lowest level of being—inanimate matter. But what is the "power" that has been lost? We call it "life." We are told by scientists that we must not talk of "life force," since no such force has ever been found to exist. Yet a "difference" between life and death exists. This cannot be denied.

Student: What is your point?

LC: Let us take a living plant. It exists from two matters: its physical existence and its life. Let's call its physical level M, and its "living force," X. So a living plant is M plus X. The factor X is of the greatest importance to us; while we can destroy it, we are powerless to create it.

Student: But more and more scientists tell us that they can create life!

LC: I was waiting for you to make that point. To the best of my knowledge, this is definitely not true. A more careful reading of what they are saying shows that they are able to create life from what appears lifeless. However, there is absolutely no evidence that we are able to create life out of something which is completely dead. What we once thought to be dead may still be alive, and it is out of that, that we create "more" life.

Student: I am not sure that I agree.

TO KNOCK A DOG UNCONSCIOUS

LC: Okay, let us assume that we are able to create life in the future. This does not mean that we know what life is. The mysterious character of X would remain and we would never cease to marvel at it. There is nothing in the laws, concepts or formulae of physics and chemistry to explain or even describe this power. In more sophisticated language: we are faced here with the problem of ontological (the branch of metaphysics dealing with the nature of "being") continuity, or simply a descent of level of "being," once the plant dies. This also applies if we shift from plant to animal life. Animals are able to do things which are totally outside the range of possibilities of the typical fully developed plant. This animal power is totally mysterious. If you want, we can call it Y. The scientific community does not even have a name for this power. It is an increase of life compared to the living plant. The best word to use is consciousness. It is easy to recognize consciousness in a dog or horse if only because they can be knocked unconscious; the process of life continues as in a plant, although the animal has lost its peculiar powers. So an animal is M plus X plus Y. Again we can destroy Y, but we cannot create it and even when we can, it stays completely inexplicable.

What happens when we try to explain human beings? What human beings are is a matter of debate. But one thing is clear: what they can do is completely beyond the range of possibilities of even the most highly developed animals. Many philosophers make the point that human beings are the only species who are not just able to think, but who are also able to be fully conscious of their thought. You can call it self-awareness. (Animals may have certain awareness, but not to the degree human beings possess this capacity.) Let's call it Z. But these are just words which do not explain a thing. It is a finger pointing to the moon. The moon itself stays mysterious. So man is M plus X plus Y plus Z. While M is physical, all the others are invisible.

EVOLUTION

Student: But has evolution not explained all this quite adequately?

LC: I do not think so. That does not mean that evolution is wrong, but the X, Y, Z factors are not explained sufficiently. Evolution is a process of the spontaneous "accidental" emergence of the powers of life. The emergence of consciousness and self-awareness, purportedly out of inanimate matter, is a spiritual phenomenon, which is totally incomprehensible to the scientific world.

Student: So physics and chemistry are unable to guide us in these areas?

IS A DOG A BARKING PLANT?

LC: Indeed, the sciences possess no concepts relating to these powers and are incapable of describing their effects. Where there is life there is form, "gestalt" (presence), which produces itself over and over again from seed, or similar beginnings. These early stages do not possess "gestalt" which only develops in the process of growth. Nothing comparable is found in physics or chemistry. To say that life is nothing but the property of certain peculiar combinations of atoms is like saying that Shakespeare's Hamlet is nothing but a property of a peculiar combination of letters! I think it is more correct to state that modern science has no method, as such, for coming to grips with life. I sometimes have the impression that people would like to say that a dog is a barking plant or a running cabbage! But this will not do. In fact, it is reported that after Plato had defined man as a two-legged animal without feathers, Diogenes plucked a cock and brought it into the Academy!

Student: But at least you admit that M—the physical dimension—is explicable.

LC: This is the other point which I wanted to make. The truth is that we do not have a complete explanation for that either. What we call an explanation is really nothing more than a description. Whatever the scientific explanation may be, there will never be an answer to the question of why? It will automatically invite another "why," and this will go on infinitely.

I am not speaking here about a First Cause or anything like that. The point I am trying to make is that since there is always another why, we never get to the rock bottom of anything and it therefore stays unfathomable. The fact that we are even capable of asking: why? is totally beyond us.

What is this capacity to ask? It indeed "exists," but we have no way of understanding this phenomenon. The point is that somewhere along the line we have to stop asking why and just accept, since there is nothing else for us to do! And that, I believe, leads us to the question concerning God's existence.

Student: Again, I am not sure I am following you. How does one get to believe in God?

THE MYSTERIOUS CAR

LC: Let me put it differently. The surest way to suppress our belief in God is to take things for granted; being indifferent to the sublime wonder of life. It reminds me of the beautiful story told by Avraham Yehoshua Heschel: "When the electric streetcar made its first appearance in the city of Warsaw, some good old Jews could not believe their eyes. A car that moves without a horse! Some of them were stupefied and frightened and all were at a loss how to explain the amazing invention.

Once, while discussing the matter in the synagogue, a man entered, who, in addition to studying Talmud, was reputed to know books on secular matters and to be well versed in worldly affairs. So they said: 'you must know how this thing works.' 'Of course I know,' he said. They were all hanging on to his every word. 'Imagine,' he continued, 'four large wheels in a vertical position in four corners of a square, connected to each other by wires. You get it?' 'Yes, we get it,' his audience said.

He continued: 'the wires are tied in a knot in the center and placed within a large wheel, which is placed in a horizontal position. 'You get it?' 'Yes we get it.' 'Above the wheel there are several wheels, one smaller than the other. You get it?' 'Yes we get it.' 'On top of the smallest wheel there is a tiny screw which is connected by a wire to the center of the car which lies on top of the wheels. Do you get it?' 'Yes we get it.' 'The machinist in the car presses the button that moves the screw that brings the horizontal wheels to move and thus the car runs through the street.' 'Ah, now we understand.'"[81]

Student: But don't you think that this is too naive a picture of man in the twentieth century?

MAX PLANCK

LC: Perhaps you are right. So let me read you a statement from the famous scientist, Max Planck, in his *Scientific Autobiography*: "The feeling of wonderment is the source and inexhaustible fountainhead of the desire for knowledge. It drives the child irresistibly on to solve the mystery, and if in his attempt he encounters a causal relationship, he will not tire of repeating the same experiment ten times, a hundred times in order to taste the thrill of discovery over and over again. The reason why the adult no longer wonders is not because he has solved the riddle of life, but because he has grown accustomed to the laws governing this world picture.

---

[81] Avraham Yehoshua Heschel, *God in Search of Man* (NY: Farrar and Straus, 1955) pp. 44–45.

But the problem of why these particular laws and no others hold, remains for him just as amazing and inexplicable as for the child. He does not comprehend this situation, misconstrues its profound significance and he who has reached the stage where he no longer wonders about anything, merely demonstrates that he has lost the art of reflective reasoning."[82]

Student: That is all very well and good, but don't we then face the problem that if nothing can really be explained, it becomes a cushion for the lazy intellect?

IMMANUEL KANT'S STARS

LC: I do not think so. What we have to realize is that we must not invent an explanation, or a better description, where such an explanation or description is impossible. It should not stifle doubt where doubt is legitimate. It must remain a constant awareness if man is to remain true to his position in this world: there is more to this world and all existence than we will ever grasp.

"Two things," Immanuel Kant once wrote, "fill the mind with ever new and increasing admiration and awe, the more often and the more steadily we reflect on them. The starry heavens above and the moral law within. The former view of countless multitude of worlds annihilates, as it were, my importance as an animal creature, which after it has been for a short time provided with vital power, one knows not how, must again give back the matter of which it was formed to the planet it inhabits (a mere speck in the universe).

The second, on the contrary, infinitely elevates my worth as an intelligence by my personality, in which the moral law

---

[82] *Scientific Autobiography* (NY, 1949) pp. 91–93.

reveals to me a life independent of animality and even of the whole sensible world—at least so far as may be inferred from the destination assigned to my existence by this law, a destination not restricted to conditions and limits of this life, but reaching into the infinite."[83]

Student: Okay, but how do you get to God who is beyond the mystery? After all, meditating upon the infinite does not immediately connect us to the religious, or Jewish understanding of God.

AN ONTOLOGICAL PRESUPPOSITION

LC: True, the certainty of the verity of God emerges as a response of the *whole* person to the mystery and transcendence of living. It is a response that rises in the depth of the mind as an ontological presupposition, which is understandable.

Student: You mean moments of insight? How does that work?

LC: I think that the most adequate answer to that is that the knowledge of God is already in us, even before we start thinking about Him. "I believe, therefore I exist" would be a more appropriate way of proving man's existence than Descarte's famous observation that man's existence is known through the principle of *cogito ergo sum* (I think, therefore I exist).

---

[83] Immanuel Kant, *Critique of Practical Reason*, translated by Abbott (London, 1889) p. 260.

Student: I have always wondered about something in relation to this. In the entire Torah there is never an attempt to prove God's existence. It is taken for granted!

LC: I do not think that it was taken for granted in the way you probably mean. After all, we just said that our belief in God derives from the fact that nothing be taken for granted. But I think what happens in the Torah is that "biblical man" was so overawed by the wonder of this world and all existence, that there was absolutely no way to deny the existence of some Higher Being. Neither does the Talmud ever attempt to prove God's existence. Only later Jewish philosophers tried to prove this, but that was possibly because of the influence of the non-Jewish world, which immersed itself in this question.

Student: All the same, why does biblical man never bother to prove God's existence?

BELIEF *THAT* AND BELIEF *IN*

LC: It relates to the English terminology: To believe *in* and believe *that*. If I say: "I believe *in* God," it does not mean that I believe *that* He exists. It really means: I trust *in* Him. The belief *that* God exists means that I *can* doubt His very existence, but I don't. It is an affirmation; a belief *that* always presupposes a belief *in*. Biblical man was mainly occupied with believing *in*, since the question of belief *that* was for him something which never came about. His belief in the existence of God was unshakable, since he saw His hand in everything.

Student: So what does the Hebrew word always used for belief, *emunah*, really mean? Does it not indicate "a belief *that*"?

LC: Not really. You are right to think that nowadays this is often the way in which the word is used, but this was not its original meaning. It really means to believe *in* and trust. That is what happens throughout biblical literature. For biblical man, God is the source of all visible and invisible existence in life as in death, growth and decay, light and darkness. It is a world where the sun rises and sets, where the stars appear, where heavy rain often pours down, where such phenomena as thunder and lightening are common. In brief, it is a world of marvels. Behind this, and in it, there is God. It is again an experience similar to electricity. It *is*. We only see its effect. We have never seen electricity, but that does not make it less real. In the same way, the religious personality sees God in everything and behind everything.

Student: But this is still not a proof of God's existence!

RABBI MOSHE CORDOVERO

LC: Indeed it is not and there is no way in which this can be achieved. That is precisely its power. Here is a most important principle at work: since God is altogether beyond us, there is no way to prove Him, because if we could, He would be confined to the limits of our minds! This would be a contradiction in terms! There is another reason why it is impossible to "prove" the existence of God. One of the defining principles of the world is that humanity is granted freedom of choice. If it were proven beyond doubt that God exists, then much of humanity's freedom of choice would be restricted. Man would be forced to follow God's instructions and one would have no option but to follow the moral code, i.e., the free choice to do bad or good, no longer having any relevance. According to this, I would go so far as to claim that if someone could prove the existence of God to me, then I could no longer believe in Him! It would, after all, not make sense that a God would take away our freedom of choice.

Let me quote you a statement by Rabbi Moshe Cordovero, one of the great kabbalists of the sixteenth century: "When your mind conceives of God, do not permit yourself to imagine that there really is a God as depicted by you, for if you do this, you will have a finite corporeal conception, God forbid. Instead your mind should dwell only on the affirmation of God's existence, and then it should *recoil*. To do more than that is to allow the imagination to reflect on God as He is Himself and such a reflection is bound to result in imaginative limitations and corporeality. Therefore put reins on your intellect and do not allow it too great a freedom, but assert God's existence and deny the possibility of comprehending Him. The mind should run to and fro—running to affirm God's existence and recoiling from any limitations, since man's imagination pursues his intellect."[84]

It could also be argued that comprehending God is like the concept of "feeling" an idea. This is impossible because touch is irrelevant to an idea. God is incomprehensible, not only because He is too profound to comprehend in the normal fashion, but also because He is of a totally different order. This was also one of the most salient points made by the Danish philosopher Soren Kierkegaard, the founder of religious existentialism. He claimed that the atheist cannot maintain that he is unable to believe in God on the basis that God cannot be proven, and so be secure in his unbelief. If God cannot be reached through the powers of reasoning, but only by *total* response of man's whole being, then the atheist, in his refusal to recognize God, is himself deciding to live a life which is not

---

[84] Rabbi Moshe Cordovero, *Elima Rabati* 1:10, p. 4b.

based on reason. It is like somebody saying that since he has little opportunity to meet the opposite sex, he decides that poets are speaking nonsense when they claim to have fallen in love!

Student: You still have not explained to me how one starts to believe in God.

LC: It is indeed a task which is most difficult to achieve. It requires climbing towards the invisible and leads along a path with countless chasms and very few ledges. The difficulty is compounded in that we will never know in advance when we actually find Him.

Student: You mean that one does not really know whether one has touched on God, or whether they have encountered some other personified form?

BUT DOES HE ENCOUNTER US?

LC: Yes, this is a difficult issue: how will we know when and where God is found?

I struggle a lot with this. We may have an encounter with God, but what we are really implicitly asking is if He has had an encounter with us! We may praise Him, but how do we know that He takes notice of our adoration? Iyov already raises this problem: "Can you, by searching, find God?" (11:7). He himself gives an answer: "God is great beyond our knowledge" (36:26).

There is a parallel situation with Avraham: he looked for God through wonder and amazement, but it was God who was to appear to him before he himself knew that God was a living "personality." In other words, it had to be a revelation *before* Avraham knew. The point being made here is that there is really no substitute for faith. Faith does not materialize out of nothing. It is not an unearned surprise, but something at which one has to work day and night. Faith is preceded by amazement, but this amazement does not automatically result in faith.

This means that faith is not easily attainable. In order to believe, we must deepen our sense of mystery, all the days of our life. However it appears that this belief only comes about, when God responds to our desire to believe.

Neither is this something which could come about through mass psychosis. Even when a revelation takes place in front of millions, as was the case at Sinai, each individual has to go through his or her own personal experience of God's answer. This is a crucial point. We cannot live in the uncertainty of whether there is or is not a living God, who is concerned with man. The answer to these questions cannot be identified casually. Faith is something which one can gain or lose at every moment of one's life.

Student: Is this how you would explain the Israelites standing at Sinai, hearing God speak, seeing the thundering and lightning, yet creating the golden calf just a few days later?

LC: There are many ways to understand this problem. I have dealt with it in one of my earlier books.[85]

But you are right that this is indeed something to which Moshe later alluded when he said: "You have seen all that the Lord did before your eyes in the land of Egypt, to Pharaoh and to all his servants and to all his land; the great trials which your eyes saw, the signs and those great wonders. *Yet the Lord has*

---

[85] Nathan T. Lopes Cardozo, "On Silence, Sacrifices and the Golden Calf" in *Between Silence and Speech: Essays on Jewish Thought* (NJ: Jason Aronson, 1992) chapter one.

not given you a mind to understand or eyes to see, or ears to hear" (Devarim 29:1–3).

In other words God warns the Israelites that although they had seen the most overwhelming miracles, there is no guarantee that this would result in a full experience of genuine faith!

Student: How so?

GOD CAN GET LOST

LC: The answer is that sometimes one realizes that one is living a religious life without real faith. One has to learn to wait, accepting that sometimes God seems to be concealed and that one has to wait for His reappearance. When God said to Moshe that He will hide His face on account of the evil which the Jews had perpetrated (*Devarim* 31:18), a profoundly poignant situation was created, a tragedy in fact—the tragedy that God can get lost!

Student: What is one to do in such a situation?

MYSTERIUM TREMENDUM AD FASCINAS

LC: There are many answers to that question. Let me share only one. It is called "religious experience." One of the great thinkers of our days, Rudolf Otto, writes in his book, *The Idea of the Holy*, that a religious experience, which is something like an encounter with God, is *sui generis*. It is not to be experienced in terms of the rational. It is like the love of music or art; one cannot explain it rationally. It is a category in and of itself.

Otto uses the word *"numen"* which means spirit—divinity residing on an object or person. His famous example is Yaacov's dream (*Bereishit* 28:10–22): "And he was afraid and said:

'how awesome is this place. This is none other than the house of God and this is the gate to heaven.'" Yaacov is not afraid that God may harm him, but the cause of his dread is the tremendous presence pervading the place where he dreamed. It is the sublimity of that moment. It is *Mysterium Tremendum ad Fascinas* (an overwhelming mystery which causes an encounter with the ineffable), and is in fact the experience of holiness. Holiness is the result of experiencing God in one's whole being; in all one does, says, thinks or feels. This experience is really God's response to man's search for Him. So belief that God exists is inexplicable to anybody who does not have that belief, but completely undeniable to those who experience it. Herein lies the dilemma.

THE PROBLEM OF EVIL

Student: Assuming that this approach works, what are we to do about the problem of evil? This, you have to agree, is perhaps the strongest objection to belief in God, or at least against the existence of a merciful God.

LC: Yes, it is. And it is a difficult issue to deal with. First of all, let us look into different arguments which may be of some help. It was St. Augustine, the great fifth century Christian thinker who articulated: either God can prevent suffering and does not do so, in which case He cannot be good, or He wishes to prevent suffering and cannot do so in which case He cannot be omnipotent.

Student: Exactly!

LC: It would be a terrible moral mistake to give simplistic answers to this question. We should not embark on a discussion of this problem without being constantly aware that we are probing an open wound and that we are arguing about the pain, blood and tears of millions of people.

Student: And the trouble is that often the easy answers to this question come from people in good health and with little to worry about!

LC: True. Let us therefore try to deal with the issue with the greatest delicacy. I will offer three answers and let it be your task to say what is wrong with them, or at least where they are problematic.

Student: I will try my best.

DIVINE DISPLEASURE

LC: Firstly, there is a view that human suffering reflects divine displeasure. In other words, God chastises man for his sins. We find many instances in *Tanach* that suggest this point of view. The most important examples are found in *Vayikra* (chapter 26) and *Devarim* (chapter 29), where God informs the Jews that if they will not observe the Commandments, they will be subject to curses and other disasters. The famous sage, Rabbi Jonathan Eibeschutz once wrote: "When we violently shake a man who has lost consciousness, we do so in order to revive him by 'chastising' him."

This is consistent with a well-known argument in Jewish tradition going back to *Tanach*: "Have I any pleasure at all that the wicked should die, says the Lord, and not rather that he should reform his ways and live?" (*Yechezkel* 18:21–23).

Student: The trouble with this argument is that more often than not it is the good who suffer and the sinful ones who avoid evil! This argument always annoys me because it sounds incredibly simplistic.

IYOV AND M. SCOTT PECK

LC: You are not the first to think so. The entire book of *Iyov* (*Job*) makes this point repeatedly. Iyov constantly stresses that the punishments, in no way, fit the crime. Indeed the Rabbis accuse Iyov's friends of sinning precisely for provoking this argument, and call it "wronging with words."[86] I believe, however, that the argument of divine displeasure should not be ignored altogether. There may be cases where God indeed sends man a message or a warning. There is a merit in it since it forces a person to examine his deeds and question his own behavior.

This is the first step towards an individual's spiritual and moral transformation. In his recent book, *Denial of the Soul*,[87] the well-known and deeply religious psychiatrist, M. Scott Peck, states that suffering is really a warning that has the potential of being a blessing. If the warning is not heeded, it could quickly turn into a curse.

He gives the example of the now treatable disease of leprosy. This was the most dreaded of medical afflictions. The reason was not that leprosy was a fatal disease, but that it caused ghastly and chronic disfigurement or deformity without people realizing it.

The cause of leprosy, Hansen's *bacillus*, is a kind of bacterium that when it infects a person, has a tendency to affect the

---

[86] *Bava Metzia* 58b.
[87] London: Pocket Books, 1997.

patient's nerve fibers. In particular, it destroys those microscopic fibers that carry the sense of pain. A leper might thus break his ankle and continue to walk as if nothing has happened because the leprosy destroyed the sense of pain in the ankle. The message that something is wrong does not reach to his brain which can cause incredible problems, such as some forms of arthritis and deformity of the joint.

The American missionary surgeon Paul Brand, who worked in India, discovered that a high percentage of devastation by leprosy is caused by this localized absence of pain. "Thank God for pain," writes Dr. Peck.[88] It is indeed important to realize, however, that such an approach could never explain all forms of suffering. It was Rabbi Yannai who was honest enough to state that "it is not in our power to explain either the prosperity of the wicked or the affliction of the righteous."[89] But that does not mean that other profound observations concerning suffering have not been offered by important thinkers.

Student: For example?

C.S. LEWIS AND THE EXTENSION OF PAIN

LC: There is the argument that there exists no extension of pain.

Student: What does that mean?

LC: Some philosophers claim that the problem of pain is not so acute, because pain can only be felt by the mind. A body does

---

[88] Ibid., p. 28.
[89] *Pirkei Avot* 4:19.

not feel pain! Only the mind alerts us that there is pain in our body. This would mean that if two people suffer, you cannot really speak about a double amount of pain, since each one can only suffer the pain present in his or her own mind. There is, they say, no more pain when two people or two thousand or two million people suffer pain. There is no such thing as the conglomeration of a thousand pains.

It was a Christian thinker, by the name of C.S. Lewis, in his provocative book, *The Problem of Pain*, who makes this point. He wrote: "We must never make the problem of pain worse than it is by vague talk about the 'unimaginable sum of human misery.' Suppose that I have a toothache of intensity X and suppose that you, who are seated by me, also begin to have a toothache of intensity X. You may, if you choose, say that the total amount of pain in the room is now 2X. But you must remember that no one is suffering 2X. Search all time and all space and you will not find that composite pain in anyone's consciousness.

There is no such thing as a sum total of suffering, for no one suffers it. When we have reached the maximum that a single person can suffer, we have no doubt reached something very horrible, but we have reached all the suffering that can be in the universe. The addition of a million fellow sufferers adds no more pain."[90]

Student: I am not so sure I agree with him, because when I see a person I love suffer, my suffering expands! So there *is* an extension of pain. If I see millions of my fellow creatures suffer, then I, too, have more pain.

---

[90] C.S. Lewis, *The Problem of Pain* (London, 1940) pp. 103–4.

LC: C.S. Lewis would respond by saying that this is incorrect, because that is *your* pain and not the pain of your fellow man! You are pained by looking at somebody else in pain, but that pain is in your mind and thus similar to the pain which you have from your toothache. Only this time, it is mental pain and not physical.

Student: Does Judaism agree with this opinion of Lewis? It sounds to me somehow far-fetched and not very relevant!

MONEY CAN BE DIVIDED, LASHES CANNOT

LC: It seems that in some ways the Jewish tradition does agree. The Talmud in *Makkot* 5a provides us with the following ruling: "In the case of false witnesses who are to be punished by receiving the imposition they desired to be inflicted on their victim (*Devarim* 29:19), the monetary impositions are shared among the offenders, but not the floggings." So, for example, if five men gave false witness against a person that he owed 500 dollars, they have to divide the corresponding money among them. Each one would have to pay 100 dollars. But if they gave evidence against a person for which he would become liable to a flogging of 39 lashes, each one would not receive a fifth of 39 floggings, but each one would receive the full 39 floggings. Besides the fact that one cannot divide 39 lashes into 5, the Talmud justifies this ruling with the following statement: "Money can be united into one total, whereas lashes cannot." It would seem that this is in accordance with C.S. Lewis' reasoning.

ONE DEATH?

Student: What about the Holocaust? Many Jews would surely object to this approach because the conclusion would ultimately be that the killing of 6,000,000 Jews does not create a greater problem concerning God's goodness, than the killing of a single Jew, or one other human being! So the Holocaust would not be any "more" cruel just because 6,000,000 happened to suffer torture and death.

LC: That is indeed true and very difficult to accept, particularly for us Jews. It is not that one man died 6,000,000 deaths, but that 6,000,000 men died one death. While I have to admit that the argument, as such, seems to be sound, I agree that it could be used to minimize the moral implication of the Holocaust.

Student: Right. It could justify the destruction of large numbers of human beings, on the grounds that it was only the killing of one man each time, and that the number plays no role.

LC: In addition, I also have difficulty with Lewis' narrow approach because it was not "just" the killing and torturing of millions of people in the Holocaust. It was also the attempt to destroy a whole nation and more besides.

WHY HAVE A UNIVERSE ALTOGETHER?

LC: Let us continue by adding another classic argument, which has been stated by numerous thinkers in different ways. This refers to a most profound question: why have a world or universe in the first place?

Student: What do you mean?

LC: Obviously, we should ask why God saw a need to create a world in the first place. I do not believe that we really have a full answer to this question since we would have to be God to know this. As one of the great Jewish philosophers, Shlomo Ibn Gabirol, in his *Keter Malchut*, once wrote: "If I knew Him, I would be Him." This is not an apologetical statement to provide us with an easy way out, but a reality that is at the core of being human. However, we can still rephrase the question: now that God has created us, what—as far as we human beings are able to grasp—could be His intended purpose for creation? What, if anything, did God tell us about the reason for our existence?

Student: What has that to do with the problem of evil?

LC: Quite a lot, because if the answer to this question is one which *demands* the existence of evil, then we would at least get a much better understanding of the purpose of evil and why we cannot do without it, however painful it may be.

Student: In that respect, you may be right, but how would the argument go?

JOHN HICK

LC: The answer to this question has been expressed in many different ways. One of the best formulations of it, I believe, is found in a book by the British Christian philosopher John Hick in his book, *The Problem of Evil*.[91] I will rephrase his words a little so as to better fit into the terminology of Jewish thought.

---

[91] John Hick, *Philosophy of Religion* (NJ: Prentice-Hall, 1983) chapter 4.

Hick's argument is based on earlier thinkers who try to make the following point: the purpose of God creating this world is not that its inhabitants would experience a maximum of pleasure and a minimum of pain. The world is a *"neshama (soul) making place,"* in which free beings, grappling with the tasks and challenges of their existence in a common environment, may become "the children of God" and heirs to eternal life. Consequently, our world has to be structured in such a way that human beings are able to reach this plateau.

Hick writes about the "counterfactual argument": "Suppose that, contrary to the fact, this world were a paradise from which all possibilities of pain and suffering are excluded. The consequences would be very far reaching. For example, no one could ever injure anyone else, the murderer's knife would turn to paper or the bullets to thin air; the bank safe, robbed of millions of dollars, would miraculously become filled with another million dollars; fraud, deceit, conspiracy and treason would somehow leave the fabric of society undamaged. No one would ever be injured by accident; the mountain climber, steeplejack, [somebody who builds a tower] or a playing child who fell from a height would float unharmed to the ground; the reckless driver would never meet with disaster. There would be no need for work, since no harm could result from avoiding work. There would be no call to be concerned for others in time of need or danger, for in such a world there could be no real needs or dangers."[92]

What this means is that there would be no possibility for any consistent law of nature. These laws would need to be constantly in flux: sometimes gravity would operate, sometimes not, sometimes an object would be hard and solid, sometimes soft. This would mean that there could be no such thing as

---

[92] Ibid., p. 47.

exact science, for there would be no enduring world structure to investigate. This would mean that by eliminating the problems and hardship of an objective environment with its set laws, life would become like a dream in which man aimlessly floats and drifts at ease. Do you understand the consequences?

Student: I suppose it would mean that the most valuable assets we have in this world—love and compassion—would be totally lost since nobody would need the assistance of anybody else!

NO RIGHT ACTION

LC: Exactly! Hick expresses it most forcefully when he writes: "In a hedonistic paradise there would be no wrong actions— nor, therefore, any right actions to distinguish from wrong. Courage and fortitude would have no point in an environment in which there is, by definition, no danger or difficulty. Generosity, kindness, the agape (Christian) aspect of love, prudence, unselfishness and other ethical notions that presuppose life in an objective environment could not even be formed. Consequently, such a world, however it might promote pleasure, would be very ill adapted for the development of the moral qualities of human personality. In relation to this purpose it might well be the worst of all possible worlds."[93]

Hick expands that suffering is ennobling and that this is the very purpose of an individual's existence. In fact, in the book of *Tehillim*, this is stated in the most clearest form: "Happy is the man whom Thou chastens, O Lord, and teaches him out of Your Law" (44:12). The point here is not just that God afflicts a person in order to recall him or her to his or her duty, but also that his or her moral value should be strengthened. This is most

---

[93] Ibid.

clearly manifested when one conquers adversity, refusing to allow it to deter one from the service of God and his fellow man. The Rabbis speak, in connection to this, of an artist testing and improving his wares, simultaneously adding to its quality as in a case of tint which starts to shine. He taps the good quality ware with his hammer to test its resilience.[94]

A man who has never suffered would have to be pitied rather than envied, for he would always have lived on a superficial plane. He would not know life's sweetness if he would never have experienced its bitterness. Iyov articulates this best when he says: "Though He slay me, yet I will trust in Him" (*Iyov* 13:1).

One could argue that there is a divine spark in man which refuses to allow him or her to be completely satisfied unless he or she submits themselves to the service of the Almighty. The Rabbis sometimes call this kind of suffering (having no connection with punishment): *Yisurim shel Ahava*, chastenings of love.[95]

FROM *TZARAH* TO *ZOHAR*

It is most fascinating to note that the Baal Shem Tov, the initiator of the chassidic movement, observed that the word *Zohar*, which means light, is related to the word *Tzarah*, anguish. In other words, the same letters in Hebrew are used to express the idea that the Jew, like all men, should channel his sufferings to achieve good, changing darkness to light, replacing *Tzarah* with *Zohar*!

---

[94] *Bereishit Rabbah* 55:2.
[95] For example see *Berachot* 5a.

Student: Okay, let us assume that we accept the answers you propose. But would anyone attempt to explain or justify the Holocaust based on these theories? Can you claim that the pain encountered there was to create a more noble man! Not only was the pain totally out of proportion to what man is physically able to endure, but most of the Nazi victims were never able to testify, because they were killed! In that case your aforementioned arguments are totally outrageous!

LC: You are right, although there are many cases where campmates in Auschwitz and in other concentration camps turned into "angels," helping, encouraging and feeding their fellow men in ways I will never be able to comprehend.[96]

Student: But these were exceptions to the rule, not the average behavior!

LC: True, but it *does* show that it is possible for some human beings to reach these heights, although many are incapable.

Student: That's all very good, but what about all the others? You are surely not going to criticize these people for not having risen to the "occasion"?

LC: God forbid! In what position am I, born after the Holocaust, to criticize? Let me rather make some other observations, which I believe have to be taken into account for whatever they are worth. Many philosophers like Lewis argue that the question concerning the Holocaust is qualitatively no different from an evil act or torture inflicted on "only" one person. As far as God is concerned, there is no difference. I

---

[96] See Eliezer Berkovits, *With God in Hell* (NY: Sanhedrin Press, 1979).

shiver from even making that statement, but there is no way to avoid it.

The question you just asked should be rephrased. We must ask whether the argument of ennoblement is still valid, when one is talking about a person who has suffered intensely.

Student: I appreciate you making the point, when you yourself have difficulties in maintaining this opinion, on emotional grounds.

LC: This is indeed one of the most difficult issues that confront us, but let us consider how many options we have. Either we deny the existence of a good God on the basis of the Holocaust, or we affirm Him despite the Holocaust. In both cases, we are in a bind. If we deny this good God, we are then left with the problem of how to explain the world with all its beauty, love and everything else there is. As we mentioned earlier, the universe leaves us standing in wonder. Alternatively, if we affirm Him, we then have to confront the issue of suffering and pain of which man is physically incapable of enduring. Both the non-believer and believer are equally confronted with a dilemma. The fact that the believer has simple acceptance in God, without any proof in the conventional sense of the word, does not make his opinion any less honest or significant than that of his non-believing friend.

Student: What are you trying to say?

LC: I am preparing you for what may sound like a ridiculous, far-fetched and apologetic argument, but one which is actually most sound.

Student: Let's hear it, and I will tell you what I think!

EDWYN BEVAN'S DOG

LC: Fine! We will have to tread on esoteric ground, simply because it is only there that our horizons will be broadened, even if I am unable to prove the "truth" of this point. But before I do that, let me tell you about a most thought provoking suggestion by Edwyn Bevan. It relates to something I said earlier about the four different "levels" of life. Bevan compares man's vision of God to a dog's perception of his human master: "In the dog's association with his master there are some fields of activity which come in the range of the dog's understanding, while there are other fields in which the dog does not and cannot comprehend what his master is about. What the dog does comes to feel and know, even with his limited intelligence, if he is a good dog and his master is a good master, is, that he is in the service of a being immeasurably superior to the dog himself: and from this intuition—mere dog that he is—he draws an intellectual and moral conclusion. His intellectual conclusion is that his master's unintelligible acts and orders are likely to be as wise as those which the dog can understand and have always proved to be.

The dog's moral conclusion is that it is his own duty to take this superior being's acts and orders in trust—always obeying the orders with alacrity and acquiescing in the acts of resignation."[97]

Student: That is a powerful illustration!

---

[97] Quoted by Arnold Toynbee, *A Study of History* (Oxford University Press, 1954) vol. 10, p. 1, n. 3.

LC: It is certainly of great help in understanding religion. What Bevan is saying is this: one cannot isolate evil as something which stands on it own. It has to be seen within the overall picture of all existence. We have to realize that, just like the dog, we can derive faith from the great deal of good there is in the world. We are able to rely on the laws of persisting nature, on beauty, on the proper function of our bodies, on love and so forth. When things go really wrong we should apply the same attitude as Bevan's dog, to trust the Master even at times that we fail to understand him.

Student: But, wait a moment, don't you think that man mainly encounters disasters and suffering in this world? Read the newspapers and watch television. It is only trouble which seems to cover the earth! So why trust in the Master?

ONLY DISASTER?

LC: I do not agree. I think that we are indoctrinated by the press and the rest of the media, that this world is mainly a place of human suffering. This is a dangerous and a one-sided perspective. With all the trouble which many people have to suffer, we should not lose sight of the fact, that percentage-wise, more things go right than wrong. It is incorrect to believe that man's life is mainly troublesome with few exceptions. Most of the time, man is able to draw faith from an infinite amount of things which go right. The trouble is that man is so fearful of that which *might* go wrong, that it spoils all the great moments that are granted to him.

This is a pessimism that might be understandable if it were realistic. It is man's psychological attitude which often denies the reality in which he lives. It is an attitude that we are able to change. There is no doubt that we have seen many people in history who were able to "see the sun," even through times when the sun was not shining on them. I do have to agree that there are many people whose lives seem to comprise only misery, to say the least. But still, the overall picture of all of mankind is one in which there is much beauty, hope and love.

Moreover, the universe-at-large seems to show such over-powering beauty and excellence, that the wisdom of a Master should definitely be acknowledged.

Student: I am not so sure about that. I'll have to think about it. In the meantime, you said earlier that you wanted to still make a "far-fetched" point. I would like to hear it.

ESOTERIC SUBCONSCIOUSNESS

LC: The "far-fetched" point is this: since we have to admit that we are, as I previously pointed out, in a "dog-like" situation here in this world, this must make us take another issue into consideration. We all know that there is something called subconsciousness; comprising thoughts of which we are not completely aware but which nonetheless influence our actions. I would like to suggest that there also exists, perhaps, a kind of esoteric subconsciousness. This touches on our esoteric exis-tence, of which we know very little, but which sends us hints coming from another world.

Student: What do you mean?

LC: I mean that we may very well be living a kind of double life. Not in the Freudian sense of our subconscious existence—although it may be attached to that too—but an esoteric sub-consciousness, in which all that we experience as evil and suffering takes on a whole new dimension. It may supply the

reason why and how we experience "impossible" and unbearable pain, as did the Jews in the Holocaust. It is the other side
of the pain which makes perfect sense but because of our
one-sided situation—or better still, our dog-like perspective,
we are never able to grasp that world. Perhaps it relates to what
some psychologists claim when they say that all pain is "only"
psychosomatic. Somewhere the deeper reason and necessity for
pain belongs to another sphere, of which we touch only the
outer shell, missing the inner core.

Student: Let's assume that you are right. But I still do not see
why you have to follow that path. There is another method of
explaining the issue of pain.

LC: What would that be?

AFTERLIFE

Student: The afterlife. Why not just simply say that in the
afterlife we will realize that all pain was for our ultimate good,
but our dog-like condition made it impossible to see.

LC: In principle, you are right and we shall come to that, but
not just yet.

Student: Why not?

LC: I find the afterlife theory problematic. While it may
explain the reason for people going through "hell" on this
earth, it does not detract from the fact that this "good" is
perceived as terrible pain at the time. Maybe the pain is a mere
illusion, but the illusion is real enough!

Student: Fine, but is your theory of esoteric subconsciousness any better?

LC: What I want to prevent is belittling the recognition of pain, in this world, or to declare it an illusion. This evil and pain might be the other side of the coin which we are unable to see. It is somehow the necessary precondition for something that needs to take place "on the other side."

Student: I have lost you.

LC: What I am saying is that it may well be necessary for evil to take place, so that an esoteric experience can become a reality somewhere else. I am trying to find a way in which I can attribute this evil without having to refer to an afterlife. My aim is to convey to people that pain is not merely punishment, or something necessary in order to become more refined. Rather, it is the consequence of living life in the here and now, which involves experiencing pain. The ultimate reason is totally unknown to us, being unable to look through the window into the other room. We are constantly perplexed by the "time" factor, which may not exist on the other side. Being timeless, in our "time-bound situation" (our physical world), requires pain.

Student: So you are saying that a spiritual "afterlife" is somehow already lived in the here and now?

LC: Yes. The expression "afterlife" is really a misnomer, because it is a timeless concept. An afterlife can only be spoken about from our limited perspective. The truth is that it is really "now-time."

Student: I am not sure I am following you here, or that what I have grasped makes any sense. I have the feeling that we are heavily involved in semantics. In any case, even if I would accept your theory, I would still ask: why did God not create the other side of the coin, i.e., the esoteric subconsciousness, without needing any compensation, in the form of pain, in this world?

CAN GOD DO THE IMPOSSIBLE?

LC: This depends on another discussion, whether or not God can accomplish the "impossible."

Student: Do you doubt that, being religious yourself?

LC: Yes, but not for the reasons you are thinking. I believe that God is indeed able to do everything, but not the impossible!

Student: Why not?

LC: For very obvious reason: since it is impossible!

Student: I am sorry, I have lost you completely!

LC: The argument is really very simple. If we say that something is impossible, we cannot say afterwards that it is possible.

Student: Why not?

CAN GOD CREATE A MARRIED BACHELOR?

LC: Because we just said that it was impossible! Let me explain, or better yet, let me ask you a question: In your opinion, do you think that God could create a bachelor who is married?

Student: Well, it depends.

LC: May I suggest the reason for your hesitation. You find yourself in a philosophical and linguistic paradox. If you say that God can make a bachelor who is married, you would have to admit that he would no longer be a bachelor. This is because the word "bachelor" means somebody not married. So, he cannot be married while at the same time, being unmarried!

Student: That is obviously true.

LC: So can God create a bachelor who is married, or not?

Student: I suppose the answer must be no!

LC: Right, and that is what I meant when I said that God cannot do the impossible. The reason is *not* that God is limited but because it is a contradiction in terms. In other words, we have violated our language. It no longer makes any sense!

Student: I see your point. Are there more cases like that?

LC: Certainly. We could ask whether God is capable of negating Himself?

Student: Definitely not!

LC: Why not?

Student: Because the definition of God is an eternal Being!

BRIBBLE, BRABBLE, BRUBBLE

LC: Yet again, you see that God cannot do everything, because it would be a contradiction in terms! Saying that God can negate His own existence is in effect like asking: can the One who can never not exist, not exist? It is like asking: can God bribble, brabble or brubble? It is meaningless.

Student: Okay, I get the point, but how is that related to my earlier question?

BENDING PAPER

LC: A lot. You see, perhaps the reason why there is pain in the world is because there is no way to have that esoteric "other side" of life without having pain in this one. Allow me to illustrate this in the following way: if I have a very thin piece of paper and I create a bend in that paper by way of my finger, would it not automatically create a "bump" on the other side?

Student: Yes.

LC: So returning to what I said earlier, could God create this bend on the paper without having the bump on the other side?

Student: No.

LC: Why not?

Student: Because it would be a contradiction in terms!

LC: Exactly. And this may give us a way of speaking about pain. If you, or better yet, God, is pushing His "finger" on the "other side" it would simultaneously create a bump on our side, which is causing the pain.

Obviously I cannot prove this, but it is possible that this is what is happening here. What I am therefore trying to say is this: as long as we are unable to see beyond this world and consequently unable to fully understand our own world (since our world may exist in direct relationship with the "ins" and "outs" of the other world), we will never know why evil takes place.

All we *can* know is that it cannot be prevented since it is the outcome of an inescapable reality somewhere else. It is not that the Holocaust was without divine purpose, but rather, that we lack sufficient information to make sense of it.

The big question, however, is why was God "forced" to create such circumstances "on the other side" which caused such a tragedy to take place on our side?

Student: Very well. There is again a lot to think about.

Before we depart today, I wonder if you would make one worthwhile observation concerning suffering which I can take home.

PASCAL

LC: Here is a notion expressed by the French philosopher Blaise Pascal: "Man's grandeur stems from his knowledge of his own misery. A tree does not know itself to be miserable."[98]

---

[98] *Pensées* (1670) p. 397.

DAY FIVE

The Trouble with Halacha; The *Weltanschauung* of Halacha; Radical Encounter; Ludwig Wittgenstein; So What?; God is of No Importance, Unless He Is of Supreme Importance; God Takes Man Seriously; Plato's *Imitatio Dei*; Glory; The Day after the Revelation; The Fireworks; Halacha Is a Divine Compliment; Why So Many Laws?; Like a Taste; No Nook or Cranny Without Halacha; The Validity of the Law; Reason or Revelation?; Is Good, Good?; Immanuel Kant; Why Are Ethics Imperative?; The Categorical Imperative; Is "Good" Teachable?; Christianity and Teaching Goodness; Does Judaism Agree with Plato?; Karl Marx; Henry Bergson's "*Élan Vital*"; Subconscious Compulsion Is Not Moral; Why Is Mankind Not More Moral?; The Holocaust and the German Intellectuals; A Completely Different Way; A Desire to Be Obligated; There Is No Law of Logic Which Will Make Man Think Logically; The Problem of Democracy; The Mind on Its Own Cannot Do a Thing; Deed and Thought Must Come Together; The Body Is Amoral; Appetite for the Good; *Mitzvot Lo Ta'ase*; All of Man's Actions Enter into His Thoughts; *Shelo Lishma*; The Positive Commandments; Habit; The Swine and the Camel; Progress or Past, What Is Kosher?; The Kosher Way; A New Awareness; The Praying Lips; To Close One's Eyes

THE TROUBLE WITH HALACHA

Student: In our conversations, we have often spoken about the central role of Halacha, Jewish law. As I mentioned earlier, I find this most troubling. Halacha requires Jews to conform to thousands of rules. It appears rigid and inflexible. The strict rule seems to have the upper hand, allowing for little self-expression. I have listened carefully to your earlier comments and I see your point, but it does not satisfy me. Your story about the chassidic Rebbe, who did not fast because he had no time to eat, is most informative, but it is insufficient without an underlying philosophy behind it that would attract a modern sensibility.

LC (Lopes Cardozo): I agree. Halacha is probably one of the most misunderstood dimensions of Judaism. I must admit that much of this is due to the fact that the philosophy of Halacha is complex, and therefore for most people a closed book. As well as needing to be a psychologist and careful reader of the Talmud, to understand it, one must also think on a profound level. Not only is this a problem in the Jewish secular community, but my experience tells me that many religious Jews themselves suffer from lack of knowledge in this field, including those who teach or learn in *yeshivot*. This is another matter that needs far more attention in Jewish education and yeshiva training. For your information, your observations do not even touch on a much more sophisticated critique of Jewish law.

Student: This becomes even more intriguing.

LC: Let me start by playing the devil's advocate and attacking Halacha from different perspectives to see how it would respond.

Student: Fine with me!

THE *WELTANSCHAUUNG* OF THE HALACHA

LC: To understand the unique position of the Halacha in Judaism, one must first clarify the basis on which it stands. One has to understand something about its general outlook

Student: That makes sense. Please proceed.

RADICAL ENCOUNTER

LC: Firstly, we have to realize that Judaism is a deeply religious tradition, which centers around God and His relationship with man. In fact Judaism teaches that the most radical encounter a man has with anything beyond himself is the one he has with God. It is "radical" in the sense that it is absolute and inescapable. It is the ultimate encounter which takes place at every moment of man's life. No minute, deed or word goes by that does not take place in the presence of God. God is an ongoing presence in man's life. Wherever man goes, whatever he thinks or does—all is open to the scrutiny of God. There is always one Intruder, one Spectator, a Listener and Reader of man's thoughts and actions—and that is the *Ribono shel Olam*

(The Lord of the Universe). This is the only definition of God which fully makes sense: the immovable Figure in our lives.

Student: I wonder how many people realize that!

LUDWIG WITTGENSTEIN

LC: Let me tell you about an insight from the famous non-Jewish (but of Jewish descent) philosopher, Ludwig Wittgenstein. He said that statistics show that most people in the West believe in God, i.e., in a biblical God, one who actually "interferes" in our lives. But if this is so, asked Wittgenstein, why are only a minority of these believing people actually religious?

Student: You mean those who actually act on their belief and whose every experience in life is infused with religiosity?

LC: Yes. Wittgenstein said that the reason is that most people add two more words to the statement, "I believe."

Student: And which are those?

SO WHAT?

LC: "So what!" They say: "I believe in God, so what?!"

Student: What do you mean?

LC: When people claim that they believe in God, most of the time they do not realize what they are saying. They do not realize that this statement: "So what" is completely inaccurate since it contradicts the first part of their claim. "So what" means that it has no direct relevance to one's life. It is like saying that one's belief in God is not something that changes my views on life or the way I conduct myself. Such a point of view is, however, totally impossible. After all, believing in God means that one acknowledges that some ultimate Being is heavily involved in one's life. Again, an ultimate and radical encounter! All our thoughts and actions take place in front of Him. This determines our relationship with everything else in the world. When God exists, then everything is touched by His existence and nothing looks the same anymore.

GOD IS OF NO IMPORTANCE, UNLESS HE IS OF SUPREME IMPORTANCE

Stated a little differently: God is of no importance unless He is of supreme importance. So how can one say: "so what"? as if it makes no difference. The truth is, obviously, that it makes *all* the difference.

Student: Do you mean to say that since man lives all his life in the presence of God, he must live a life which reflects the ongoing encounter?

LC: Correct! In fact your observation reveals one of the foundation stones of Halacha. Halacha is basically an answer to a most profound question: How will I be able to live a life of integrity and honor in the ongoing presence of God? Or, in slightly different language: if I live in the presence of the King, how do I behave as spiritual royalty?

Student: That makes a lot of sense.

GOD TAKES MAN SERIOUSLY

LC: That is not all. There is another important base upon which Halacha stands. God takes man seriously. Man's deeds and thoughts count in His eyes. Judaism argues that if God created man with the potential to think, to make up his mind and to behave according to his choices, it stands to reason that man's deeds and thoughts are significant. Why would God create man with the capability to choose and act accordingly if He doesn't take him or her seriously?

Student: What about the animals? Don't they have the same options? They think and act! Yet the Torah does not give them the same elevated treatment of honor and seriousness as it gives man.

LC: There is a crucial difference. Animals do not possess the faculty of making moral decisions. Both Torah and science confirm that there is no sense of moral consideration within animals. This dimension is unique to man.

Student: Please carry on.

PLATO'S *IMITATIO DEI*

LC: What one has to realize is that the encounter with God is based on the premise that man is created in the image of God.

This means that man has a most unusual connection with God about which He seems to care. This concept is known in the general world as *imitatio dei*, which was introduced by Plato.[99]

---

[99] Plato, *Theaetetus*, 17/6a–b and Laws 1v/99.

Student: What does that actually mean?

LC: It is best expressed by the Talmud in a famous statement: "The Torah says: 'and unto Him you shall cleave.' But is it possible for man to cleave to the divine Presence? Is it not written: 'For the Lord your God is a devouring fire....' However the meaning is: cleave to Him by imitating His characteristics. As He clothes the naked...so you clothe the naked. As He visits the sick...so you do the same...."[100]

Student: In other words, it is not His essence which is spoken of here, but His attributes.

GLORY

LC: Correct. The point is that God can only be known by His relational attributes, i.e., by those parts of His ways to which man can relate, since man is only capable of "imitating" these qualities. Beyond this, there is no similarity between God and man. In the book of *Yirmiyahu* (9:22–23), this matter is well described in the following way: "Thus says the Lord: let not the wise man glory in his wisdom, neither let the mighty man glory in his might, let not the rich man glory in his riches. But only in this should come glory: that he understands and knows Me, that I am the Lord who exercises mercy, justice, and righteousness on earth, for in these things I delight, thus says the Lord." So the relational attributes, such as mercy, justice, and righteousness, become the example to emulate.

---

[100] *Sotah* 14.

Student: But why is it necessary to have God ask man to imitate Him? Why not have Him reveal Himself as the God-head without making any further demands on man?

THE DAY AFTER THE REVELATION

LC: Because our belief in God does not ensure our dependence on Him, nor does it guarantee a close connection with Him. Revelation alone does not get us very far. God may have revealed Himself to man at Sinai, but the question is what happens after the revelation is over. Only the requirement of "imitating" God's example of behavior, through His law, guarantees a bond between God and man which will endure even after the revelational experience has passed.

This revelational experience is sustained through our compliance with Halacha. By emulating His attributes, God remains real to us. When the Sinaitic revelational experience has faded, God continues to speak to man via the Halacha. The powerful voice of God at Sinai remains thousands of years later.

THE FIREWORKS

Student: But why not have a continuous revelational experience of God in other ways, as took place at Sinai? Why not keep the Jews "standing at Sinai," for the rest of their lives and just continue the "fireworks" as detailed in the Torah?

LC: This, I would argue, would undermine the very purpose of human existence. The whole point is that even when no longer experiencing the direct heavenly voice, man should still maintain the same relationship with God. Sinai is "abnormal," in the sense that it is not conducive to normal human functioning. It is not a great art to admit God's existence and the need to serve Him when His fireworks continue to sparkle and burn. The art is to find Him, when things *are* normal, when we are busy with our day-to-day life. This is the challenge with which man is continually confronted. It is precisely for this reason that it is so difficult to be truly religious. Judaism constantly makes the point that one should be part of society and not close oneself off from the world by living on top of the mountain. It is within the laws of nature and the normalcy of society that one has to find God. This may be the reason why Sinai is considered by tradition as the lowest of all mountains. It had to be a mountain that man could "ascend," so as to experience the exclusiveness of God.

Yet, at the same time it had to be translatable into the common life of men. The mountain could therefore not be too high! So too, the laws had to be "down to earth."

Student: If I understand you correctly, you are saying that the giving of the Torah and the Halacha are greater manifestations of God taking man seriously than the revelation alone.

HALACHA IS A DIVINE COMPLIMENT

LC: The requirement of the law is a vote of confidence of God in man. It is a divine compliment. We alluded to this before when we spoke about the differences between Judaism and Christianity.

This is expressed in a famous statement of the Rabbis: "Beloved is Israel, for the Holy one Blessed be He surrounded them with commandments."[101]

---

[101] *Berachot* 6b.

WHY SO MANY LAWS?

Student: But what is the purpose of all this? Why have so many laws? What is it that the law wants to accomplish above all that which you mentioned earlier?

LIKE A TASTE

LC: Good point! We are treading on dangerous ground. While we will never be able to fathom all the intentions of God, Jewish thinkers have constantly emphasized that we have an obligation to discover God's intention as much as possible within the limits of the human mind. That is the reason why the sages always spoke about the *ta'ame hamitzvot*, not the *reasons* of the commandments but about their "taste." Just as one cannot "know" meat by eating it, so too, we do not know the "ultimate" reasons of these commandments, though we could definitely get a taste of their significance.

Student: Are you saying that the commandments are foremost ethical directives, which man can experience as though tasting something?

LC: To a certain extent this is true, but I hasten to add that this is not entirely correct. I am not convinced that all the laws are reflections of the need for ethics. There may very well be other motives at work, of which we may know only some, while others remain beyond us.

Student: I also see many laws existing primarily for ethical reasons, but there are quite a few ritual laws that do not seem to have any ethical value.

LC: True. And it is these laws which pose the greatest challenge when we are looking for some divine purpose. But as we shall see, there *is* purpose to them.

NO NOOK OR CRANNY WITHOUT HALACHA

Student: But besides this problem, I am still bothered by the amount of laws! There seems to be no nook or cranny into which Halacha does not penetrate. What is the spiritual significance of all these laws? I have been told that the law instructs the Jew how to dress, and even specifies which shoelace he should tie first. This seems absurd!

LC: We definitely have to understand all that, but I think you overlook a most important point. Even ethical commandments require a great deal of explanation.

Student: Why?

LC: Because they introduce a major philosophical-religious problem!

Student: Which one?

THE VALIDITY OF THE LAW

LC: The question of the validity of the law.

Student: What do you mean?

LC: This is the problem. Various philosophers have asked what is the law's validity or better, what are the criteria we set in determining their values?

Are they valid because they conform to the laws of logic, or because they are willed by God?[102]

Student: What is the problem?

REASON OR REVELATION

LC: There are two schools of thought. One states that the good must be recognizable, seen as good through the means of human reason. In other words, its value comes from its own inherent quality. Consequently, the ultimate evaluator is reason itself. The other is of the opinion that the law has validity because it is willed by God.

Student: So, according to the first school of thought, the law revealed by God has an understood validity of its own, which is not dependent on its revealed nature. While the second school claims that its validity is solely dependent on its divine revelation.

LC: Exactly.

Student: But that would raise a question! If the law has validity of its own—even without revelation—what is the purpose of revelation? Man could have initiated the laws himself, through his own intellect.

LC: That is exactly the problem to which I alluded. There are thinkers who would argue that since reason, as the final evaluator, would make the need for revelation superfluous, one

---

[102] See Eliezer Berkovits, *God, Man and History* (NY: Jonathan David, 1965) chapter 10.

must argue that the law, being of a God-given nature, must, by definition, be beyond all human reasoning.

IS GOOD, GOOD?

Student: So the good is good because it is the will of God. Without the will of God there can be neither good nor evil.

LC: Correct. Good is good because God determined it to be so. But, if God would have said the opposite, then what is now known as good would be known as evil!

I do not have to tell you that this is highly problematic. It would mean that what we now call evil is not so from a reasoned standpoint, but only because God decided accordingly. God could have said the reverse. Yet, once we reject this approach, we come back to our earlier problem: why have a revealed law when reason will be its ultimate arbitrator?! This matter has been an ongoing debate between both Jewish and non-Jewish philosophers. It seems like an insurmountable dilemma.

IMMANUEL KANT

Student: I heard that Immanuel Kant, the great German philosopher, as well as the Deists, about whom we spoke before, declared that only reason could be the source of authority.

LC: That is true: Kant stated that "The true and only religion contained only such laws...of whose absolute logical validity we may become aware of ourselves...which we therefore acknowledge as revealed by pure reason."[103]

---

[103] Immanuel Kant, *Religion Within the Limits of Reason Alone*, II and IV.

Student: Obviously, this is not a solution from within religion itself, since religion must claim that there is a need for revelation. Secondly, it sounds quite arrogant when man's intellect becomes the ultimate arbitrator. Who says that man has the intellectual power to decide independently, based solely on his own reason?

LC: That is indeed what some religious thinkers observe, but whatever the solution to this problem is, it is clear that it is not only the ritual laws that create philosophical problems; but also those laws belonging to the category of ethics.

Student: In that case, what is one to do?

LC: Firstly, we have to deal with two other issues. One is the question of why man should be obliged to live by the demands of ethics; and secondly, we need to examine human behavior in the light of that obligation.

WHY ARE ETHICS IMPERATIVE?

Student: You mean to say that we need to discover the reason why ethics are an imperative?

LC: Yes. What we have to realize is that something may be right from an ethical point of view, but who says that we are *obliged* to listen to this demand? We need to discover a way in which we are able to induce man to act in accordance with this ethical obligation.

Student: A man could well argue, for example, that compliance with ethics is not as important as experiencing pleasure. I agree that one may have to pay the price for not behaving ethically, but suppose this person does not care about the price and feels that the advantage of pleasure is more attractive!

LC: Exactly! How can it be proven that one ought to care about ethics in the face of great pleasure? This question is even more pertinent when we adopt the opinion of some philosophers who claim that ethics is intuitive. Why then should anybody have to act accordingly? After all, one has the option of refusing to listen to one's own ethical instinct.

THE CATEGORICAL IMPERATIVE

This is one of the weak points in Kant's famous *Categorical Imperative*. It states that man has an inner ethical voice, which he should follow. At best, Kant showed that it is an a priori requirement, in accordance with the intellect, to act according to this principle of pure reason. But he completely overlooked the most important thing, which is that man would be *obligated* to act according to this famous rule. Obligation is considered to be the most important value in ethics.

Student: So you are actually saying that it is neither categorical nor imperative?

IS "GOOD" TEACHABLE?

LC: Indeed! But not only that. This also leads to a second problem. Presuming that we are in agreement over the obligatory source of all ethics, the question still remains: how are we going to induce man to act accordingly?

The finest rules of human conduct are worthless if man does not follow them! This echoes Plato's attempt to respond when asked if goodness is teachable.[104] Like Socrates, he was of the opinion that goodness is the result of grasping the "supreme idea" and its contemplation. Goodness, in his eyes, is an extension of knowledge itself, and, like all knowledge, is teachable.

Student: So is evil to be understood as the result of lack of knowledge?

LC: Yes. According to Plato there is something called "involuntary evil." Consequently, all evil is due to ignorance, and therefore involuntary. We see this concept running throughout the whole of secular humanism. It believes that all evil is the result of a lack of education. Everything would be alright if people were to have adequate enlightenment!

CHRISTIANITY AND TEACHING GOODNESS

Student: Would Christianity also agree with this attitude?

LC: No, or at least not classical Christianity. If anything, it teaches the opposite of this Socratic teaching. For Christianity, it is essentially futile to teach goodness effectively.

Student: Why?

LC: Adam and Chava's succumbing to temptation rendered man incapable of achieving good from his own strength. Man would be lost without God's merciful compassion. Here, too, we discover a kind of "involuntary evil," but for a completely different reason: this evil is not due to ignorance. Man's nature

---

[104] Plato, *Dialogues; Meno; Protagoras; The Republic and Laws.*

simply lacks the power to be good. He cannot improve on his own—he relies on redemption.

Student: As we discussed earlier, this is something to which Judaism will always object.

LC: Correct. The escape from responsibility, as we saw before, has never had any place in the Jewish tradition; indeed, it opposes avoiding responsibility!

DOES JUDAISM AGREE WITH PLATO?

Student: Does Judaism agree with Plato that good is teachable and that it is a matter of the mind?

LC: Not really. It will perhaps agree with Plato that it is teachable, but not through the means of the intellect.

Student: How then does Judaism claim to achieve this?

LC: Before we come to the Jewish solution to this problem, I want to mention the fact that different philosophical systems have tried to respond to this matter. Let me just note one or two of them; it will help us appreciate the Jewish response a little better.

Student: That seems to make sense.

KARL MARX

LC: One obvious example is the approach of Karl Marx. For Marx, there is hardly any need to teach man goodness. Neither would it be of much use, since these ideas in themselves are powerless. In Marx's eyes, the emphasis needs to be placed on the material condition of man. Once man lives under proper and comfortable material conditions, all will be well. Man will then automatically turn into a good citizen and there will be no more worries.

Student: This seems to me to be a completely unsatisfying perspective. In fact, history has shown that material satisfaction usually *deters* one from noble deeds!

HENRY BERGSON'S "*ELAN VITAL*"

LC: That is right. Yet while reality proves Marx wrong, history does not solve the question of how man is to become good. It seems to have a blind belief in the essential goodness of man. But this cannot be proven and when stated this way, comes across as quite dogmatic.

Let me mention one more serious attempt to deal with the problem. It is found in writings of the French philosopher Henry Bergson, and specifically in his work, *The Two Sources of Morality and Religion*. Here, Bergson, who was a Jew by birth, introduced his famous principle called "*Élan Vital*."

Student: What is that all about?

LC: Henry Bergson agreed with Christianity that man is really unable to create his own moral criteria. He thus rejected the approach of Socrates and others that claimed that all morality can be induced from reasoning. But Bergson did not opt for the notion of grace, as in Christianity. He introduced the idea of "*Élan Vital*," which is a kind of inborn moral subconsciousness formed through compulsion. In a closed society, he states, this compulsion comes about through social pressure and somehow works like instinct. In a more open society, it comes about through the genius and inspiration of saints and prophets, like the creation of "new species," which consequently exercises an irresistible attraction.

Student: That does not seem to be a bad way to solve our question.

LC: I agree that this certainly is one of the best attempts made, but there remains a problem. While Bergson clearly saw that the conscious acceptance of an ethical code does not guarantee man's ethical behavior, he seemed to overlook the fact that once something becomes a compulsion, it can no longer be considered ethical.

Student: Why not?

SUBCONSCIOUS COMPULSION IS NOT MORAL

LC: Because the moment it becomes a subconscious compulsion, it ceases to be part of the foundation of ethics, whose whole basis is built on man's ability to make decisions as a result of freedom of action! Ethical obligation presupposes freedom of will and action.

Student: In other words: man acts ethically when he chooses between two or more alternatives and decides to conform to certain values. So one can only speak about morality when there is freedom to act otherwise. Once one is compelled to do something, one can no longer speak about having chosen in favor of ethics.

LC: Obviously, we often decide about moral issues, without being fully conscious of them. This is, however, due to earlier conscious decisions, which have become part of our nature. These kinds of decisions have moral value, since the framework for such decisions, based on free will, was created at an earlier stage. This is however different from Bergson's "*Élan Vital.*" In the last case, there are external pressures which cause people to behave the way they do. They are not the results of earlier decisions of the individual.

WHY IS MANKIND NOT MORE MORAL?

Thus, the issue remains unresolved by Bergson. Also, according to Bergson, we are confronted with a disturbing question: if standards of morality are compulsive, why do people not behave more morally than they do?

Student: The issue is even more complex, because historical record does not show that greater enlightenment or intellectual advancement has led to an increase in man's moral behavior.

LC: I suppose that Bergson would respond that this is true, and that we need more saints!

THE HOLOCAUST AND THE GERMAN INTELLECTUALS

Anyway, it is self-evident that an increase in man's knowledge is in no way conducive to better moral standards. We saw this most recently during the Holocaust, where German intellectuals were instrumental in creating the concentration camps and gas chambers.

LC: True.

Student: In this light, I wonder if man is not just simply an immoral being, as classical Christianity teaches. If that is the case, then there is little hope for man to adequately deal with moral problems on his own

A COMPLETELY DIFFERENT WAY

LC: You would be right in regards to Christianity, but Judaism has a completely different way of dealing with this issue. From the Jewish perspective, although man has a strong inclination to immorality, man is nonetheless capable of being moral.

Student: I wonder how!

LC: Judaism's stance suggests that there is a solution to the ethical dilemmas which general ethics is incapable of addressing. Its main point is that most thinkers or religions do not properly understand the very foundations of ethics. Philosophers work with the assumption that once an ethical principle is reasonable, there is no need to prove it is obligatory. They believe that reason has enough authority to command and power to compel.

Student: This is what we spoke about before: since the law is reasonable, what is the reason for revelation; if the law is not reasonable, what is the good of revelation? So they claim that there is no reason for revelation even to occur.

LC: Yes, but what they did not realize is that reason is the faculty of understanding, of recognition and interpretation, and no more than that. As I indicated before, reason cannot, as such, obligate anybody.

Student: So what can obligate?

A DESIRE TO BE OBLIGATED

LC: The will, the desire.

Student: So there can be no obligation unless there is a desire to be obligated!?

LC: That is right. Reason knows no desire, though man may desire what is reasonable. What ought to be, should perhaps be reasonable—not because it is always reasonable, but because someone desires it to be the actualization of that which is reasonable. As such, all authority of reason is hypothetical.

THERE IS NO LAW OF LOGIC WHICH WILL MAKE MAN THINK LOGICALLY

Student: It seems that you are implying that if man should prefer foolishness to wisdom, there is nothing in the laws of nature that can compel man to think and act logically.

LC: This is the reason why I said that Kant's famous *Categorical Imperative* fails to live up to its own claims. One can say that one should respect the Categorical Imperative but that can happen only as the result of desire. Only after forming this desire can one speak of obligation. Obviously, not everything that is desired or willed is good, but without will there can be no acceptance of obligation. With that conclusion, we can begin to understand the need for some kind of revelation. We may claim, indeed, that all law derives its authority from some form of revelation. This is the foundation of law: the Lawgiver must make his will known to establish his law and there must be an enforcement policy, to make the public aware that this is a serious matter, from which there is no escape. This applies, too, in countries with the highest levels of democracy. Without an authority stating that the law is law, there is no law.

In a democratic setting, the population is itself the one that creates this obligation through the desire to have some suggestion become a binding norm. This is also true in the case where a minority opposes the majority. In a democratic country, it is also the will of the minority that the law should be like the majority.

Student: So are both aforementioned schools of thought right as well as wrong?

LC: Those who believed that a law could not be subject to the test of reason were right. And those who declared that a law, not given by God, could never claim to be absolute were right in the sense that it cannot attain an absolute obligation by itself. Simultaneously, both schools were wrong because they confused logical validity with ethical obligation. Here is the point: we consider "the good" to be an obligation, through the will of God. Without this acceptance, it remains a "suggestion." Logical validity may beckon it, but it will never escape the problem that it is not yet an absolute obligation.

It is interesting to note that Maimonides seems to have been aware of this dilemma when he wrote in his codex "*Mishne Torah*,"[105] about the need for non-Jews to keep the seven Noahide Laws, which are the foundation of all human ethics. He states that those non-Jews who live by these laws are the (spiritual) "sons of Noach" and are "the pious of the nations."

---

[105] *Mishne Torah, Melachim* 8:11.

But he also adds that this is only so when they keep these laws because of God's will, and not because they make logical sense and are valid as "natural law." Interestingly, this statement seems to contradict Maimonides' famous philosophical work, the *Moreh Nevuchim, the Guide for the Perplexed*. There he states that the highest service of God is that attained through the intellect.

Student: But since there is often no real difference between both positions—collective reasoning or divine revelation—what then, after all, is the real practical difference? When an earthly lawgiver obligates a nation to live by a law, then it becomes law. Why is there a need to have God as the authority? When man decides that something is to become an obligation—so it is!

THE PROBLEM OF DEMOCRACY

LC: One of the differences is that a law, which is enforced by a human authority, is always open to compromise or even complete change, as in a democracy. In other words, it will always lack the quality of absolute obligation. Ultimately, the laws are as changeable as the desires of those who originally implemented them, or their inheritors. Only in the case where they are willed by God, and are thus beyond the authority of man, are they definite obligations. One may further argue that all human law is somehow relative ethics; law serving as the subjective desire of man. It is essentially utilitarian.

Only God can give a law that somehow expresses a divine desire, which possibly is an end in itself.

Student: Okay, but what about the question of whether or not moral good is teachable?

THE MIND ON ITS OWN CANNOT DO A THING

LC: The first thing to realize is this: the mind on its own is incapable of any action. The spirit, as such, is impotent. It can only act in relation to the material world, or in the case of the human being, with his or her body. No one has ever accomplished anything based solely on *contemplation*. There must be some kind of cooperation between body and mind. Matter alone is inanimate. Mind alone is, at best, noble paralysis. Action can only effectively be realized when mind and body interact. Without this interaction, reality will only be a jungle of wild and blind forces going nowhere. This is even more true when speaking of ethics.

Student: You mean to say that the ethical deed can only represent itself through the close cooperation between both body and mind, as well as agreeing over what needs to be accomplished?

DEED AND THOUGHT MUST COME TOGETHER

LC: Without that, nothing can be achieved. In an ethical act, deed and thought must unite. We could go one step further and say that we could not even think without the existence of the brain organs, which are material.

Student: In other words, the ethical deed is the result of the mind deciding upon a desired goal, and the body being the practical means of attaining it.

THE BODY IS AMORAL

LC: Yes. The spirit of man may recognize ethical aspirations on an intellectual level, but the physiological condition of man is the only one which can translate this into reality. What you also have to realize is that the human body is powerless to achieve ethical goals by itself. The body, as such, is indifferent to the ethical. It has no interest in mercy or righteousness. The body does not know of any moral code. It is amoral.

Student: So the only way for man to function would be for the body and soul to make room for each other. I suppose this requires self-limitation and, perhaps, a certain degree of self-denial.

LC: However, both body and soul are primarily "interested" in satisfying their own needs. They are selfish. This is precisely man's ethical dilemma. Man must somehow live with both of them. This is what makes us human.

Student: So why not grant Plato his right to claim that the human soul is confined to the body, as we discussed before? Or to put it more succinctly: the soul uses the body?

LC: Maybe Plato was right about this. Where Plato errs is that he believed that sufficient knowledge would guarantee that the soul would make proper use of the body. Knowledge, though, is never the exclusive cause of action. Aristotle already made that point when he stated that the mind is "never found producing without appetite."[106]

---

[106] Aristotle, *On the Soul*, 111/9–10.

Student: But isn't the "appetite" faced with the problem of having many competitors?

LC: That may be true, but ultimately, nothing happens without there being one kind of appetite or a combination of many, which will cause the mind to activate. There must be some kind of urge and its effectiveness depends on the outcome between conflicting appetites. This brings us back to the proposition by Marx, namely that an idea only becomes potent when it captures the imagination of the masses. In that sense, Marx was right when he opposed the Socratic human approach. Where he went wrong is his claim that there is no independent realm of values and ideas.

Student: How does Judaism respond?

APPETITE FOR THE GOOD

LC: The first thing is to again realize Judaism's optimistic notion which claims that God has confidence in man. But in order to make man understand and act on this, there is the need for an appetite of "the good." Judaism is of the opinion that such a possibility exists, or more specifically, claims there is an inclination in man which calls for such appetite. We call it the *yetzer hatov*, the good inclination, which, like its opponent, the *yetzer hara*, the evil impulse, is rooted in one's heart.

While it is true that the good inclination is something all people have, the *yetzer hara*, according to the Jewish tradition, is in many ways much stronger than the *yetzer hatov*.[107] It is therefore necessary to foster emotional forces that promote and empower the good inclination. This means that "good" needs and appetites have to be strengthened, and this creates a kind of education which, requires a completely different educational structure from that recommended by Socrates and Plato. We must continually strive to find a way through which the physical side of man becomes the tool to realize this goal.

Student: You mean that the body must somehow be opened to the needs of the soul without losing its "own" independence?

LC: Yes. Emotional drives must be induced so that the body works in conjunction with the soul in fulfilling its desires. We also have to realize that there are two tasks here which need to be fulfilled in order to achieve this. Firstly, we have to sublimate some of the egocentric inclinations within human nature. In order to achieve this sublimation, certain inhibitions are necessary. Sublimation can only take place when natural wishes are channeled in such a way that they become refined. This does not involve subduing these inclinations, but rather channeling of these forces. These inclinations have to be guided in such a way that they create space for something more noble, without losing the inclination itself.

Student: You already hinted at this at the very beginning of our discussion.

---

[107] *Nedarim* 32b.

MITZVOT LO TA'ASE

LC: Yes. These inhibitions are called *mitzvot lo ta'ase*—interdictory or prohibitory commandments. Through these *mitzvot*, possibilities are opened up, through which the body can prove itself in a higher dimension. Here we touch on the second no less important task, namely to educate the body. Without the body, nothing can be done. It is the indispensable instrument for all action.

Student: But how do you educate the body? As you have already observed, one cannot convince the body by speaking to it.

ALL OF MAN'S ACTIONS ENTER INTO HIS THOUGHTS

LC: At this point, Judaism offers a very different theory to that of Socrates and Plato. The body can only be taught by making it *do* things. One does not learn to swim by going to the library and reading books on swimming. The only way to learn to swim is to simply get into the pool and start to swim! So too with anything else. Mentality, says Judaism, is, to a very great extent, created by action. What a man does enters into his thoughts. That is the key in understanding the importance of the positive commandments, or as we call them in Hebrew: the *mitzvot aseh*.

Student: Are you saying that one *becomes* that what one *does*?

LC: Yes, all of what man does enters into his emotions and feelings. When one does the right things, one will also be led to think the right thing. When one does the wrong thing, one will, after a time, start to have bad thoughts.

Student: I am not sure I can agree with that. Experience shows that there are many people who may be doing the right thing but definitely do not seem to think or feel it. Some, in fact, are real hypocrites!

SHELO LISHMA

LC: This is definitely true. For this too, Judaism introduces another dimension. It claims that one must *desire* to become affected by the deed and to allow the deed to enter into one's subconscious feelings and emotions. We call this action "*shelo lishma*" until it becomes "*lishma*," starting "*not* for its own sake," until slowly it is done for "its own sake." This means that when still in a stage of "*shelo lishma*," one already desires it to become "*lishma*." Without that, there is no chance that anything will change within oneself.

There is still another aspect to this process: the need for training. In this respect, it is no different from any other form of human behavior. Take the case of military training. One can only teach soldiers *as if* they are in a war. Only in this way will they slowly adjust to war conditions and know how to act once a real war breaks out.

Student: But it will never be the same as real war!

LC: That is true, but there is also a positive aspect to it. In training, one can still make mistakes, without creating a disaster, or for that matter, killing somebody or getting killed.

Student: But what is it you're trying to show? What has this to do with our topic of how to teach the human body to be open to ethical behavior?

LC: It is of great importance, because ethical training could only develop through the "as if" condition. In order to teach the Ten Commandments, one must first be observant of less severe prohibitions, such as the Dietary laws. After that, we can read the Torah which tells us of the prohibitions of killing and stealing. What has to be understood is that one does not learn how to control oneself or to elevate one's passions unless one goes into some kind of a battlefield. What can definitely not be done is a direct attack on the amoral body, as it is like sending untrained soldiers onto the firing line. Emotions can only be subjugated by even stronger emotions.

THE POSITIVE COMMANDMENTS

Student: How do the positive commandments contribute to all this?

LC: There are different stages in understanding these laws. Let us assume for a second that the positive commandments are also part of the "as if" condition and have no real value beyond this. For argument's sake, let us state, for example, that there is really no value as such, in keeping the Dietary laws. The only importance then would be that we observe them "as if" the kind of food we eat matters. Or take a positive commandment such as the daily laying of *tefillin*, the phylacteries. There seems no real need for man to observe it, but we act "as if" it is very important.

Student: Let me interrupt you: are you suggesting that there is no intrinsic value in these commandments?

LC: Not at all. My point is that even when we argue that the commandments have no intrinsic value, in and of themselves, but only a value insofar as the "as if" condition is concerned, there is still much to learn from them. It is like a soldier who is engaged in a camouflage exercise. His helmet is adorned with branches and leaves. He does not dare to move lest an enemy take a shot at him. The truth is that there is no enemy around. Similarly, he aims a rifle, loaded with phony bullets, and shoots at a target which is also make believe. The great value, however, is obvious; if he really has to confront an army he is well prepared. He has learned discipline. This supports the story I told you about the chassidic Rabbi who fasted, by default, only because he found no time to eat on *Yom Kippur*, as he lost all interest in taste on *Tisha Be'Av*.

Student: I certainly remember the story. You made the point, then, that through the observance of the commandments, one would internalize them to such an extent that the external commandment became an inner voice and instinct. One has really transformed one's personality into a living Torah. But you are, once again, focusing on the negative commandments while we are speaking about the positive ones.

LC: It is not very different. For example, we make *kiddush* over wine on Friday night. By repeating this ritual week after week, we slowly create a subconscious condition that eventually becomes almost automated, whereby we are told that Friday night is a time to make *kiddush*. It becomes like second nature, although never to the point that man loses his freedom of choice.

HABIT

Student: Wait a moment! We are faced with an old problem—that we are no longer acting out of a religious requirement, but out of habit. I cannot see how this would add to our religious consciousness.

LC: This is indeed a good point and is the risk involved when living a halachic life. But all life is a risk. In Judaism, the great art is in making sure we avoid the problem of habit by constantly reminding ourselves, on the conscious level, of what we are trying to do. When our subconscious starts speaking to us, telling us that we are in need of doing a *mitzva*, our conscious will save us from doing this purely out of habit.

Student: Is this possible?

LC: Certainly, though it is not something that comes easily. Here lies the great *avoda*, the great work cut out for each one of us. We call it *kavana*, intention or concentration while doing the *mitzva*. I would like to add that this is facilitated by "understanding" the *mitzva*. One understands the possible message behind the *mitzva*, something we call the "*ta'am*." As I said before, this term is wrongly translated as the reason for the commandments. It really means the "taste" of the *mitzva*, since it is impossible to know for sure what intention God had when he gave these *mitzvot*.

Student: In other words, it is speculation.

LC: Yes, but it is part of the very process in which Judaism operates. It is considered a separate *mitzva* when we try to understand the possible reason why God gave this or that commandment. It is a complex issue that I suggest we leave for another occasion.

Student: Fine, but you owe me at least one example of such a "*ta'am*" before we return to our original discussion.

THE SWINE AND THE CAMEL

LC: Okay. Let me share with you a most fascinating insight related to the Dietary laws. You may know that there are several animals which we are not allowed to consume. They are animals that do not have split hooves and don't chew cud. (There are considerable differences between the commentators over the correct anatomical interpretations of these signs.) Animals missing either of these signs are not considered fit for kosher food (*Vayikra* 11). Now, among these animals, there are several who stand out for their unusual anatomic make up. For example, one is the *chazir*, the swine or pig, and another one is the camel.

The swine is not kosher because it has only one of the two anatomical signs required to be a kosher animal. It has cloven hooves, but does not chew the cud. The camel, however, has a reverse condition. It chews the cud but has no cloven hooves. So neither are kosher.

Our sages, who have delved deeply into the possible "reasons" why kosher animals need both signs (and we will discuss this perhaps another time), ask the obvious question: what is the symbolic meaning of having only cloven hooves but not chewing the cud; and what may be the reason behind an animal being non-kosher because it chews its cud but does not have cloven hooves. A midrashic compilation states that the camel is the symbol of the Arab world (till this day the Arab World uses the camel as one of its major means of travel) while the swine is identified with the Roman Empire, or if you prefer, Western Civilization.[108]

Student: Why?

PROGRESS OR PAST, WHAT IS KOSHER?

LC: That is precisely the question. Let me tell you something most interesting. The split hoof is a symbol of progress. It is through this anatomic form that an animal is able to move easily forward, even when there is pressure in the opposite direction. There is a strong basis for its hoof to move quite fast. This is not the case with those animals that do not have cloven hooves. They may, like the camel, move forward fast, but only as long as there is no real opposing pressure.

Chewing cud is something else altogether. It is the symbol of bringing that which has already been in the past back to the present. An animal chewing cud will reconsume its food several times by chewing on it. This is the reason why these animals have long intestines and several stomachs. In other words, the camel symbolizes the past, since it reconsumes what has already been, while the swine symbolizes progress, the future. The swine, which does not chew the cud, tells us to look to the future without taking too much notice of the past. While the camel will chew its cud, i.e., it will constantly revert to the past, not focussing on the future. It may be that that this is one dimension of the Arab world. Although there is a lot of beauty in it, it also seems to be a culture of nostalgia, of what "used to be." It often draws its pride from the past and boasts of it as

---

[108] *Yalkut Reuveni, Vayikra* 11:4; see Rabbi Joel Schwartz, *Lekach Tov*, p. 90.

one of the culture's shining features. The Arab world of a long time ago was indeed a most advanced culture, blessed with great thinkers, poets and artists. But since then, it somehow lost its touch with progress and became increasingly past orientated. I suppose that the authors of this midrash were of the opinion that even in the days when Arab culture was at its peak, it already had a strong affiliation with past events and was never fully committed to the future. (Obviously this does not mean that there are no great Arab scientists working on the future, but it means that on a national level, there is more emphasis on the past than on the future.) This may be the reason that the camel was identified with the Arab world and with the past.

Student: Well, is this not true about the Jews as well? Are they not as much past oriented as the Arabs?

LC: I think that that is definitely true, but let us also take note of the second part of the midrash. We see the reverse of the camel when we look at the swine. Here there is little interest in the past. The swine does not chew its cud, but is always on the run, in the sense that it has split hooves which symbolizes progress. This is very much the ideology of the Roman Empire, and by inference, Western civilization. This ideology has little respect for the ancient world, often looking down on it, considering much of the past to be outdated, even simplistic and primitive. It does not like turning to the past to learn from it. But if neither of these approaches are right, what is left?

Student: No doubt a combination of both.

THE KOSHER WAY

LC: Right! There is no future without learning from the past and there is no past so great that one can continue to rely on it and just let it be. Based on this principle, our Rabbis acknowledged the need for both signs in our Dietary laws. One has to live within the framework of a tradition, requiring us to look to the past, but only as a prerequisite for future progress. It is only the combination of these signs, owned by the swine and the camel, which produces a "kosher" ideology. Therefore, both signs are required for an animal to be kosher. Cloven hooves and chewing cud! This also answers your question concerning the Jews. It is true that they are just as committed to the past as the Arabs, but what the Torah comes to teach them is that this alone is insufficient. One has to be occupied with the future, with progress, in order to survive and make a contribution towards mankind. In other words, it is not that the midrash instructs us that Jews *are* progressive, but that they *should* be progressive. By the way, bear in mind that Arabs are also forbidden to consume the meat of the swine.

Student: Okay, but are you claiming that when one eats kosher food, one should actually taste this message in one's consumption?

LC: I agree that this is not an easy task. Perhaps I should introduce another dimension. Since we have trained ourselves not to eat the meat of the swine or the camel, we have in fact laid the subconscious foundation of this message (of the need for both past and progress) without our being fully aware of it. In other words, the act of abstaining from this kind of food sends "hidden" messages to the human mind, on an unconscious level. An inner knowledge, perhaps a kind of intuition, is provided that these kinds of food should not be consumed.

By the way, we should not forget that *kashrut* laws teach us, among other things, that we cannot just be blasé when it comes to food. We should take notice of the moral implications of consuming any food. This is also emphasized when we make a blessing before and after food. The whole process of eating is given dignity. Let me stress again that nowhere do we find a denial of one's need for food. The limitations and rules are only partial, in order to elevate the art of eating to a higher plane. This also applies to sexuality, or any other bodily pleasure.

Student: I am not yet sure that I get your point concerning the positive Commandments, and especially the ritual laws. What is so significant about them? The points you've made up until now are somehow understandable, but I cannot see how they are so crucial as to become of ultimate importance.

A NEW AWARENESS

LC: In that case, allow me to elaborate. Another aim of these laws is to give us a new awareness—one that is basically foreign to our entire organism. It is the heightened "awareness of the other." The purpose of the prohibitions is to be able to say "no" to our self-centered demands; while the positive commandments are to say "yes" to a higher spiritual order, which is different from our "natural" condition. By observing these laws, one breaks down the exclusiveness of man's organic selfishness. These laws make us focus on something beyond ourselves—an acknowledgment that there is more to existence than our own selfish needs and desires. The trouble is that we cannot easily make the "body" reconcile itself with this. It demands training, but this can only succeed when we understand the nature of our bodies.

Student: What do you mean?

THE PRAYING LIPS

LC: I mean that the body can only be educated when the foundation of the subconscious is laid. That, in turn, can only be accomplished when we create a certain instinctive and habitual reaction within our bodies. The way in which this happens within the Jewish tradition is by creating a habitual pattern of certain bodily reactions and conduct. Through this the body opens itself to something other than ourselves, which should eventually lead to the recognition of the ultimate Other: God.

Let us return to the example of the *kashrut* laws. Religious and sometimes even non-religious Jews are overcome with nausea when they see or are asked to eat certain non-kosher foods, such as the meat of swine. This is not a "normal" reaction, and certainly not part of the original condition of mankind. Many people in the world do not exhibit any kind of repulsion for this genre of food. So it shows an existence of a will of an outside source which has created a new psychological structure. This nausea is a result of a "re-education" of our natural desire for food, guided by the will of God. Don't misunderstand me. I am definitely not saying that this exhausts the meaning of this specific law.

The Rabbis themselves tells us that: "a person should not say, I do not eat pork because I dislike it. But rather he should say I *do* like it, but what can I do, since the Lord of the Universe forbade its enjoyment."[109] Neither does this contradict what I just suggested. Let me give you another example, one with which I have often been troubled. It is the problem of habitual prayer.

How many of us do not suffer from prayer in which our minds and hearts are not engaged? Our lips say the words perfunctorily while our minds are wandering somewhere else. While this is indeed far removed from the desired ideal of prayer, we should not underestimate what really happens. We have created a condition in which our lips pray "on their own." This is quite an achievement. By nature, our bodies know nothing of prayer. But through training we have slowly created another dimension to ourselves, which created a subconscious "habit" to pray. If we could only invest in it and give it our full intention, we could turn this into a most uplifting experience; into real prayer. After all, we already laid the foundation for this and opened our bodies to the "other."

In the Talmud it says that we owe a debt of gratitude to the head. It bows as prescribed, without a conscious order from our mind to do so, when we reach that part of our prayers where we need to bow (the *modim* prayer).[110] This is not ideal. But let us not forget that this in itself has tremendous value. We must never forget that what ultimately counts at the end of the day is a person's actions and not his thoughts! This is the positive submission to the Ultimate!

---

[109] *Torat Kohanim, Vayikra* 20:26.
[110] Jerusalem Talmud, *Berachot* 6b, 7a.

Student: If I understand you well, you claim that the inhibitive disciplines within Judaism serve to curtail egocentric impulses. The result is that the other unspent emotional energies can be channeled through a different outlet—through the positive commandments which creates an encounter with the Other.

LC: Very well said! It is the combination of the "as if" condition, together with its discipline, and the transformation of the energy, which has now become free. The way has been paved open for the higher planes of our existence. Otherwise man would not be ready to absorb and appreciate the non-egocentric order of his other existence through higher values and concerns.

Student: Okay. I think that is enough for me to digest for the moment. No doubt I will have to come back to this at another time.

TO CLOSE ONE'S EYES

LC: Just one more observation before we depart for the day. Let us never forget that *mitzvot* are to sanctify, and are not for ceremonial purposes. The esthetic satisfaction they offer is even more meager when compared to art or music. There is a minimum of "show" in Jewish observance. Ceremonies are for the eyes, but Judaism is an appeal to the spirit.

Avraham Joshua Heschel once wrote that the only ceremony once conducted in the Temple and still observed today in the synagogue is the blessing of the priests, but then the congregation is required to close its eyes.[111]

---

[111] See Avraham Joshua Heschel, *I asked for Wonder: A Spiritual Anthology*, edited by Samuel H. Dresner (NY: Crossroad, 1983) p. 87.

DAY SIX

The Palestinian Problem; Unfairness; Eurovision Song Contest; Israel Is a Mistake; Politics Has a Short Memory; Abba Eban's Mistake; Grace After Meals: First Mankind, Then Israel; Destroying Israel's Morality; Rabbi Yehuda HaLevi and *Chutzpa*; The God of Israel Is the God of History; How Many Miracles Took Place at the Red Sea?; Zionism Is the Belief of Secularists in Miracles; *Yihye Beseder*; Miracle Obsession; Zionism Without Yehuda HaLevi?; Maimonides and Balance; Stability; Only Torah Is the Guarantee; Jerusalem Could Get Lost; The Love for the Land; Step by Step Judaism; Three Kinds of Antisemitism; Sara's Mistake; Antisemitism is Rooted Within the Family; The Courage of the Sages; Rabbi Samson Rafael Hirsch and Sara; Arabs Are Half-Jewish!; The Lack of Identity; Did God Not Agree with Sara?; Permanent Damage; Amalek; Timna's Conversion; Rabbi Yehoshua Ben Perahyah and Jesus; A Wave of the Hand Is Enough to Create a New Religion; Spinoza and Uriel De Costa; Afterlife Again; Old-Fashioned; Change of Attitude; The Meaninglessness of Existence; The State of Waiting; I Will Not Smoke So That I Can Buy a Car; Is Heaven a Bribe?; Worship Without Reward; "Hear, O Israel" and Its Contradictions; Rabbi Akiva; Juxtaposition; Elisha Ben Avuya and the Promise of Long Days; Two Levels of Judaism; Karl Marx's Critique of Religion; The World Creates Reward in the World to Come; The "*Mitzva*" of Being an Atheist; The Prophets' Obsession with Justice; Cornering the Market; There Is No Afterlife in the Torah; Communism Is Like Catholicism; Sinai Is Disturbing; Moshe Forgets the Torah at Sinai; Sinai Has No Bank Machine; God Walks with Man through the Marsh of Life; The Commandments Presuppose Non-Obedience; Weak or Strong?; We Were Dead Longer Than Alive; The Risk of Not Waking Up; Changing Garments; Dealing with Pain; In the Presence of God; Shabbat Shalom

THE PALESTINIAN PROBLEM

Student: Good morning. Let me change the topic of our conversation by asking your opinion about the Palestinian problem and the peace negotiations. What do you believe is the solution? It seems to have become a major issue for the security of Israel and the future of its existence.

UNFAIRNESS

LC (Lopes Cardozo): The Palestinian problem is a highly complex issue. It is most difficult to stay "objective" about it. Too many issues of the past are embroiled in it, many of them being highly emotional. Let us first of all understand that, from the Israeli point of view, a tremendous unfairness is taking place. Even the most moderate Arab States do not full-heartedly accept the existence of Israel. If some do, it is more out of political necessity than out of love for the Jewish people. There is even a reluctance to acknowledge that Jews require a place of their own, and that historically, Israel is the country of origin from which they were forced out thousands of years ago. Neither have the Arabs (among others) understood the ongoing and unique love Jews have for this land. This is a love, which rather than wilting over the centuries, only

blossomed, all the way through to the fruition of modern
Zionism. This is one of the most phenomenal experiences in
the history of mankind. Perhaps it is the very lack of precedent
that makes the Jewish claim such a bitter pill to swallow.

EUROVISION SONG CONTEST

Student: Indeed, if one watches the media, Israel is constantly
attacked, far beyond the issue of what kind of government is in
power. When something as innocuous as the performance of an
Israeli pop group in an international music competition appears
on TV, Jordan Television switches off the Eurovision Song
Festival. Even mere sporting events cannot be seen on Arab
television when Israelis are involved. All too apparent in their
intention are the profoundly anti-Israel sermons expressed in
mosques, and found in schoolbooks throughout Arab countries,
as well as the vitriolic anti-Jewish hate campaign in their
literature.

LC: Yes, it is all deeply disturbing, although, with
tongue-in-cheek, I would have preferred that Israel, rather than
Jordan, had decided not to broadcast the European Song
Festival! I do not believe that we belong in such "festivals," it
not being conducive to our mission in the world. But that is
another story.

ISRAEL IS A MISTAKE

Indeed, the Arab world sees Israel as an alien entity in the
Middle East. In their estimation, Israel is a mistake, an aberra-
tion, which will, in due course, have to disappear. All this is so
shocking to the Jewish mind and heart, so that a normal
dialogue seems totally out of the question. Our thousands of

years of hoping and yearning to return to this land are totally ignored or rejected by the Arab world. This is traumatic for all Jews.

Student: According to many historians, I have also been informed that the Palestinians were never a distinctive group. They were unheard of in history until now. Aside from these historical facts, one wonders if there is not enough land in the Middle East to allow for a Palestinian state far away from Israel's borders.

POLITICS HAS A SHORT MEMORY

LC: All of this may probably be true, but it is no longer relevant. By now, the Palestinians see themselves as a nation, having full rights to the land we call Israel. Somehow people seem to have a very short memory. Historical facts seem to have been totally forgotten. Yet, I do not believe it will help to try and force this argument back to the fore. The nations of the world will not hear of it and Israeli leaders on all sides of the political spectrum have for years ignored the problem, failing to give an adequate response. It is a closed book for most of them. So the question is: what do we do *now*, when all this has become an absolute reality?

The Palestinians see themselves as a nation as does the world. There is no point in trying to turn back the clock, when there is nobody reading that clock!

Student: True.

LC: The reality is now completely different. For Jews, the issue is an enormous moral-religious dilemma. Our future confidence and moral well-being as a special nation will be totally jeopardized if we are indifferent to the Palestinian's desire for self-determination: even when that determination is perhaps totally unjustified.

Student: What do you mean?

LC: We have two options. Either we recognize their fundamental desire to be a nation with a land, thereby seeking to accommodate them, while simultaneously building safeguards so as not to weaken our own national security. Or we can create a society that dominates over a million and a half vehemently resentful people by force.

Even if you argue that we have the power to choose the second option, our Jewish religious morality will be ultimately undermined, and in its wake, our very reason for existence. For two thousand years, we never dreamt of becoming a nation that would itself rule another people—albeit against the nation's will—and therefore be forced to take strong military measures against another nation. The end result will be the destruction of the centrality of Israel in world Jewry. This was certainly not a Jewish or Zionist aspiration!

Student: Perhaps, but many people would respond that there is no alternative. They will argue that we have no choice but to hold onto the West Bank and the Golan Heights, otherwise we will be left without any Land of Israel.

ABBA EBAN'S MISTAKE

LC: I understand their point of view and have no easy answer. I cannot judge the security issue, but we must not confuse security needs with questions of political control or with grandiose visions of Jewish historical destiny. If a smaller

Israel would be better able to live up to its Jewish moral-religious standards, without placing itself in real danger, we will have to opt for that, because it is more important to be moral than to inhabit all of the land.

This, by the way, seems to be the opinion of the rabbinical leaders of the "Ultra-Orthodox." It reminds me, by the way, of a debate I saw on television between some well-known Rabbis and Mr. Abba Eban, the former Foreign Minister of Israel. He was severely attacked for his documentary, "Heritage," in which he portrayed a purely historical and sociological understanding of Judaism. To allow his viewers an understanding of the cultural dimensions of Judaism, he showed great monuments of the past, such as the Temple mountain, Mount Sinai, and others. One of the Rabbis commented that this was precisely his mistake: Judaism's essence is precisely that which cannot be shown. It is a religion of spirit and morality; so creating a documentary about its physical historical monuments is a mistake. Although the Rabbi may have overstated it, I think that this is an important point. We are the people of spirit and morality. That is our life force. The external manifestations of that spirit is secondary.

This again shows that the land is a means, not an end in itself. In no way does this mean that we do not see Israel as tremendously important. We cannot have Judaism without a place called Israel. The different monuments Mr. Eban showed in his documentary are of some importance, but they could never reveal Judaism's message. Likewise, a larger or smaller Israel will not make much of a difference as far as our mission in life is concerned.

GRACE AFTER MEALS: FIRST MANKIND, THEN ISRAEL

It is interesting to note that this point is clarified in our bene-
dictions recited during the *Grace after Meals*. First we thank
God as the Creator and Sustainer of *all* human beings and life.
In the second blessing, we thank God for having given us the
covenant, the Torah and the land. In the third blessing, we
express the yearning for rebuilding Jerusalem and the Kingdom
of David. In other words, Halacha teaches us that only after we
have acknowledged our solidarity with humanity is it appropriate to give thanks for our particular spiritual identity. The
renewal of Judaism, and the strengthening of our commitment
to Torah, must flow from our deepest awareness that all human
beings are sustained by God's gracious love.

DESTROYING ISRAEL'S MORALITY

There is still another matter at hand. The issue here is not
black-and-white. It is not a problem between good and evil in
the traditional sense of the word. It is the conflict between two
positive values: living morally and the assurance of our security. It is balancing the dignity one accords to human beings
with the need for self-survival.

The question can be summarized as follows: how much can
I risk and still survive? In other words: how much am I allowed
to sacrifice for the sake of justice? The answer is grounded in
several views concerning the miraculous nature of the people
of Israel.

Student: Can you explain?

RABBI YEHUDA HALEVI AND *CHUTZPA*

LC: We have to go back to one of the great Jewish philosophers, Yehuda HaLevi.

Student: What about him?

LC: Rabbi Yehuda HaLevi lived in the twelfth century and is a prominent figure in Jewish philosophy. He alludes to the fact that at the foundation of the existence of the Jewish people lies the concept of miracle. In his magnum opus, *The Kuzari* (chapter 1), which is written in dialogue form, the Rabbi is asked by the king: "Whom do you believe in?" The Rabbi responds and says: "I believe in the God of Avraham, Yitzchak and Yaacov." The king then asks: "Why not say that you believe in the God who created heaven and earth? Or, for that matter, the God of nature?" The Rabbi responds in a most unusual way: "The God of nature is the God of the philosophers. The God of the Jews is the God of history."

Student: So?

THE GOD OF ISRAEL IS THE GOD OF HISTORY

LC: Well, that means that Yehuda HaLevi sees a God who is not bound by the principle of necessity. He is the God who creates revolutions, takes a people out of their bondage, performs miracles all along and overturns historical process. He is a God of radical surprise and innovation. He can, and will, do anything—especially for His beloved nation! If that is the case, then Israel's future is open and anything can happen. You can see this clearly in our *Haggada*, which we read on the Seder night of Passover.

HOW MANY MIRACLES TOOK PLACE AT THE RED SEA?

One of the strangest insertions in the *Haggada* is the competition it records between the Rabbis concerning the number of miracles that took place when the Jews left Egypt, and were at the Red Sea. One says ten, another one claims fifty, while a third insists on two hundred and fifty! It is clear that these Rabbis increase the miracle potential so as to emphasize that this is what Jewish history is all about: miracles! It seems that this is the very nature of Judaism and the Jews. Surprise and hope!

ZIONISM IS THE BELIEF OF SECULARISTS IN MIRACLES

Student: I think you have a good point there, but how is this connected with our Israel–Palestinian conflict?

LC: I will tell you. It lies at the very core of the problem, because a great degree of Zionism—even secular Zionism, is built on this notion.

Student: Why?

YIHYE BESEDER!

LC: Because Zionism really means to do the impossible, that which is, by other criteria, unrealistic! The whole Israeli State was born and raised on that belief: you create a State, you establish an army, you stand up against millions of your enemies and you keep going as if nothing is a "real" problem. My Israeli friends tell me that there are two popular phrases in the Israeli vocabulary: *yihye beseder* and *gam zeh ya'avor* ("everything will be alright" and "this too will pass"). Even the secular Zionists cannot survive without the concept of miracle. They allude to a camouflaged kind of belief in the God of Israel, while officially denying it. This is the reason why secular Zionism is basically a religious enterprise!

MIRACLE OBSESSION

Student: This is alright on the surface, but this very attitude is becoming dangerous. Things are not going so smoothly any more in the Jewish State. The Palestinians cause increased problems. The Mossad has recently been involved in operations which failed, getting Israel into diplomatic hot water. Local Israeli politics encounter trouble at the UN. Serious accidents happen because people were not vigilant enough concerning safety measures and so on. So, the problem still remains: Yehuda HaLevi and others created a vision of Jewish History for which we are now paying the price. If he would not have written all this, secular Israelis would not have responded in the way they do!

ZIONISM WITHOUT YEHUDA HALEVI?

LC: I think you are overlooking a most important fact: secular Israelis, who are now responsible for the foundation of the State, would otherwise have never started the enterprise! There would never have been something called Zionism, not even secular Zionism. If not for their belief in miracles, there would never have been a modern Zion.

Student: That may be true, but it does not diminish the fact that this miracle ideology is getting out of hand!

LC: True. Therefore, I believe that we really need to modify Yehuda HaLevi's approach, or at least its application, and realize that his view is not the only Jewish way to understand Jewish history.

Student: Are you claiming that others disagree with him?

MAIMONIDES AND BALANCE

LC: Yes. Another great Jewish philosopher seems to have taken a different stand in this matter. I think it would be beneficial to try to merge his philosophy together with that of Yehuda HaLevi, creating a "new" approach to our problems.

Student: Who is this other great Jewish philosopher?

STABILITY

LC: Maimonides! He is of the opinion that Jewish history is not just the history of a miracle, but also of God's natural laws of "stability." Interestingly, for Maimonides, Avraham found God through philosophical reflection on nature. He does not announce a miracle, but the great power behind the mystery of the cosmos. For Avraham, according to Maimonides, it is God's predictability and causal necessity and order which make Him so powerful. The words, "I will be who I will be" (*Shemot* 3:14), mean: I am the principle of necessity and stability. Maimonides' question is therefore: how much room in the world is there for freedom, and to what extent is it possible that God will make miracles happen?

Student: That approach differs from that of Yehuda HaLevi!

LC: It certainly does. What this means for our discussion is that while miracles and the supernatural are doubtlessly part of Israel's history, it does not mean that one can therefore just rely on miracles all the time. "Stability-reality" also plays an important role. I suppose the ramifications for today would be that Maimonides would warn us not to rely too heavily on the miracle of the State of Israel's existence, while also bearing in mind the logic of historical necessity.

Student: In other words, be more careful about the way we try to solve the Palestinian problem.

LC: Right. Only when we combine the theories of Yehuda HaLevi with those of Maimonides can we stand on firm Jewish ground, allowing us to find an answer to this conflict. I should, however, make the point that Yehuda HaLevi's approach may well be related to another issue to which I alluded beforehand, which plays a major role in the outlook of many members of Israel's *charedi* community. I believe that, although impossible to prove, this attitude should not be dismissed lightly.

Student: I am eager to hear.

ONLY TORAH IS THE GUARANTEE

LC: As I have previously mentioned, from the perspective of Judaism, the land of Israel is a means and not an end. It was given to the people of Israel on the clear condition that it would be used as a country in which Jews would be living a full Jewish life, as ordained by the Torah and Halacha. The aim would be to send their monotheistic moral message to the nations of the world. This raison d'être seems to be central throughout the sum total of the Jewish tradition. There is no escaping it. King David captured it well when he wrote: "He gave them lands of peoples, and they inherited the toil of nations, so that they might safeguard His statutes and observe His teachings" (*Tehillim*: 105:44–45). For the religious mind, this means that Jews will only be able to hold on to the land as long as they fulfill their religious and moral responsibilities. When Jews do not live up to their mission, a possibility arises that Israel will be lost. The Jewish people could lose the land of Israel.

This may sound ludicrous to the secular mind, but it cannot be denied that the Torah repeatedly makes this point. For the religious, the pressure to concede land is God's response to the secularism of the State of Israel. It is the result of a nation losing its own identity.

In some religious circles, there is a strong feeling that secular Zionism, which was once so successful, is now showing serious cracks in its ideology. It was unable to bring Israeli society to a greater commitment towards Judaism. (We see this clearly in the Israeli army, where there are growing motivational problems and feelings of betrayal by Zionist philosophy.) Within religious circles, there is a sentiment that the ongoing transfer of land from the West Bank to the Palestinians is not so much the work of this or that political party, but rather stems from divine objections to the way in which Jews value and fulfill (or not fulfill) their mission.

JERUSALEM COULD GET LOST

Student: This is a most serious statement.

LC: It reminds me of an important observation made by Rabbi Samson Rafael Hirsch of Frankfurt: "From time to time in the course of the centuries, God allowed His everlasting people to touch the earth again. He put it to the test to see whether it had become ripe for the Torah State on earth, whether it had at length learned to devote itself unreservedly and exclusively to the Torah, and whether it could preserve this devotion...in freedom and abundance and in independence and power. But up to now, Israel had always given signs that it has not yet reached that point. True it has shown, that, while having no footing on earth, it can commit itself with cheerful confidence to the celestial wings of the divine law. But it has also shown that as soon as it touches the soil and thinks that it has firm ground under its feet, it runs the danger of abandoning the divine law and revering as gods, alongside the Torah of its God, the political independence, the social freedom and the civil rights which this soil provides. It turns the danger of devoting its life to them and finding room for the Torah only in its synagogues, committing afresh all the old transgressions which brought on the *Churban* (destruction) of its state and temple. Again and again, God has straightaway allowed this soil to vanish from under its feet."[112]

Student: Frightening!

LC: Yes, it is. Rabbi Hirsch seems to be of the opinion that the people of Israel are always in danger of losing the land. It is much too early to understand the divine criteria which presently govern the State of Israel, but for many religious people, the writing is on the wall. Even the consensus that Jerusalem should stay undivided would not guarantee its future, once metaphysical issues start to play a role. The great battle over Jerusalem has yet to begin. Even with all the statements made by Israel from across the religious and political spectrum,

---

[112] Quoted in *Jewish Observer* of Agudat Israel of America, January, 1999.

expressing unequivocally that Jerusalem can never be divided, there is still no way of determining whether or not Israel will be forced into such a division at a later stage. Let us not forget that Rabbi Yehuda HaLevi's observations which I mentioned before only apply when the people of Israel live as fully committed Jews.

Student: But such return to full observance will never take place! Does this mean that the Israeli State is doomed to disappear once more?

THE LOVE FOR THE LAND

LC: Let me quote the well known sage, Rabbi Zalman Sorotskin, who, in turn, cites Rabbi Shmuel David Walkin.[113] In *Vayikra*, at the end of the section spelling out all the trouble which could befall the people of Israel when they do not observe the commandments, the following statement is found: "Then I will remember the covenant with Yaacov, and My covenant with Yitzchak, and also My covenant with Avraham I will remember, and the land I will remember."

Rabbi Sorotskin explains how the structure of the verse alludes to its meaning. First God will recall the merit of the covenant of Yaacov as the highest level of divine service, which is the study of Torah, thus absolving the people of Israel of punishment. In case, however, the Jews do not find themselves on that level, God will remember them even when they are no longer studying Torah, but are involved in the meticulous observance of the laws between man and God, as symbolized by the life of Yitzchak, who is known as the man full of the awe of God. When even this level is not maintained, God

---

[113] *Oznayim laTorah, Vayikra* 26:4.

will still remember the Jews for living by the laws that regulate the relationship between man and his fellow man, which was Avraham's main mission. And finally, if even this fails, God will still not abandon His people because: "And the land I will remember." What, asks Rabbi Walkin, does that mean? His response is that even when the Jews sink so low as to no longer observe the commandments between man and his fellow man, God will still remember them for their love of the land of Israel, for which they sacrifice their lives, in order to safeguard the security of its inhabitants. God will not reject them.

Student: That is a beautiful idea!

LC: The implication for today seems to be the following: now that many of our Israeli soldiers have sacrificed their lives for this land, which God has granted us to develop, we must now strive for the next stage. This would be the level of Avraham, which requires enormous effort into our relationship with our fellow men. Once we have achieved that goal, we should strive for the level of Yitzchak, and ultimately to the highest level which is that of Yaacov.

STEP BY STEP JUDAISM

Student: So, step by step, we should commit ourselves and find the road back to God and Judaism.

LC: Yes, God does not ask us to do this all at once. As long as we are moving forward and getting a little closer to Him, we become ever more deserving of the land of Israel.

Student: This supports your previous comment concerning the need to emphasize the commandments between man and his fellow man, this being a common denominator between all Jews and Israelis. But speaking of the Palestinian people and the problems between us and them, why is there such animosity between the Arabs and the Jews? Does it have any religious meaning?

THREE KINDS OF ANTISEMITISM

LC: Here you touch on a crucial point that requires an unusual answer. An answer that comes from the Talmud, and which is also stated by our biblical commentators. In the biblical and talmudic traditions, there exists three kinds of antisemitism. There is Arab antisemitism, Amalekite antisemitism (which is somehow identified with the antisemitism in the West), and there is Christian antisemitism. The last two are deeply interwoven. We can examine how, according to the Talmud and Jewish commentators, these forms of antisemitism came into existence.

Student: Let's hear.

SARA'S MISTAKE

LC: Let us start with Arab antisemitism. Ramban (Nachmanides) traces this back to the first Arab we come across in the *Tanach*, Ishmael, the son of Avraham and Hagar, his handmaid. If you remember, it was Sara who suggested that Avraham marry Hagar, after realizing that she, Sara, was not bearing any children. After Avraham marries Hagar, the latter gets pregnant straightaway and this causes her to look down on Sara. Sara complains to Avraham about her. "Then

Avraham said to Sara: 'See, your handmaid is in your own hands, do to her that which is good in your eyes.' Then Sara was hard on her and she [Hagar] fled from before her"(*Bereishit* 16:6).

Discussing the way in which Sara treated Hagar, Ramban observes: "Sara our mother sinned in dealing harshly with her handmaid and Avraham, too, by allowing her to do so. God heard her afflictions and gave her a son, who was destined to be a lawless person, *who would bring suffering on the seed of Avraham and Sara with all kinds of affliction.*"

This is a most unusual observation. To condemn Sara and Avraham for what they had done is startling. Most commentators are not willing to go along with Ramban and feel that one cannot accuse people of that stature for what they did. But whatever lies at the root of this difference of opinion, one cannot deny that Ramban appears to have spoken prophetically.

Student: And if Sara would have behaved differently and treated Hagar with respect, would things have been different? Would Jews and Arabs have got on better with each other?

LC: That is very possible. In fact, other commentators seem to make that exact point. But there is another dimension to it which I think we have to consider very carefully. Ramban seems to allude to the fact that the problem of Arab antisemitism is rooted "in the family."

ANTISEMITISM IS ROOTED WITHIN THE FAMILY

Student: What does that mean?

LC: That this kind of antisemitism is of our own doing and that Arab antisemitism was started by members of Avraham's household. It did not originate from outside!

Student: That is a most disturbing observation, to say the least, but one we better take seriously!

LC: Indeed, such a statement has enormous implications.

Student: Are you suggesting that the Arabs are therefore justified in what they are doing against our people?

THE COURAGE OF THE SAGES

LC: Not at all. They are responsible for all their deeds. But, if we ask how it is that many of them live with a deeply rooted animosity against Jews, Ramban seems to supply us with an answer. It is very, very disturbing. But this commentary highlights the courage of the sages, and in particularly the Ramban. There are few world traditions which are prepared to criticize their spiritual heroes to such an extent. It shows their unflinching commitment to the truth.

Student: That is indeed true.

RABBI SAMSON RAFAEL HIRSCH AND SARA

LC: Most interesting is Rabbi Samson Rafael Hirsch's comment on this episode. He seems to follow in the footsteps of Ramban, but adds another intriguing dimension to the story. He writes: "But she [Sara] had forgotten that what she had wished for was an impossible thing, that a woman, who had become a wife to Avraham and a mother to his child, could not, simultaneously, be a slave. Avraham's proximity and Avraham's spirit would break the feelings of slavery, would awaken the feeling of equality of all human beings; would arouse the urge of freedom and break all chains."

Student: Fascinating!

LC: There is more. Rabbi Hirsch continues: "the nation descended from Avraham and Hagar is half-Jewish. God has given us, the Jewish nation, a mission with a dual aspect:

A. *Emunah* (faith), theoretical truths which we have to accept and intellectually develop.

B. The law, the commandments, which in harmonious agreement with these truths of belief form complete life in accordance with the dictates of the divine Will.

On one level, specifically the theoretical one, the Arabic nation holds a high place in the ranks of mankind. They developed the Avrahamic Godliness, with such fine acuteness that the concept of the unity of God in the works of many Jewish philosophers, as far as they are developed philosophically, rest predominantly on the works of Arab writers. These contain *emunah* but without the commandments. In Judaism, however, it is insufficient to only have spiritual thoughts of the unity of God. To the '*Shema*,' (Hear Israel, the Lord your God is One) must be added the phrase '*Ve-ahavta*' (the verse regarding loving your God), the practical submission of all human forces and efforts with one's 'entire heart, soul, and might....'"[114]

Student: Most interesting!

---

[114] Commentary on *Bereishit* 17:14.

ARABS ARE HALF-JEWISH!

LC: What is most intriguing is Rabbi Hirsch's observation that Arabs are half-Jewish. Not only is this quite controversial and halachically problematic (although a lot could be said about it in relation to the question of converting children who have a Jewish father and a non-Jewish mother), but is also interesting because of its "universal" attitude, in which the Arab nations have a most important role to play. But all this "went sour" because of what happened "at home." So, the struggle with the Arab nations now becomes abundantly clear.

THE LACK OF IDENTITY

Since they are half-Jewish, Arabs are confronted with a problem, one which we all know too well: a lack of identity. Ishmael and his Arab descendents are half-Jewish, which means he is also half-Gentile. He falls in the pit of "nowhere land" and trapped in such psychological torment, becomes a difficult, frustrated man, with a dichotomy of identity.

According to Ramban and Rabbi Hirsch, this could all have been prevented, if Sara would have been more compassionate to Ishmael. But she was not, and we are thus left with a difficult personality who will cause trouble for us in the future. In other words, Ishmael walks away with deeply buried resentment at everything that happened to him and to his mother in the house of Avraham and Sara. We seem, in accordance with Ramban, to be paying the price for this thousands of years later!

DID GOD NOT AGREE WITH SARA?

Student: In fact, not only is Hagar harshly treated by Sara, but later on, too, Ishmael is sent away by Avraham! What I do not understand, however, is that on that occasion Avraham shows tremendous reluctance in sending Ishmael away.

It is God who tells Avraham to listen to the voice of his wife and send Ishmael away. So God agreed, and in fact instructed Avraham to do exactly what Ramban accused him of doing!

PERMANENT DAMAGE

LC: I was waiting for you to ask this question! I will tell you what I believe the answer to be. Seemingly, God is telling Avraham that there is no way back any more. You cannot turn the clock back. In other words: because Avraham allowed Sara to do what she did against Hagar without protest, permanent damage has been done. Now, years later, Avraham is once more asked by Sara to take further steps against Hagar, this time stressing the need to remove Ishmael. Avraham refuses, but God tells him: Too late! The damage has already been done years ago. This time it is better that you make Hagar and Ishmael leave, because keeping them at home after all that had happened will only aggravate the situation for all parties. This is the real tragedy of the story. One cannot undo early mistakes! Now one has to live with them!

AMALEK

Student: Okay, this may account for Arab antisemitism, but what of the antisemitism present in the West which you identified with Amalek?

LC: Here too we find a similar, most disturbing, observation by our sages. The Talmud asks why Amalek became antisemitic.

Student: Before you continue, who is Amalek?

TIMNA'S CONVERSION

LC: Amalek was the grandson of Esav, the brother of Yaacov. His father was Eliphaz. Now we all know that there was a great deal of tension between Esav and Yaacov. Things deteriorated to such an extent, after Yaacov "stole" the blessings from Esav (although Esav had in fact sold him his birthright at an earlier occasion), that Esav wanted to kill him. Esav is portrayed as the arch-enemy of Yaacov and becomes a prototype of antisemitism. This is startling enough in itself. But the sages in the Talmud tell us how Amalek became his grandson and somehow "outdid" his grandfather's antisemitism. We are told that Eliphaz was married to a non-Jewish lady called Timna. How, though, did she became his wife? The Talmud explains: "Timna was the daughter of kings. She came to Avraham, Yitzchak and Yaacov and they would not accept her as a convert, so she went and became the concubine of Esav, saying: it is better to be a handmaid to this nation than a noble woman elsewhere. From her came forth Amalek who caused sorrow to Israel. Why? Because they should not have turned her away!"[115]

Student: So your point again is that the cause lay in "the family"?

LC: Correct.

---

[115] *Sanhedrin* 99b.

Student: But you are saying more than this. You are claiming that the resentment is a direct result of the mistakes of our ancestors.

LC: Yes, it is. Besides, it is unclear to me why Avraham and the others rejected Timna. I also wonder if the Talmud is hinting that we should not be overly strict when non-Jews approach us to convert, but that is a topic on its own about which we have already spoken.

Student: What about Christian antisemitism?

RABBI YEHOSHUA BEN PERAHYAH AND JESUS

LC: Let us have another look in the Talmud. In a section once censored by the Christians (but which the new editions of the Talmud again carry), we find a discussion of the reasons why Jesus became an apostate. I quote: "Our Rabbis teach us: Always let the left hand repel and the right hand invite, unlike Elisha...and not like Rabbi Yehoshua ben Perahyah, who repulsed Yeshu (Jesus) with both hands.... When Yannai the king killed our sages, Rabbi Yehoshua ben Perahyah [and Jesus] fled to Alexandria of Egypt. On the resumption of peace, (Rabbi) Shimon ben Shetach sent a message to him: 'From me [in Jerusalem] the city of Holiness, to you Alexandria of Egypt, my sister: My husband stays in your midst and I sit forsaken.' He [Rabbi Yehoshua ben Perahyah, together with Jesus] arose, went and found himself in a certain inn, where great honor was afforded him. He said: 'How beautiful is this *Achsania* (Inn).' Thereupon Yeshu (Jesus) said: 'Rabbi, her eyes are narrow!' [The word *Achsania* has two meanings: inn or innkeeper, Jesus seems to misunderstand Rabbi Yehoshua and understood him to speak about the female innkeeper!] He, [Rabbi Yehoshua] said to him: 'Villain, do you have the habit of looking at women?' He sent out four hundreds trumpets and excommunicated him. He [Jesus] came before him many times and said to him: Receive me [let me repent and accept me!]. But he would not acknowledge him. One day, he [Rabbi Yehoshua] was reciting the *Shema*, when he [Jesus] came before him. He was intending to receive him [and forgive him], and made a sign to him. He [Jesus] thought that he repelled him [thinking that the sign was dismissive]. He went and hung up a tile and worshiped it [out of protest]. He [Rabbi Yehoshua] said to him: 'Return.' But he replied: 'I have understood from you that every one who sins and causes the multitude to sin has no chance to repent.' And a teacher said: 'Yeshu, the Nazarene practiced magic and let astray and deceived Israel.'"[116]

Student: So, Christianity came into existence because Rabbi Yehoshua ben Parahyah repelled Jesus!

A WAVE OF THE HAND IS ENOUGH TO CREATE A NEW RELIGION

LC: There is much in this narrative that I do not fully understand, but the Talmud does seem to be suggesting here that this incident played a role in the development of Christianity. I do not believe that if Rabbi Yehoshua would have been more flexible, Christianity would not have come about. Perhaps, it would have been different and it would not have planted the roots of so much antisemitism. What is fascinating is that the sages were prepared to make this point openly. Again, we see great courage. It reveals integrity.

---

[116] *Sanhedrin* 107b.

I should add here that the identity of Yeshu as Jesus, of the New Testament, is in dispute. While there are some serious historical problems regarding this, it is not the issue at stake here. No doubt, the sages wanted to make a most profound statement about how careful we need to be in treating our fellow men, even when their words are of a heretical nature. With a simple wave of the hand, one is unconsciously able to bring about a revolution or a new religion, even creating animosity for thousands of years!

Student: And you are saying that it happened again "in the family"?

SPINOZA AND URIEL DE COSTA

LC: Yes, I am. It needs a lot of reflection to understand this, and I am still struggling with it. Whenever I read this talmudic text, I am reminded of the rejection of Spinoza and of Uriel de Costa by the leaders of the Portuguese Spanish Synagogue in Amsterdam in the seventeenth century, as discussed earlier. These leaders, too, seem to have taken a similar stand as Rabbi Yehoshua ben Parahaya. If they would only have been more careful, many problems could have been averted.[117]

AFTERLIFE AGAIN

Student: Let me once more change topics. One of the paradoxes contained in Judaism is the issue of the afterlife. There seems to be a strong "other-world" element in Judaism. The end of the fourth chapter of *Pirkei Avot* clearly teaches that this

---

[117] See *Mekor Baruch* by the famous talmudist, Rabbi Baruch HaLevi Epstein (author of *Torah Temima*). Translation appears in *Recollections* (Southfield, Mich.: Targum Press, 1989) p. 190.

life is only a preparation for the real life hereafter and that it is the afterlife which really counts. At the same time, you told me that there is a tradition telling us that one will have to give account of all legitimate pleasures in this world which one denies oneself.

LC: That is true. Judaism definitely holds a very strong belief in the afterlife while simultaneously emphasizing the importance of this world. What is the problem?

OLD-FASHIONED

Student: It seems to me that a modern person cannot take something like the afterlife seriously. It may be appropriate for the belief system of the Middle Ages, but for us moderns, it is a little too old-fashioned and primitive.

CHANGE OF ATTITUDE

LC: I would have to disagree with you. If you follow the literature on this topic carefully, you will see that many thinkers are giving the afterlife far more credence than you think. This is true even among non-Jewish secular thinkers.

Student: Why is that?

LC: The First and Second World Wars have made many thinkers re-evaluate the issue of an afterlife. These wars shattered the idea that mankind finds itself in a constant progress towards higher moral standards, which was very much the general belief before these wars, due to the influence of the writings of the German philosopher Hegel. No one today, however, can deny that man's depravity was horribly revealed in these wars. There is the feeling that it is impossible that this mundane life of ours is all there is.

Student: Why not?

THE MEANINGLESSNESS OF EXISTENCE

LC: Because we may have to come to the conclusion that without an afterlife, life is meaningless. What I mean to say is that life in this world carries so many problems and so much pain, that if there is not some higher spiritual meaning, then it is all senseless.

Student: But perhaps it indeed has no meaning!

LC: That is possible. But remember our earlier discussion. If life is indeed totally meaningless, than we still have to address the question of *why* it is there in the first place. In that case it would have made more sense if life did not exist at all. Nothingness is more consistent with meaninglessness than is existence.

Student: So we are returning to the mystery which we spoke about before.

THE STATE OF WAITING

LC: Not only that, but it is also my belief that deep inside us we all know that there is more to life than mundane reality. It seems as if we are subconsciously in a constant state of "waiting" for something else, something beyond searching for that which cannot be reached in this world. We appear to live in

this "waiting" state until the moment—and even at the time—
of our death.

Student: Is this not like Freud, who stated that religion is
"wishful thinking"?

LC: This may be true, but I believe that it is really too simplistic. Freud's opinion that religion is wishful thinking and only
an illusion is, in my estimation, an inadequate explanation of
why man feels the need for religion.

I WILL NOT SMOKE SO THAT I CAN BUY A CAR

Student: Don't you think that it is ignoble for a man who does
good to desire reward for this? The whole notion of reward and
punishment and an afterlife is nothing more than an attempt to
store up good deeds in a kind of spiritual bank, out of which
the calculatingly virtuous may draw? Is it not similar to the
man who gives up smoking for a while in order to save money
to later buy himself a car? He denies himself certain pleasures,
undergoing pain and discomfort, in order to ensure himself
more intense delights at a "later" stage.

IS HEAVEN A BRIBE?

LC: Again you have a point, but I think it is lacking as an
explanation of the whole concept of belief in afterlife. The
aforementioned Christian author, C.S. Lewis, wrote: "Again
we are afraid that heaven is a bribe, and that if we make it our
goal we shall no longer be disinterested. It is not so. Heaven
offers nothing that a mercenary soul can desire. It is safe to tell
the pure in heart that they shall see God, for only the pure of
heart want to. There are rewards that do not sully motives. A

Day ☼ ☼ ☼ ☼ ☼ ☼

man's love for a woman is not mercenary because he wants to marry her, nor his love for poetry mercenary because he wants to read it, nor his love for exercise less disinterested because he wants to run and leap and walk. Love, by definition seeks to enjoy its object."[118]

Student: This is a valid point.

LC: There is more. Let us not forget that the religious person does not only want eternal bliss for himself, but also for his fellow man. If it is virtuous to want human happiness to be increased here on this earth why should it be ignoble to desire an increase of eternal happiness? Again, if God—as no doubt monotheistic religions believe—happens to be, despite all the pain, a benevolent and omniscient God, who would not have lacked anything before He created man, would He then not want to have man live a complete happy life? And since, for reasons we have discussed, this cannot be achieved in this world, would He not make sure that this will at least take place at a later moment in man's spiritual life? In other words, eternal life somehow vindicates God's justice.

Student: This at least makes sense from within the framework of Judaism.

WORSHIP WITHOUT REWARD

LC: Let us also not forget that the Jewish tradition knows about worship without any reward whatsoever.

---

[118] C.S. Lewis, *The Problem of Pain* (London, 1940) p. 133.

There is the famous observation of our sages: "Be not like servants who serve their master in order to receive a reward, but be like servants who minister to their master without expectation of receiving a reward."[119]

Student: This really goes back to what you just quoted in the name of C.S. Lewis.

"HEAR, O ISRAEL" AND ITS CONTRADICTIONS

LC: That is correct. This is also hinted at in the first and second chapters of the "*Shema*."

Student: You mean the "Hear, O Israel" prayer, which continues with the obligation to love God with all one's heart, soul and might?

LC: That is right. As you know, this is not so much a prayer as it is a statement of belief. The introductory statement: "Hear O Israel, the Lord your God, the Lord is One," is followed by different sections appearing in our prayer book which contain, without doubt, the most forceful and fundamental statements about Judaism. There are three parts to these sections of which the first two seem to conflict with each other.

Student: How?

---

[119] *Avot* 1:3.

RABBI AKIVA

LC: Well, the first paragraph reads: "You shall love the Lord, your God with your whole heart and with all your soul and with all your might" (*Devarim* 6:5).

The fascinating point here is that it is categorical, an absolute demand for which there is absolutely no reward promised. It is a *mitzva*, which is valid in and of itself. You may know Rabbi Akiva's famous comment on this when he said: "with all your soul, even when He takes away your soul," that is your life.[120]

A different representation is found in the second paragraph of the *shema* called: "*Vehaya*," in which explanations are given for the *mitzva* to love God and to serve Him: "If you listen to My Commandments...I will give rain in your fields...take care, lest your heart be deceived and God will become angry with you...and there will be no rain...and you will perish from the good land..." (*Devarim* 11:13–21). In contrast to the first paragraph, these verses promote reward and punishment.

JUXTAPOSITION

Student: So, how do we understand the juxtaposition of these two passages?

ELISHA BEN AVUYA AND THE PROMISE OF LONG DAYS

LC: It seems that they relate to two great concepts which co-exist in Judaism, both of which are legitimate: *lishma*, "for its own sake" and *shelo lishma*, "not for its own sake." I have mentioned both these before. Both are ways to serve God and,

---

[120] *Berachot* 54a.

as such, the Torah recognizes them both. The first passage relates to the more ultimate way in which to serve God: for its own sake, without any desire to receive reward; the second one—the more common motivation—is "*shelo lishma*," not for is own sake, but for the sake of some kind of reward.

This distinction relates to the difference of attitude between Rabbi Akiva and his famous colleague, who later became known as Acher, the "other one"—Elisha ben Avuya. The Talmud quotes Rabbi Akiva's aforementioned statement that "with all of your soul" means "even when He takes your soul," i.e., with your life. This corresponds to the first passage of the *Shema*: no reward, just *lishma*, for its own sake. Elisha ben Avuya, however, became Acher—the "other one"—after an incident mentioned elsewhere in the Talmud (i.e., his name is no longer mentioned because he walked out on the Jewish tradition)!

There it reports that he was walking past an orchard whose owner told his son to climb a tree where a bird's nest lay. The boy was to send away the mother and take the eggs, as is commanded in the Torah. The child did his father's bidding, thus fulfilling two *mitzvot* simultaneously: honoring one's parents and sending away the mother bird. Regarding both of these commandments, the Torah states: "That your days may be prolonged" (*Devarim* 5:16). But just as he was climbing, the child fell from the tree and died. Elisha then exclaimed: "Where is the long life of this one?"[121]

Student: In other words, Elisha ben Avuya believed that the Torah did not live up to its promise and consequently he decided to reject Judaism and turned into Acher, "the other one."

---

[121] *Kiddushin* 39b.

LC: Yes. He seems to be right. After all, how could God allow this to happen when He had promised that one would be blessed with long life? However, if one thinks about this more carefully, one must conclude that all this depends on our earlier observations concerning "*lishma*" or "*lo lishma*." When the Torah promises that one would enjoy a long life it is speaking about reward. It is consistent with the second paragraph of the *Shema* which states that one will be rewarded for the observance of the *mitzvot*. Thus, observing a *mitzva* with the ulterior motive of a reward is acting not for its own sake, "*lo lishma*." But when somebody performs a *mitzva* for its own sake, this means that there is no expectation that a reward will be forthcoming. This is exactly the message of the first paragraph of the *Shema*. This does not mean that there will definitely not be a reward. Perhaps there will be, but there is no guarantee that it will *definitely* follow. Otherwise, it would not be categorical.

The story of Elisha ben Avuya is, therefore, most significant. Elisha ben Avuya should have known that the explanation of the boy's death is not that the Torah did not live up to its promise, but that this incident reflects a case of *lishma*, in which God was not bound to grant him a long life. Perhaps the boy observed these *mitzvot* for their own sake and was therefore not entitled to receive this blessing.

Student: Don't you think that all this is a little far-fetched? How can it be that a young boy would observe these commandments for their own sake?

LC: I believe that the Talmud, by quoting this story, is making a most serious point. It refers to these two levels of faith (*lishma* and *lo lishma*) and through this story, demonstrates how essential these are to the Jewish tradition. It deliberately had to discuss a case of a young boy so as to emphasize that even in the case of an innocent child honoring his father and fulfilling the *mitzva* of sending a mother's bird away, there is still no way to claim that one is entitled to a reward of long life. Theoretically speaking, there is a possibility that all this was done *lishma*! The story warns us not to fall victim to a simplistic reading of the Torah.

Student: But God did not have to withhold this reward from this child!

LC: True. But it is essential to understand that if God would have given him his reward, the very message of the story would have been totally lost! Do not forget that the purpose of the story is not to relate merely what happened, but to teach us about the foundations of the Jewish faith. To me, the recounting of the story of Elisha ben Avuya is a remarkable example of the courage of the sages. They were not afraid to be challenged about their own beliefs.

TWO LEVELS OF JUDAISM

Student: So to return to your earlier comments: Judaism knows two levels of faith. One contains the "not for its own sake" and the other "for its own sake."

LC: That is right and what is so interesting is the fact that it is clear that the "not for its own sake" has, without doubt, the upper hand in most of the Torah. There are many more passages that promise reward and punishment than those which speak in terms of faith for its own sake. In fact there are almost no passages where the "*lishma*" condition is subject to further elaboration. Somehow this means that the Torah is most realistic about the nature of the vast majority of humanity. In other words, one could argue that the Torah makes concessions to human weakness, although not to the same degree as Christianity suggests, as was discussed earlier.

Student: Very well, but to return to the issue of the afterlife; the bitterest complaint against this doctrine is the fact that it diverts man's concern from contemplating world evils, encouraging him to tolerate poor social conditions.

KARL MARX'S CRITIQUE OF RELIGION

LC: You refer to Marx's critique of religion, often paraphrased as "religion is the opium of the masses."

Student: Right, and this is a serious critique. Marx claims that religion is a tool for the preservation of the economic and social status quo. After all: according to religion, man's final bliss is to be found in the hereafter. I think he is quite right when he accuses religion, and therefore the belief in God, of encouraging indifference to economic struggle in the here and now. His main point is that religion persists in telling the poor people that they should not worry about their poverty, because they will ultimately be rewarded for this in the world-to-come. The more you suffer in this world, the greater your reward in the next world! It also encourages rich people to abstain from helping the poor, since this would really lead to the poor peoples' "downfall" in the world to come, by diminishing their reward in the afterlife. Economic changes and enhancement are completely stagnated, if not outright undermined, by this attitude. In this way, religion becomes a danger to the welfare of mankind!

LC: Yes, it does. And I believe that Marx was absolutely right in pointing this out.

Student: So?

LC: So the answer is that this may well apply to many different religions, including Christianity, but definitely not to Judaism.

Student: What do you mean? Does Judaism not proffer a strong argument for the afterlife and reward and punishment?

LC: Yes, it does, but for exactly the reverse reasons you just mentioned in the name of Marx.

Student: How?

THE WORLD CREATES REWARD IN THE WORLD TO COME

LC: Because Judaism is of the opinion that one only gets rewarded in the world to come when one tries one's very best to advance the betterment of man in *this* world, i.e., by specifically creating a better social environment. When one does not, then there is reason to believe that one may find oneself in great trouble in the hereafter.

THE "*MITZVA*" OF BEING AN ATHEIST

Let me say that this very argument is the reason why some chassidic masters used to say that, at times, it is even a "*mitzva*" to be an atheist.

Student: Pardon?

LC: Judaism happens to argue that one can never neglect the poor by telling them that God will look after them! When it comes to the inferior conditions of one's fellow man, one should be like an atheist. This means that one should act as if God does not exist and help the poor where ever possible.

Student: But what has this to do with the afterlife?

THE PROPHETS' OBSESSION WITH JUSTICE

LC: Everything! Just as one cannot argue that God will look after the poor, thus alleviating us from the burden of helping them, so, too, is one unable to claim that one should be indifferent to his condition since he will be rewarded in the world to come! If you look in the Torah, you will find that many commandments deal with the improvement of social conditions. How often does the Torah demand social justice, loving-kindness, and charity? Likewise the prophets are known for their harsh critique of injustice; they seem obsessed by it. The sages of the Talmud were also pioneers in the field of social justice, stressing the equality of all men, and fought to protect society against exploitation.

Student: Can you give me some specific examples.

CORNERING THE MARKET

LC: Certainly. In the talmudic tractate of *Bava Metzia* (50b), the problem of profit motive is discussed. The conditions of overcharging and undercharging of a sixth of the market price are laid down. If these laws were violated, the sale may be canceled! Similarly, discussions are recorded concerning the middleman's profit (*Bava Batra* 91a); the profit on commodities such as eggs, wine and various kinds of flour, where prices need to stay low since they are essential to human life, or of "cornering the market" (ibid., 90b); the issue of the employee who has the right to retract half way through his work (*Bava Metzia* 77a). Elsewhere, the Talmud states that the buyer of property sold by the court, so as to pay the debts of a bankruptcy, must sell it back to the person who went bankrupt if the latter was able subsequently to pay the money to purchase the property back again![122] There are many more examples.

Student: I see.

THERE IS NO AFTERLIFE IN THE TORAH

LC: I should also mention that in the entire written Torah there is no mention of the afterlife, perhaps because it anticipated Marx's criticism! Even the rewards spoken about in the Torah relate to reward in *this* world in a literal manner, as we mentioned in connection with the second chapter of the "*Shema.*"[123]

Student: So Marx would have been proud of Judaism, had he known the Talmud!

COMMUNISM IS LIKE CATHOLICISM

LC: Maybe. Who knows? But since we are already speaking of Marx, let me make the following point: it should be noted that, historically, Marxism itself has become a "religion." The

---

[122] *Bava Metzia* 16b.
[123] There are, however, some allusions to the afterlife (for example, *Bamidbar* 16:30).

various religious practices that Marx so violently condemned became part and parcel of his own movement!

The Rector of the Collegium Russicum of the Vatican, Gustav A. Wetter, in his book: *Der dialectische materialismus, Seine geschichte and Sein System in der Sovjetunion* made the point that there is a great similarity between Catholicism and Communism.[124]

He shows that both philosophies see this world as a place of much evil, which requires redemption. Likewise, their ideologies are stated in four texts of canonization. In Catholicism, they are in the Gospels of Matthew, Marc, Luke and John. In Communism, the texts are Marx, Engel, Lenin and the ongoing "latest interpretation." Both are being reserved, defended and explained by the infallible authority of the party: the Holy Office and the Politburo. They can never be criticized, but only followed. They must also be protected from heretical ideas, ensuring that their teachings remain "pure" and that people who are guilty of heresy can be excommunicated. The Church and the party are the pillar of truth, their mission is "soul saving," and there is no salvation outside their teachings—in other words, the whole world must be captured by its faith and converted to its truth. There is little doubt that *Daas Kapital* replaced the Bible within the world of Communism.

Student: I have been told that Marx's burial place in London used to be a place of pilgrimage for thousands of communists!

LC: Indeed, Communism became a kind of religion, with perhaps, even more dogma than Christianity. But to return to Judaism, I would argue that the revelational experience at Sinai

---

[124] Vienna, 1952. Quoted by Hans Kung, *Bestaat God?* [Dutch] (Hilversum: *Gooi en Sticht*, 1978) p. 269.

seems to lack a spiritual dimension, which is another proof of its this-world oriented philosophy.

SINAI IS DISTURBING

Student: What do you mean? Was this not the ultimate religious experience, at least as far as Judaism is concerned? What more can one expect than a whole nation hearing the word of God?

LC: Nevertheless, there is something unusual about it. The Sinai experience seems to differ from what we would today call a mystical experience. While I admit that the whole experience must have been highly enigmatic, it is, at the same time, most disturbing that the Torah describes it in totally non-mystical terminology.

Student: What are you trying to say?

LC: If you look in the Torah, God's disclosure on Sinai lacks any mystical dimension. Rather, it is stated in the form of a *mitzva*, a commandment. We are told about thunder and lightening, but not a word is uttered about what "happened." It just states that God "spoke," as if this was the most normal thing, and He "just" told the Israelites what He wanted them to do. That's it! No introduction on His part. No word about who He really is. Just a down-to-earth demand of what He wants from them! This is hardly appropriate for a religious experience of such grand proportion and attraction.

Student: Is not the whole of Kabbalah (Jewish mystical tradition) full of mystical "speculations" of what happened at Sinai?

LC: True, but in the *written* Torah there is hardly a word about it, as if it refuses to involve itself in such experiences. It is not important to know *what* exactly happened, but rather to be aware *that* it happened. One should also realize that it was of great overall significance.

Student: And you bring this as proof of your earlier point: that Judaism is mainly interested in human actions in the mundane world, and can thus be seen as a counterpoint to Marx.

MOSHE FORGETS THE TORAH AT SINAI

LC: Exactly. Besides this, there is a remarkable midrash which tells us that when Moshe was on the top of Sinai he tried to remember what God had taught him, but constantly failed to do so. "All the forty days that Moshe was at Sinai, he studied Torah and forgot, studied and forgot. Finally he said: King of the Universe, I have studied for forty days and I do not know a thing. What did God do? When Moshe finished the forty days, God gave him the Torah as a gift as it is written: 'And He gave it to Moshe.'"[125]

Student: What does that mean?

LC: What it means is that Moshe was somehow unable to internalize the Torah on top of Mount Sinai. He could not remember it. This may be because there was no way that he could immediately implement it.

Student: Why not?

---

[125] *Midrash Rabbah, Shemot* 41.

SINAI HAS NO BANK MACHINE

LC: Because Sinai is not of this world! It has no bank where you can change your money; nor a neighbor who can give you a headache. Neither does it contain fields on which you can grow barley. In other words, Moshe could not immediately translate what he learned into action. Therefore, he failed to remember. Whatever we can learn about life will only stay with us when we can do something with it in the here–and–now. Moshe had no opportunity for that. Once more, the point is made that the *nature* of the revelational experience is of little importance, since it is not able to relate to this world. What counts is that God spoke to man and told him what to do.

Student: So why give it to him on top of Mount Sinai?

LC: I suppose that man had to first "climb the mountain," showing his absolute desire to accept the will of God. God does not offer His will on a silver platter. Man has to fight and struggle for it. Only then is he able to receive it.

Only with sweat and hard labor is one able to receive the Torah. The midrash does not tell us that "all was lost" but that, while Moshe was learning, the message of the Torah could not fully penetrate into his heart. Still, the final step of comprehension could only come about after God had performed a miracle of "giving" the Torah to Moshe, as Moshe had no opportunity to translate its lessons into action. Again, this demonstrates how much the Torah and its commandments are part of this world. It is also the place, par excellence, where God's will is to be performed. Denial of this world is the denial of the *mitzvot*! In addition, this midrash adds another dimension to this.

Student: And that is?

GOD WALKS WITH MAN THROUGH THE MARSH OF LIFE

LC: That God is prepared and willing to accompany man through all the problems of our earthly existence. While accepting man's shortcomings, the Torah denies the possibility of man's hopelessness in this world.

Student: We discussed this already before.

LC: That is true, but I think it is important to emphasize this point in a different way. God shows complete involvement and trust in the affairs of man.

Student: You have said this before, too!

THE COMMANDMENTS PRESUPPOSE NON-OBEDIENCE

LC: Yes, but understand the implications: the very essence of the Torah acknowledges the possibility of human failure. Implementation of the Torah is built on the premise that man could fail. The commandments presuppose non-obedience! Sinai shows real people who are vulnerable and weak. And still, God is prepared to get involved.

WEAK OR STRONG?

Student: But now you contradict yourself! In an earlier part of our discussion, you made the point that, in the eyes of God, man is *not* weak and vulnerable. Now you say the reverse. In fact, you said then that this is Judaism's strongest critique of Christianity!

LC: There is a major difference. What I am saying here is that despite man's weaknesses, God keeps on believing in him. God communicates to man through Halacha, that despite all his weaknesses he is still great enough to act in accordance with the Halacha. Halacha recognizes man's weaknesses and creates a way through which one is able to overcome his weaknesses within the boundaries of his ethical behavior. Classical Christianity, however, maintained that the situation is hopeless and that the halachic requirements are beyond man's grasp. It is a subtle yet unbridgeable difference!

Student: True. We touched before upon the issue of the afterlife. Allow me to return to this. Most people are scared of death. It's a real mystery. Could you address this?

WE WERE DEAD LONGER THAN ALIVE

LC: Well, for a start, I think it is most important to remember that we are actually more used to death than to life.

Student: Pardon?

LC: Let us not forget that we have been dead longer than alive, at least in the way in which we experience life in this world. Expressed slightly more unconventionally: before we were born, we were actually dead. In our prenatal state, we were dead for "millions" of years. As such, death is not "unknown" to us! There is a second dimension to this. Our sages have made the point that when we sleep, we actually experience a sixtieth of death. Death is, in a certain sense, a daily experience. When we sleep we touch death. Recognized as a most wonderful thing, we normally look forward to going to sleep.

The experience of dozing off is seen by most people as superb. This is most astounding, perhaps even bizarre, if one considers the fact that it is an experience of semi-death. Why are we not scared of sleep?

Student: Well, perhaps there is some kind of longing for death, being free of all responsibilities. Also, we know that we usually get up again the next morning!

THE RISK OF NOT WAKING UP

LC: I do not think that it is as simple as that. Firstly, one can never be sure that one really will wake up. Secondly, is it not odd that many of us look forward to sleep more than anything else? As you alluded, there must be some form of craving to have a "death experience." The only thing that allows us to see this in a positive light is the fact that we know we will re-awaken in another few hours! But that as well is accompanied by a great anticipation of falling back asleep again just a few hours later! There may be yet another dimension to this. Is it not somehow true that we die every second? Every moment of our lives is over "within a second," never to return again. Every moment creates a new life experience, which leaves the one before behind as death. Just like our body constantly renews itself as old cells die and are replaced with new ones, so, too, is the experience of our existential life.

Student: I am not sure I get you.

CHANGING GARMENTS

LC: Let's put it another way and turn the tables on what we just said without actually contradicting ourselves. According to

Judaism, and many other religions, when we die, we actually continue to "live." We have simply done away with the "garments" of this world. We just change "stations" or "clothes" and continue on our "road." But one thing we must admit. This experience is also ongoing while we are alive. We change garments every second, not in full bodily form, but in a minor way. Nevertheless we leave behind many experiences, which will never be relived. If one really thinks about it, then one will realize that our day-to-day experience does not differ greatly from our death experience. It is just more radical! Basically involving the same process!

Student: But is not our knowledge of what will happen in our day-to-day experience the very reason for our supposed tranquility? After all, we know what is planned will most probably happen a second, minute or even days later from now. That is quite different in the case of death.

LC: You have a point. But I would like to ask how much of this is really true? How much do we really know for sure, even in our day-to-day life. I agree that there are facts on which you and I can rely, such as sunrise and sunset. (Although, according to the philosophers, one cannot even be one hundred percent sure about these!)

Most of the time we utilize a lot of guesswork, without being sure of very much. How often does a day which we had so carefully planned completely change because of the occurrence of some totally unpredictable minor incident?

Student: True.

DEALING WITH PAIN

LC: Let me add yet another point to this. We spoke before about pain. I believe that this is the greatest problem related to death. It is not so much death itself which we dread, but the possible pain which accompanies it or precedes it. As I've already suggested, pain can be perceived differently, in a way that makes it more tolerable to endure.

I have applied this different perception of pain for about a year, at a time when I myself was in intensive pain. The problem with pain is that it does not dissipate as fast as we would hope. If pain—even intensive pain—would be over in a moment, it would definitely be easier to cope with. But because it takes hours, days or even years to disappear, it often becomes unbearable and exhausting. In other words, the foremost problem with pain is its *duration*. If we could forget about an earlier pain and have no memory of it, the situation would be drastically different. If we could stop being "plagued" by our memory, pain would be much more bearable. It would only be there for a fleeting moment as far as our memory is concerned.

However, since we *do* have a memory, which can take us back many years, we claim that "there is no end to pain." But what if we train ourselves so that we see every moment as completely new? This is similar to my suggestion that death renews itself every moment of our life. Every earlier moment would then truly be the past and would no longer "loom over" the present.

Student: You mean to say that if we could ignore earlier pain and block it out as if it was a pre-life experience, as if it took place in another life, or "in death," it would be easier to tolerate?

LC: Yes, and then, the pain would actually exist for only a moment! With this frame of mind, we should be able to train ourselves in such a way that we only have pain in the present, but never in the past. It is a totally different mind set. Pain would not become a condition that turns us crazy.

Student: Rabbi Cardozo, it is getting late and next week my University examinations begin. I have to stop our conversation, though I would have really liked to continue. Let me suggest that this was only "round one" and that I hope that more opportunities of further "rounds" will present themselves in the near future. There is so much I would still like to discuss. Let me ask you to make one last observation, some kind of final message, to carry with me for the time being. What would you say?

IN THE PRESENCE OF GOD

LC: Allow me to remind you, as I must also remind myself, that perhaps the most important dimension of this discussion is the fact that it took place in the presence of God. One can only speak about God in the presence of God. That is what king David meant when he said: "I have set the Lord before me at all times" (*Tehillim* 16:8). Sometimes we believe that our lives are too painful and too absurd. But we should never forget that our lives, our deeds and our thoughts, take place in the presence of God. This means that there is meaning beyond absurdity, that every small deed counts and every word has power. Wherever we go we carry God with us. This is a great privilege, but even more, a great responsibility. As I mentioned before: God is of no importance, unless He is of supreme importance.

SHABBAT SHALOM

As for now, let us enjoy Shabbat—the sanctification of time in a turbulent sea of worldliness. Shabbat Shalom!

About the Author

Rabbi Dr. Nathan Lopes Cardozo, Dean of the David Cardozo Academy for Jewish Studies and Human Dignity, lectures regularly at over fifty institutions of Jewish and secular learning around the world. He is often hosted by programs with affiliation ranging from the Orthodox Union and Union of Sephardic Communities to Oxford and Harvard Universities. Regarded by many as a type of ambassador of Jewish conscience, he has, over the past twenty-five years, attracted a large number of students with his unconventional style. His fresh approach to many topics of social concern and his unswerving honesty continue to engage Jews and non-Jews alike.

Rabbi Cardozo studied at the Center for Advanced Rabbinical Studies of Rabbi Unterman and at the Mir Yeshiva, receiving rabbinical ordination from Gateshead Talmudic Academy. He also holds a Doctorate in Philosophy. Author of *The Torah as God's Mind, The Infinite Chain, Between Silence and Speech,* and *The Written and Oral Torah,* Rabbi Cardozo pens many essays on Judaism and prepares a popular weekly Internet column called *"Thoughts to Ponder."* He resides in Jerusalem with his wife, children and grandchildren.

To contact Rabbi Cardozo, send an email to:
Cardozo@UrimPublications.com

Publication of this book was assisted by the

**David Cardozo Academy
for Jewish Studies and Human Dignity**
'Machon Ohr Aaron
7 Cassuto Street
Jerusalem 96433 Israel
Tel: 02 641 4077
Fax: 02 642 6076
Email: nlc@internet-zahav.net
Website: http://www.cardozoschool.org/index.htm